LATIN AMERICAN HISTORICAL DICTIONARIES SERIES

Edited by A. Curtis Wilgus

1. Moore, Richard E. *Guatemala*. rev. ed. 1973.

2. Hedrick, Basil C. & Anne K. *Panama*. 1970.

3. Rudolph, Donna Keyse & G. A. *Venezuela*. 1971.

4. Heath, Dwight B. *Bolivia*. 1972.

5. Flemion, Philip F. *El Salvador*. 1972.

6. Meyer, Harvey K. *Nicaragua*. 1972.

7. Bizzarro, Salvatore. *Chile*. 1972.

8. Kolinski, Charles J. *Paraguay*. 1973.

Historical Dictionary of Paraguay

by

Charles J. Kolinski

Latin American Historical Dictionaries, No. 8

The Scarecrow Press, Inc.
Metuchen, N. J.   1973

Library of Congress Cataloging in Publication Data

Kolinski, Charles J
    Historical dictionary of Paraguay.

    (Latin American historical dictionaries, no. 8)
    Bibliography: p.
    1. Paraguay--Dictionaries and encyclopedias.
I. Title.
F2664.K64   989.2'003   72-13238
ISBN 0-8108-0582-0

EDITOR'S FOREWORD

Paraguay has had a tragic and fascinating history. During her first half century she had three picturesque dictators: Dr. Francia turned the country into a hermit nation and isolated it from the world, while the next two dictators, father and son, ruled the country as their personal fief. The son, Francisco Solano López, with Napoleon for his guide, bathed the country in the bloodiest war in South American history--the War of the Triple Alliance. This was the culmination of the jealousies and rivalries of Brazil, Argentina and Uruguay over their weak neighbor, Paraguay, which tried without success to obtain direct access to the sea through adjacent countries. The final territorial struggle came in the 1930's in a war with another neighbor, Bolivia, when the Chaco War resulted in more than doubling the national territory. Landlocked and unhappy, the people and governments of this nation during the past 100 years have been divided by two cultures and two languages: the Spanish and the native Guaraní, used in public and private activities and in official publications. Both foreign economic assistance and alien immigration have benefitted, yet complicated, the national progress, while numerous political factions have often nullified gains otherwise helpful to the whole country. In the middle of the present century another strong man appeared on the national scene, and in 1954 Alfredo Stroessner took over the government which he holds today.

In looking about for a compiler for this Historical Dictionary of Paraguay it seemed only logical to select Dr. Charles J. Kolinski, since 1964 Professor of Latin American Studies at Florida Atlantic University, Boca Raton. In 1961 and 1963 he was granted the M.A. and the Ph.D degrees by the School of Inter-American Studies at the University of Florida. In 1965 that University Press published his doctoral dissertation, entitled Independence or Death: The Story of the Paraguayan War, the best and only detailed account in English of this fearful and bloody struggle. This was a culmination of his interest in Latin America which began when he was a student in the late 1930's at George Washington University.

iii

For twenty years, beginning in 1940, Dr. Kolinski was a member of the United States Foreign Service with assignments at Sao Vicente, Cape Verde Islands; Glasgow, Scotland; Lisbon, Portugal (six years); Rio de Janeiro, Brazil; Guayaquil, Ecuador; and Asunción, Paraguay. He has been in most of the Latin American countries and has traveled extensively in Europe. For 12 years during his service abroad he was concerned with economic affairs, chiefly transportation and communication--civil aviation, highway and railroad affairs. He retired from the Foreign Service in 1960, with the rank of Consul and Second Secretary, to devote full time to his Latin American interests. In World War II he served as Naval Lieutenant (j.g.) with the 12th Fleet, based at London, England, and as a Port Officer at Glasgow, Scotland.

While a Foreign Service Officer, he was a regular correspondent for the Foreign Commerce Weekly, contributing both country studies and specialized trade, transport and industry reports. He has published scholarly articles in the Hispanic American Historical Review, for which he was Editorial Assistant from 1960 to 1963, the American Historical Review and other professional periodicals. He has also contributed articles on Paraguay to encyclopedias. These activities and others led to his serving in 1966 as Consultant to the AID project in the Dominican Republic and as Consultant-Advisor to the Peace Corps Program for Paraguay at New Mexico State University. For his various research travels he has received special grants, one to Paraguay to complete this book.

Dr. Kolinski has undertaken the assignment given to him, as to other compilers of volumes in this Series, of selecting the material for inclusion in this volume which he considered logical, justifiable and comprehensive, remembering that the work is not an encyclopedia but an historical dictionary. Persons who use this guide will, I believe, agree that he has admirably accomplished his task.

A. Curtis Wilgus,
Emeritus Director,
School of Inter-American Studies
University of Florida.

PREFACE

Largely isolated from the world until the modern jet
age, and still regarded as the Last Frontier of the Americas,
Paraguay has nevertheless continuously exerted a strange
fascination upon the foreign traveler who visits there. More
often than not, Europeans and North Americans come away
with a confirmed fondness for and deep interest in the land
and its peoples. I must confess that I suffered, and will no
doubt always suffer, from this delightful affliction.

To one who knows Paraguay and the Paraguayans, the
land is a near Arcadia or Paradise at South America's geographical heart, and its peoples possess a record of historical evolution without parallel in its high drama and pathetic
tragedy. Probably no nation in the world reflects the mould-
ing impact of the great eras which produced modern Paraguay: the Spanish conquest of southern South America which
originated at Asunción; the age of the Jesuits and their "Empire within an Empire"; the era of the great authoritarian
leaders--Dr. Francia and the two López, father and son;
the smashing debacle of the nineteenth century Triple Alliance
War, Latin America's greatest and bloodiest conflict; and finally, the unique demographic rebirth of Paraguay in two
generations to revindicate its 1870 tragedy in triumphant victory over Bolivia in the desolate Chaco.

This story, however, is often a difficult one to tell
because of the dearth of historical records and the barriers
in understanding a nation which was both isolated and nearly
unknown. The Historical Dictionary of Paraguay seeks to
resolve these problems. It offers what is hoped will prove
a many faceted and comprehensive survey of terms and def-
initions which will encourage a sound knowledge of Paraguay
and the Paraguayans, their geography, economic resources
and development; their society, customs and literary and
artistic growth; and above all, their moving history. If the
effort represents an aid to both the scholar and the layman
interested in Paraguay, then I shall feel I have repaid in a
modest way the many kindnesses received from our Paraguayan friends.

It is a particular pleasure to acknowledge the constant encouragement and assistance provided me by Dr. Edgar L. Ynsfrán, Asunción attorney-historian and formerly Minister of the Interior. Over a 12-year period which included two extended visits at Asunción, he directed me in my research quests, provided me with the facilities of his magnificent library, arranged field trips for me, and endured innumerable tedious hours of evaluating my findings. Above all, the warm hospitality shown by his family in receiving my wife and me as members of their household remains an unforgettable and charming memory.

Others at Asunción who must be remembered are Benigno Riquelme García, Paraguay's "catálogo andante," or walking history catalog; Carlos Alberto Pusineri Scala, capable director of the Casa de la Independencia; Andrés Aguirre, the revered historian of Acosta Ñú and Paraguay's boy soldiers; Dr. David Lofruscio, archetype of Asunción's foremost gentlemen and scholars; and Drs. Julio César Chaves, Efraím Cardozo, Hipólito Sánchez Quell, and Juan B. Gill Aguinaga, all representing the best of Paraguay's modern historiographical sector. A note of gratitude must also go to General Alfredo Stroessner, President of the Republic, who offered his personal services, encouraged me to explore his country and generously provided a military plane to facilitate our visit to the old Chaco War battlefields. Too numerous to mention are the many others of all levels, both at Asunción and in the "campo," who invariably greeted us as their most welcomed friends.

The excitement and stimulating historical field investigations arising from such friendships could not have occurred without the assistance provided by a summer 1971 research travel grant awarded by Florida Atlantic University. Research travel under the grant, in addition to archival work at Asunción, included visits to the Alto Paraná region, the old Jesuit Misiones district, the Humaitá Triple Alliance War zone, and the Mennonite Chaco colonies.

Finally, this work is dedicated to Peg--friend, wife and accomplished fellow Paraguayan adventurer.

C.J.K.

Boca Raton, Florida.
September, 1972

ABACOTE, CHIEF. Chieftain of the Agacé Indian tribe whose
hostile activities plagued the Spanish at Asunción in the
1540's.

ABAMBARE, CACIQUE see also LAMBARE. Chief of an
Indian tribe living in the vicinity of today's Asunción.
Abambaré first resisted the arrival of Juan de Salazar
and his Spanish conquistadores, and subsequently joined
with them in efforts to subdue neighboring Indian tribes.

ABAMPAE. One of three sectors into which land around
Jesuit Indian reductions was divided. Abampaé was
the sector in which crops produced remained the property of the grower.

ABC. One of Asunción's three current daily newspapers,
founded in 1968. A tabloid of usually neutral political
stature, it rivals La Tribuna in terms of circulation.

ABENTE, VICTORINO, 1846-1935. Spanish national who
emigrated to Paraguay shortly after the Triple Alliance
War. Paraguay, his adopted home, was the subject of
his popular and widely read poetry. Best known for
his El salto Guairá and La tejedora de Ñandutí.

ABENTE HAEDO, VICTOR, 1882-1939. Nephew of poet
Victorino Abente. Journalist, poet and politician.
Member of the Chamber of Deputies, and Senate,
minister of the interior and professor at the Colegio
Nacional.

ABIPON INDIANS. One of the several Chaco Indian tribes
encountered by early Spanish explorers.

ABREU, CAPTAIN DIEGO DE. Rebellious Spanish officer
at Asunción in the late 1540's whose activities stirred
unrest and hampered the government of Martínez de
Irala.

ABREU, LIEUTENANT JOSE DE. Portuguese officer sent

1

by the commander of Brazil's Rio Grande do Sul province in May, 1811, to offer aid to Spanish Governor
Velasco at Asunción. His arrival and the report that
the governor had agreed to Portuguese occupation of
the Mission area across the Paraná River from Itapúa,
were developments which hastened the May, 1811, independence revolution.

ACA CARAYA. Famed Paraguayan army escort cavalry
    regiment whose record dates to the War of the Triple
    Alliance. Noted for their uniforms featuring helmets
    adorned with monkey tails, from hence their name in
    Guaraní. Their impressive "charge" along Asunción's
    Avenida Mariscal López is still a featured attraction
    of military parades.

ACA MOROTI. One of Paraguay's three elite cavalry regi-
    ments during the Triple Alliance War, the others being
    the Acá Carayá and Acá Verá. Non-existent today,
    troops of this unit wore white helmets adorned with
    white horse tails.

ACA VERA. One of Paraguay's three elite cavalry regiments
    during the Triple Alliance War, the others being the
    Acá Carayá and the Acá Moroti. Non-existent today,
    troops of this unit wore distinctive shining metal hel-
    mets.

ACADEMIA DE LA LENGUA Y CULTURA GUARANI see
    also BERTONI, GUILLERMO TELL. Founded in 1949
    by Guillermo Tell Bertoni for research into the origins,
    development and usage of the Guaraní language. De-
    veloped from an earlier organization founded in 1920
    and named the Sociedad Cultura Guaraní.

ACADEMIA LITERARIA. Founded in 1841 during the Second
    Consulate of 1841-1844. Major step in the renewal of
    higher educational facilities following the void during
    the regime of Dr. Francia.

ACADEMY OF GUARANI CULTURE see ACADEMIA DE
    LA LENGUA Y CULTURA GUARANI.

ACARAY RIVER. River draining east central Paraguay
    which enters the Paraná River slightly above Puerto
    Presidente Stroessner about 210 miles east of
    Asunción at the Brazilian border. Its strong rapids
    near the confluence with the Paraná were selected as

the site for Paraguay's first hydroelectric project,
completed in 1964, and now supplying Asunción with all
its power requirements.

ACEVAL, BENJAMIN, 1845-1902.   Statesman and educator.
Credited with the founding in 1877 of the Colegio Nacional de la Capital, one of the first projects toward
the promotion of Paraguay's current higher education
system. Representative to the Hayes Arbitration negotiations regarding ownership of the Chaco, and negotiator of the Aceval-Tamayo boundary treaty with Bolivia.

ACEVAL, EMILIO.   President of Paraguay from 1898 until
his removal from office in 1902.

ACEVAL-TAMAYO TREATY.   Signed with Bolivia February
16, 1887, but not ratified.   An early attempt at resolution of the Chaco sovereignty problem which contemplated acceptance of extreme Bolivian claims including
territory bordering on the Paraguay River.   Provided
for division of the Chaco into three sections: one each
to be awarded each nation, and the ownership of the
third to be decided by arbitration.

ACOSTA, FATHER MANUEL DE.   First rector of Asunción's
Jesuit College following the inauguration in 1610 of
Latin classes.

ACOSTA ÑU, BATTLE OF   see also   CAMPO GRANDE,
BATTLE OF.   On August 16, 1869, the rearguard of
the retreating Paraguayan army, composed largely of
teenage adolescents engaged in a bloody action with
Brazilian troops at this point about six miles north of
the interior city of Eusebio Ayala, 45 miles from
Asunción.   The heroic actions and death of most of
the young soldiers became a national epic.   The anniversary of the battle is now celebrated as a national
holiday known as the "Día del Niño," or "Children's
Day. "

ACUÑA, HECTOR DE.   Spanish soldier sent by Governor
Alvar Núñez Cabeza de Vaca in the early 1540's to
explore the Lake Xarayes region in Mato Grosso to
the north of Paraguay.

ACUÑA DE FIGUEROA, FRANCISCO.   1790-1862.   Uruguayan composer who wrote Uruguay's national hymn in
1828, and who is also credited with having composed

Paraguay's national hymn probably in 1846.

ADELANTADO. Term used in early Paraguay to signify "Gobernador" or Governor.

ADMINISTRACION NACIONAL DE ELECTRICIDAD (ANDE). Only generator and distributor of electric power in Paraguay for public consumption. A government enterprise, ANDE is also the only state-owned organization which has reflected a profit in recent years. Its operations are expanding with the completion of the Acaray hydroelectric project located near Puerto Presidente Stroessner and the Paraná River.

ADMINISTRACION NACIONAL DE TELECOMUNICACIONES (ANTELCO). Established under Law No. 56 of October 24, 1948, the National Telecommunications Administration is a government-supervised monopoly for the operation of telecommunication services in Paraguay. It superseded the operations of the International Telephone Company, whose properties were expropriated in 1947.

ADMINISTRATIVE ORGANIZATION OF PARAGUAY see DEPARTMENTS.

AGACE INDIANS see also **ABACOTE, CHIEF.** A Guaraní tribe living south of Asunción along the east bank of the Paraguay River whose hostile activities plagued Spaniards at Asunción in the 1540's.

AGUA RICA, FORTIN see **SAMAKLAY** and **MASAMAKLAY.** Site of an incident in the Chaco preluding the war with Bolivia.

AGUEDA. Mentioned in the last will of Domingo Martínez de Irala as his Indian servant-mistress by whom he had a daughter, Isabel de Irala. Isabel was twice married. A son by her first marriage to Gonzalo de Mendoza was Captain Hernando de Mendoza, a founder of Buenos Aires, and a son by her second marriage to Captain Pedro de la Fuente was Pedro Hurtado, a noted soldier and colonial official in the Plata provinces.

AGUERO, JUAN FRANCISCO. Paraguayan national residing in Buenos Aires who in 1810 was commissioned by the Buenos Aires Junta to proceed to Asunción on a mission to explain the background, events and policies emanating from the May movement against Spanish rule.

AGUERRI, FATHER JUAN DE.   Bishop of Buenos Aires,
favorably inclined toward the Comunero movement, who
was temporarily in Asunción in 1733.   Elected governor
by the Asunción commune following the battle of Guaya-
hibití and the death of Manuel Agustín de Ruiloba.   Un-
equal to the task, he soon departed from Paraguay
leaving the position to Cristóbal Domínguez de Obelar.

AGUIRRE, ANDRES, 1902- .   One of interior Paraguay's
most noted historians, residing at Eusebio Ayala (Barrero Grande) and specializing in the later phases of the
Triple Alliance War, particularly the Battle of Acosta
Ñú, fought in the vicinity in 1869.   Known also for his
poetry and oratorical skill.

AGUIRRE, ATANASIO CRUZ.   Uruguay's Blanco Party president in 1864 and early 1865 who mistakenly expected
Paraguayan support against the Argentine-backed Colorado Party faction led by Venancio Flores.   Collapse of
the Aguirre government and the Flores victory were
direct events leading to the Triple Alliance War.

AGUIRRE, COLONEL CESAR see REVOLUTION OF 1947.
Rebel army officer in command of the early stages of
the 1947 Revolution in the Concepción area.

AGUIRRE, CAPTAIN JUAN FRANCISCO,   -1811.   With
Félix de Azara, a member of the commission which
sought unsuccessfully in the late eighteenth century to
establish frontier limits with Brazil.   A native of
Asturias, Aguirre left a diary of his 1784-1796 experiences in Paraguay which remains a unique source
record.

AHO-POI.   Paraguayan hand-made embroidered textiles customarily made in the area of the city of Villarrica.
Also the name presently applied to embroidered shirts
custom-made from this material.   Ahó-Poí and Ñandutí
lace are Paraguay's two principal textile handicrafts.

ALBAIA INDIANS.   Presumably a tribal branch of the fierce
Chaco Guaycurú Indians who engaged in raids upon the
northern zone of eastern Paraguay about the time of the
Spanish conquest.

ALBERDI, JUAN BAUTISTA.   Prominent nineteenth century

Argentine statesman, author of the Argentine Constitution
of 1852, and foe of General Bartolomé Mitre, who
championed the cause of Paraguay during the Triple Alliance War. His pro-Paraguayan essays mirrored the
wide anti-war sentiment in Argentina's provinces.

ALBORNO, PABLO, 1917-   . One of Paraguay's most
widely-known painters, specializing in impressionism.

ALBORNOZ, MIGUEL. Alleged in some historical records
to have been one of the early tutors of Francisco
Solano López.

ALBUQUERQUE, BRAZIL. Mato Grosso Brazilian port
along the upper Paraguay River which, with the nearby other ports of Coimbra and Corumbá, was a supply
depot and an objective of Paraguay's northern invasion
force in the early stages of the Triple Alliance War.

ALCALA, JOSE RODRIGUEZ see RODRIGUEZ-ALCALA,
JOSE.

ALCALDE. Spanish term used in Paraguay and elsewhere
in Spanish America for the principal authority in urban
areas. Similar to the position of mayor. In Paraguay's interior cities and villages the "comisario" is
the official holding this title.

ALEN, COLONEL PAULINO. Commander of the Paraguayan
garrison at Humaitá in 1868 during the Triple Alliance
War, who preferred suicide to surrender when the
allies succeeded in encircling his position.

ALFARO, FRANCISCO. An inspector sent to Paraguay in
the early 1600's by King Philip III who aroused discon-
tent among the colonists by his orders against oppres-
sion of native Indians.

ALFARO, JUAN. Recorded as the author of a letter in 1821
to Corrientes contacts which was intercepted and which
apprised Dr. José Gaspar Rodríguez de Francia of the
ill-feeling against him by Spaniards resident at Asunción.
Wholesale arrests and imprisonment of such persons
was the immediate result.

ALFONSO, BASTIAN. Engineer and craftsman credited with
ship and church construction in Paraguay's early colonial era.

ALIGUATA-ZENTENO, BATTLE OF. One of Paraguay's
    major Chaco War victories occurring at the close of
    1933. Commencing in October, a large Bolivian army
    was forced into a retreat of rout proportions which
    finally ended in its unconditional surrender at Campo
    Vía. Bolivian losses included over 8,000 officers and
    men as well as enormous supplies of war material.
    Brigadier Estigarribia was promoted to General of Divi-
    sion, while on Bolivia's side German General Hans
    Kundt was replaced by General Enrique Peñaranda.

ALIHUATA, FORTIN. Paraguayan fortified Chaco outpost on
    the southern front, and scene of heavy fighting in the
    1932-1933 early stages of the Chaco War with Bolivia.

ALIHUATA TRAIL see ALIHUATA, FORTIN. Paraguayan
    supply line linking several "fortines" or military out-
    posts on the southern front in the early stages of the
    Chaco War.

ALLEN, JAMES AND EZRA. American balloonists who
    came to Brazil after the Civil War and offered their
    services to the Brazilian army in Paraguay during the
    Triple Alliance War. Their ascents for aerial observa-
    tion purposes at the siege of Humaitá marked the first
    use of such equipment in Latin America.

ALMEIDA, FRANCISCO, 1882-1960. Asunción-born sculptor
    who studied in Rome and Paris. Noted for having pro-
    duced the sculptures of Dr. Francia, Carlos Antonio
    and Francisco Solano López, and of Marshal Estigarri-
    bia, which adorn downtown Asunción's Pantheon of the
    Heroes. Sculptor of other similar statues of historic
    figures at interior cities.

ALON see AYALA, JOSE DE LA CRUZ. Politically ori-
    ented youth organization of Paraguay's Liberal Party.
    So named in honor of José de la Cruz Ayala, a noted
    liberal leader of the late nineteenth century who used
    the pen-name "Alón." Also the name of a politically
    oriented periodical which was first published in 1903.

ALONSO, CRISTOBAL. Harness-maker and a craftsman
    among the Spanish arrivals of the early colonial period.

ALONSO, COMANDANTE MARIANO ROQUE see ROQUE
    ALONSO, COMANDANTE MARIANO.

ALOS Y BRU, JOAQUIN. Appointed governor in 1781. Noted
for his efforts to contain Portuguese expansion northwest toward the Chaco in regions claimed by Paraguay.

ALSINA, ADOLFO. Member of a group of Paraguayans in
1874 who plotted to obtain Argentine approval in an effort to eliminate allied occupation of Paraguay after the
Triple Alliance War.

ALTO PARANA RIVER see also PARANA RIVER. Term
frequently used in histories and geographic studies of
Paraguay to denote that portion of the Paraná River
northward either from its confluence with the Paraguay
River or from the port of Encarnación. Thus, for example, the Friendship Bridge eastward from Asunción
at the Paraguay-Brazilian frontier, crosses the Alto
Paraná River. Occasionally referred to as the Upper
Paraná River.

ALTOS. Small village located in the Cordillera de los Altos
near the summer resort of San Bernardino on Lake
Ypacaray, about 40 miles northeast of Asunción. Once
a significant colony site for late nineteenth century
German immigrants.

ALVAREZ, JUAN. Blacksmith who accompanied the Pedro
de Mendoza expedition to Paraguay.

ALVEAR, CARLOS M. DE. Supreme Director of Buenos
Aires who sought unsuccessfully in the early years of
the Dr. Francia era to obtain Paraguayan aid in expanding the Buenos Aires army.

ALVEAR, MARCELO T. DE. Argentine president in 1924
who promoted an unsuccessful plan for mediation of
the growing Paraguayan/Bolivian Chaco dispute.

ALVEAR Y PONCE DE LEON, DIEGO DE, 1749-1830.
Spanish government official and member of the special
commission assigned to define boundary limits between
the Spanish colonies and Portuguese Brazil pursuant to
the 1777 Treaty of San Ildefonso. Wrote a five-volume
diary of his travels in Paraguay and La Plata which is
a valuable source record.

AMAMBAY, CORDILLERA OF. Low-lying mountain range
of the Paraná plateau near the Brazilian border in ex-

treme northeastern Paraguay. Crossed by the remnants of Paraguay's army in its 1869-1870 retreat. In
its foothills near the border city of Pedro Juan Caballero exists the point known as Cerro Corá, where
Marshal President López was killed March 1, 1870.

AMARAL, JOSE MARIA DE. Brazilian minister at Asunción
in 1857 who abruptly left his post following alleged
acrimonious discussions with Carlos Antonio López of
navigation rights along the Paraguay River.

AMARILLA, EDUARDO, 1874-1940. Son of Hilario Amarilla,
famed Paraguayan artilleryman of the Triple Alliance
War. Journalist who edited El Cívico as of 1895, and
a reporter for El Nacional, official paper of the Liberal Party. Agent from 1914 to his death for the
Buenos Aires newspaper La Razón.

AMARILLA, MAJOR HILARIO. Hero of the Triple Alliance
War and famed as the Paraguayan army's expert with
rocket launching devices and other artillery.

AMARILLA FRETES, EDUARDO, 1908-   . College and
university professor, and historian. Author of numerous books, articles and newspaper studies of historical
subjects including the Paraguayan and Chaco Wars, and
the early independence era.

ANDE see ADMINISTRACION NACIONAL DE ELECTRICI-
DAD.

ANDINO, GENERAL JOSE. Commandant of a detention camp
system in the Chaco during the World War II period at
which anti-Axis and anti-government suspects were reportedly held.

ANGOSTURA. Paraguayan river battery and defensive fortification constructed at the terminal of the Pikysyry
trench line on the Paraguay River below Villeta south
of Asunción. Surrendered in December, 1868, to allied troops by Colonel George Thompson, the British
commander of the Paraguayan garrison, at the close
of the Lomas Valentinas campaign of the Triple Alliance War.

ANTELCO see ADMINISTRACION NACIONAL DE TELE-
COMUNICACIONES.

ANTEQUERA Y CASTRO, DR. JOSE DE, 1690-1731 see
    also COMUNERO REVOLT. Born in Panama. Famed
    leader of Paraguay's Comunero Revolt, 1717-1735, re-
    garded as the most significant uprising against Spanish
    rule prior to the early nineteenth century independence
    movements. Sent to Asunción by the Audiencia of
    Charcas to investigate accusations against Governor
    Reyes Balmaceda, Antequera deposed the governor and
    assumed control of the government. Pressured by
    royalist forces from Buenos Aires, he returned sub-
    sequently to Lima where he was imprisoned by the
    Viceroy, reportedly on instigation from Jesuit sources.
    Antequera and a "Comunero" companion from Paraguay,
    Juan de Mena, were executed in Lima in 1731 on
    charges of sedition and rebellion against the king.

ANUNCIACION, FATHER GABRIEL DE LA. Brother of early
    explorer and author Ruy Díaz de Guzmán who, with his
    brother Francisco de Guzmán, accompanied the first
    Franciscan missionaries in Paraguay and taught them
    Guaraní.

APA RIVER see also APA RIVER BRIDGE. Northern
    frontier boundary with Brazil since the Triple Alliance
    War. Previously, Paraguay had claimed territory to
    the Branco River farther north, but these claims
    clashed with those of Brazil which held the Apa to be
    the frontier.

APA RIVER BRIDGE. Located along the Apa River, the
    northern border of Paraguay facing Brazil, and con-
    necting the two Bella Vista towns of Paraguay and Bra-
    zil. An important new highway connection inaugurated
    in 1971. The area was a major disputed boundary
    zone between Paraguay and Brazil prior to the Triple
    Alliance War. It was also the locale of the Retreat
    from Laguna, a Brazilian wartime defeat.

AQUI. Popular Asunción illustrated news and current local
    events bi-weekly magazine published since 1968. Con-
    tains material not usually appearing in daily newspa-
    pers.

AQUIDABAN RIVER. River system arising in the area of
    the northeastern border city of Pedro Juan Caballero
    which flows westward to enter the Paraguay River
    shortly to the north of the port city of Concepción.

Near one of its eastern branches, the Aquidabán-Nigüí, the last action of the Triple Alliance War was fought March 1, 1870, at Cerro Corá.

AQUIDABAN-NIGUI RIVER   see also   CERRO CORA.   A tributary of the larger Aquidabán River, and located about 80 miles northeast of Concepción near the highway from that city to Pedro Juan Caballero.   The final action of the Paraguayan War at Cerro Corá occurred in its vicinity on March 1, 1870.   Marshal President López was shot to death on its banks at the action's close.

AQUINO, JULIAN,   -1868.   Technical director of Paraguay's State Printing Department, editor of Semanario, and secretary of the Asunción police in 1868.   Executed at San Fernando during the last stages of the Triple Alliance War on charges of conspiracy against Marshal President López.

ARACARE, CHIEF.   Indian chief who accompanied Martínez de Irala on a Chaco expedition and was subsequently executed for treachery.

ARAGUAY RIVER   see   PILCOMAYO RIVER.   Original name in early colonial times for the Pilcomayo River.

ARAGUAYA, BARÃO DE.   Brazil's representative in Paraguay following the end of the Triple Alliance War in 1870.

ARANDA, COLONEL BERNARDO   see   FRENTE DE GUERRA. Army chief of staff and one of the leaders of the Fascist-inclined Frente de Guerra which allegedly influenced the Higinio Morínigo government during the World War II period.

ARBITRATION DECISION OF OCTOBER, 1938.   Following the definitive Chaco Peace Treaty of July 21, 1939, the October decision by the arbitration college composed of the United States, Argentina, Brazil, Chile, Peru, and Ecuador officially established the limits of Paraguay-Bolivia Chaco jurisdiction.   Paraguay received nearly double the land area contemplated by the earlier treaties of 1879, 1887, and 1891, while Bolivia was excluded from the Paraguay River except for free port privileges at Puerto Casado.

ARCE, FORTIN. Bolivian fortified Chaco post. Taken by
    Paraguay's army in October, 1932, in an early offen-
    sive drive of the Chaco War.

ARCHIVO NACIONAL DE LA ASUNCION. Paraguay's state
    archives located in Asunción. Dating from 1596, it
    contains a wealth of documentary material which is,
    however, not chronologically complete. Whole sections
    of the archives were seized by allied troops during the
    closing stages of the Triple Alliance War and taken to
    their respective countries as war trophies. The Rio
    Branco Collection in Rio de Janeiro, for example, com-
    prises considerable archival material taken by Brazilian
    troops after the battle of Piribebuy, August, 1869.
    Following the war, the government appointed José
    Falcón to reorganize and reopen the Archivo Nacional.

ARECAYA PUEBLO. Indian village site northeast of
    Asunción, and a center of rebellion against the Spanish
    colonists in the 1650's.

AREGUA. Small town located about 20 miles east of Asun-
    ción along the Presidente Carlos Antonio López Railway
    and near the shores of Lake Ypacaray. Founded in
    1538 by Domingo Martínez de Irala, and now noted both
    for its well-preserved colonial-style houses and as a
    popular summer resort.

ARGENTINA, LA see also DIAZ DE GUZMAN, RUY.
    Written by Ruy Díaz de Guzmán and the first published
    history of the Río de la Plata area, embracing the pe-
    riod from the expedition of Juan de Solís on to the
    founding of the Paraná River port city of Santa Fe.
    President Carlos Antonio López had an edition of this
    first work published in 1845.

ARGENTINE-PARAGUAYAN COMMISSION. Provided for by
    a convention signed December, 1936, and negotiated by
    Paraguay's new Febrerista government in an effort to
    improve commercial relations with Argentina. Largely
    ineffective due to the short life of the Febrerista re-
    gime.

ARIAS DE SAAVEDRA, HERNANDO (HERNANDARIAS), 1560-
    1643. One of colonial Paraguay's most outstanding
    governors and the first "criollo" or native-born Para-
    guayan to be appointed to this position. "Hernandarias,"

as he is also known, pursued a vigorous policy of colonization and development in Paraguay, and sought especially to promote the welfare of the Indian tribes and their incorporation within the colonial social structure. The introduction of the Jesuit mission system occurred during his 20 years of administration. Governor of Paraguay five times. By royal order his portrait was included in the "Sala de Ilustres Varones de Indias" in Seville's Casa de Contratación.

ARMENDARIZ, JOSE DE see CASTEL FUERTE, MARQUES DE. Viceroy of Peru during the Antequera-Comunero episode.

ARMENTA, FATHER BERNARDO DE. Franciscan missionary living on the Brazilian Atlantic coast at Santa Catarina, and who accompanied the 1541 Alvar Núñez Cabeza de Vaca expedition overland to Asunción as a guide-linguistic aide. Subsequently arrested for alleged treason against the governor when he sought to leave Paraguay.

AROSTEQUI, JUAN. Member of the ill-fated 1820 conspiracy group against Dr. José Gaspar Rodríguez de Francia, Paraguay's El Supremo.

ARREGUI, BISHOP JUAN DE. Bishop of Buenos Aires who traveled to Asunción in the early 1730's and became embroiled in the Comunero movement. Temporarily a figurehead governor appointed by the Comuneros, he became disenchanted with the movement and escaped back to Buenos Aires.

ARTAZA, POLICARPO, 1895-   . Poet and journalist. Owner of the pro-Democratic Liberal Party newspaper El País· which was seized by the Morínigo government in Paraguay's pro-Axis era during World War II.

ARTIGAS, JOSE GERVASIO. Uruguay's national hero famed for his determined policy to liberate his nation from both Argentine and Brazilian hegemony. Fleeing from enemies in 1820, Artigas and some 500 followers sought asylum in Paraguay. In a remarkable out-of-role act, Dr. José Gaspar Rodríguez de Francia authorized his entry, the grant of a small pension, and specified that he could reside indefinitely at San Isidro de Curuguaty, a remote village in extreme east central Paraguay.

Artigas remained in Paraguay, never caused any trouble, and died there at the age of 92.

ASOCIACION ALIADA AMERICANA. Pro-Democratic and pro-Allied organization in Paraguay during World War II.

ASOCIACION FEMENINA NACIONAL-SOCIALISTA. Reportedly a German-financed women's organization of pro-Nazi sympathies in Paraguay during the World War II era.

ASOCIACION INDIGENISTA DEL PARAGUAY see INDIAN ASSOCIATION OF PARAGUAY.

ASOCIACION NACIONAL DE EX-COMBATIENTES. Chaco War veterans association which enjoyed strong political prestige particularly immediately before and during the short-lived Febrerista administration of 1936-1937.

ASOCIACION NACIONAL REPUBLICANA. Known popularly as the Colorado Party. Founded September 11, 1887, by General Bernardino Caballero, and since 1947 modern Paraguay's strongest, most important political party. It espouses a conservative ideological philosophy based upon a nationalistic regeneration of Paraguay's traditions and past. It closely supports General Alfredo Stroessner since 1954, and the army in turn requires that all officers be members of the Colorado Party. It publishes the daily newspaper La Patria, and its headquarters comprise one of downtown Asunción's largest and most modern office buildings. Its regime as the major political party has not been threatened since President Stroessner assumed office in 1954.

ASOCIACION PARAGUAYA see also LEGION PARAGUAYA. Original Paraguayan exile organization opposed to President Francisco Solano López. Founded at Buenos Aires in 1864 by Carlos Loizaga, Colonel Fernando Iturburu and others. In 1865 its members organized the Legión Paraguaya, an armed unit which became part of the allied army but saw little action during the Triple Alliance War.

ASUNCION see also SALAZAR Y ESPINOSA, JUAN DE. Capital of Paraguay founded August 15, 1537, by Juan de Salazar y Espinosa. Recorded as the first permanent Spanish settlement in southern South America.

Situated on a high bluff at a bend in the Paraguay River
slightly to the north of the confluence of this river with
the Pilcomayo River and the Argentine-Paraguayan
Chaco border. Current population estimated at 400, 000
or about one-fifth of the national population. Located
approximately 1, 000 miles upstream from Buenos Aires
on the Paraná-Paraguay river system.

ATENEO PARAGUAYO. Short-lived Asunción cultural organization founded in 1883. Revived in 1933 through the
fusion of the Instituto Paraguayo and the Gimnasio
Paraguayo. Its objectives are those of stimulating the
cultivation and diffusion of the sciences, arts and physical education.

ATIRAHU, JULIAN. Paraguayan musician and composer of
the mid-nineteenth century whose works are noted for
their reflection of Jesuit influence.

AUDIENCIA. The highest tribunal of justice in Spanish America in the colonial period. Paraguay, for a period,
was included within the Audiencia of Charcas or Alto
Perú, today's Bolivia.

AULA DE FILOSOFIA. Philosophy school, most important
Paraguayan institution of higher learning at mid-nineteenth century. Founded in 1856 by Ildefonso Antonio
Bermejo, Spanish intellectual whose services were
contracted for in Paris during the modernization program stimulated by Carlos Antonio López.

AURORA, LA. One of the most important literary projects
initiated up to mid-nineteenth century. A monthly review of developments in the arts, sciences and literature under the direction of the Spanish intellectual
Ildefonso Antonio Bermejo, it was first published on
October 1, 1860. Among its contributors were Natalicio Talavera, Mariano del Rosario Aguiar, Gumer-
sindo Benítez, Mateo Collar, Juan Bautista González,
Andrés Maciel, José del Rosario Medina, Américo
Varela, Domingo Parodi, and Marcelina Almeida.

AUSTRALIAN COOPERATIVE SOCIETY see also LANE,
WILLIAM AND NUEVA AUSTRALIA. Formed in the
1890's by William Lane, an Australian Socialist-journalist, for the purpose of promoting a communal-type
socialist colony experiment in Paraguay. Dissention

and unwillingness among members of the group to follow a purely socialist life pattern caused a split shortly
after arrival in Paraguay.   Surviving colonists formed
two separate colonies which were only moderately successful.

AVALOS Y MENDOZA, JOSE DE. Prominent and wealthy
Asunción businessman whose scheming against Governor
Reyes Balmaceda during 1717-1721 was a factor in
stimulating José de Antequera y Castro, the future
Comunero leader, to come to Paraguay. The untimely
death of Avalós was a serious loss to the ambitions of
new Governor Antequera.

AVAY, BATTLE OF. Following the battle of Ytororó opening the Lomas Valentinas campaign, Paraguayan and
Brazilian cavalry units met in a final clash at Avay,
near the riverport of Villeta on December 11, 1868,
one of the last significant battles of the Triple Alliance
War. Refusing to surrender, Paraguay's remaining
cavalry units were eliminated in close quarters fighting.

AVEIRO, COLONEL SILVESTRE, 1839-1919. Secretary/
clerk to both Carlos Antonio and Francisco Solano
López, and supervising official of the trial courts or
tribunals which heard the cases of those suspected of
treason against President López during the 1868 conspiracy period. One of the few Paraguayan army officers who survived the final action of the Triple Alliance War at Cerro Corá, March 1, 1870. His Memorias militaries, 1864-1870, represents one of the few
first-hand wartime accounts of Paraguay's side.

AVILA, MANUEL, 1850-   . Triple Alliance War veteran,
journalist and government official. One of the founders
of the Liberal Party, and first director of the Correos
y Telégrafos, Paraguay's postal department. Author
of several monographs on Triple Alliance War episodes.

AYALA, LIEUTENANT CIPRIANO. Bearer of Paraguay's
declaration of war on Argentina to Buenos Aires on
April 8, 1865. Arrested subsequently while seeking to
return to Paraguay.

AYALA, ELIAS, 1871-   Prominent figure in Paraguay's
Liberal Party history. Noted for his participation in
the Revolution of 1904 terminating a long period of Col-

orado Party administration.   Also author of an outstanding study of the Chaco entitled Paraguay y Bolivia
en el Chaco Boreal.

AYALA, ELIGIO, 1880-1930.   One of Paraguay's most able
Liberal Party presidents, holding office during 1924-
1928.   Especially known for the several major reforms
effected during his administration, particularly in public
finance.   Educator, author and statesman.   Though internal tranquility and progress marked his regime, his
last years in office coincided with the opening incidents
of the Chaco War with Bolivia.

AYALA, EUSEBIO, 1874-1942   see also   EUSEBIO AYALA,
CITY OF (the interior city at which he was born).
Intellectual, statesman and politician noted for his
studies abroad particularly in international finance and
law.   Paraguay's capable Liberal party leader and the
nation's president from 1932 through the period of the
Chaco War until the Febrerista coup of 1936.   Regarded as the "most complete Paraguayan of his times."
Died at Buenos Aires.

AYALA, FORTIN see also NANAWA, BATTLE OF.   Formal
name for Paraguay's southernmost Chaco military base
and outpost of the Chaco War.   Known more widely
as Nanawa, the area was the locale of some of the
war's bloodiest and most prolonged fighting.

AYALA, JOSE DE LA CRUZ, 1854-1892   see also   ALON.
One of the founders of the Liberal Party and a popular
journalist/political commentator in the post Triple Alliance War period.   His pen-name, "Alón," was later
given to a politically oriented youth organization of the
Liberal Party.

AYALA, COLONEL JUAN B.   see also   TOLEDO, BATTLE
OF.   Commander of Paraguay's forces at the Chaco
War battle of Toledo fought February 27, 1933.   One
of the more vicious of the war's major battles, Toledo
proved a serious defeat for Bolivia's German General
Hans Kundt.

AYALA-MUJIA PROTOCOL.   Understanding between Paraguay
and Bolivia in 1913 looking to settlement of the Chaco
problem by arbitration if necessary.   The agreement
lapsed due to inability on both sides to reach a settlement.

AYOLAS, JUAN DE. Spanish captain in the Pedro de Mendoza expedition who in 1536 ascended the Paraná and
Paraguay Rivers in search of a new route to Peru.
Presumed killed by Chaco Indians in 1539 near the new
outpost of Candelaria on the Upper Paraguay River.

AZARA, FELIX DE, 1746-1821 see also AGUIRRE, JUAN
FRANCISCO DE. Spanish official sent to Paraguay in
the 1780's to define boundary limits with Portuguese
Brazil pursuant to the provisions of the 1777 Treaty of
San Ildefonso. Remained in La Plata and Paraguay for
16 years, returning to his native Spain in 1801. His
memoirs and his several books on the history and geography of Paraguay are valuable source records of the
era.

AZCURRA, CORDILLERA OF see CORDILLERA DE
AZCURRA.

- B -

BADO, CAPTAIN JOSE MATIAS. Famed Paraguayan Triple
Alliance War hero noted for his abilities as a reconnaissance scout. Wounded and captured by the allies
in 1868, he preferred to die rather than to accept medical aid. A town on the Brazilian border in extreme
northeast Paraguay is named after him.

BAEZ, CECILIO, 1862-1941. Jurist and expert in history
and sociology whose prolific works are among the best
known on the subject of Paraguay's cultural evolution.
Held numerous government and diplomatic posts, and
served as provisional president in 1907-1908.

BAEZ, COLONEL FEDERICO GUILLERMO. Prominent political figure in the early post-Triple Alliance War
period. Provisional President of the Convention of
1870 which agreed upon the terms of the Constitution
of 1870.

BAEZ, PEDRO J. Author of an interpretive study published
in 1953 entitled Paraguay--un país que muere? (Paraguay, a dying Nation?).

BAEZ ALLENDE, AMADEO, 1903-   . Jurist, diplomat
and historian. Author of numerous historical studies,

notably on aspects of the evolution of Paraguayan educational facilities.

BAHIA NEGRA. Riverport located along the Paraguay River
in the extreme north Chaco region about 400 miles
above Asunción. Strategically important as a base and
departure point for expeditions toward Bolivia in the
colonial era, and as a Paraguayan base during the
Chaco War.

BALANSA, DR. BENJAMIN. A French scientist born in
Narbonne, France, who in 1873 was sent to Paraguay
by the Museum of Natural History in Paris to study
native flora. Selecting the interior village of Yaguarón
for his work site, he built a distillery and succeeded
in developing a process for distillation of petit grain
oil, used as a base in the preparation of quality per-
fumes. Paraguay is still the world's major supplier of
this commodity. Balansa died in Hanoi, Tonkin, in
1889.

BALDOVINOS, DR. MARCOS. Member of a conspiracy plot
against José Gaspar Rodríguez de Francia who disappeared as a prisoner in the mass arrests ordered by
El Supremo in 1820.

BALLIVIAN, BATTLE OF. Capture of the inhabited point
of Ballivián on the Pilcomayo River on November 17,
1934, constituted another significant Paraguayan Chaco
War victory following that of El Carmen the previous
day. Both were important offensive actions in Paraguay's 1934 drive toward Bolivia's Andean foothills.

BANCO DE ITAPIRU, ACTION OF see also ITAPIRU,
ACTION OF. Low-lying sand bank in the middle of
the Paraná River, near the Paraguayan Itapirú river
outpost in extreme southwestern Paraguay. Locale on
April 10, 1866, of a hard-fought action of the Triple
Alliance War in which Paraguayan forces failed to delay
allied plans to cross the Paraná River. Known also
as "Ilha da Redençăo" and "Ilha Cabrita," the island
or sand bank disappeared shortly after the war.

BANCO NACIONAL DE FOMENTO. Paraguay's National
Development Bank, established by Decree-Law No. 281
of March 14, 1961, to promote and finance projects
for domestic agricultural, livestock, forestry, indus-

trial, and commercial development. One of the principal vehicles for the furtherance of internal improvement programs.

BANDEIRANTES. Portuguese pioneers who in the sixteenth and seventeenth centuries spread westward from the São Paulo area to Mato Grosso and the Paraguayan border in search of slaves, gold and diamonds.

BANDEIRAS see also BANDEIRANTES. A variant of the term "Bandeirantes," referring to the mameluke or "mameluco" bands of half-breed Brazilian raiders who plundered much of eastern and northern Paraguay in the sixteenth and seventeenth centuries in Indian slave raids.

BANKS, BENJAMIN, 1889-1957. Businessman, financier, banker and government official. Minister of Hacienda during the Chaco War noted for his oratorical skill in parliamentary sessions. Died at Buenos Aires.

BAÑUELOS, DOMINGO. Outspoken, pro-Democratic president of Paraguay's University Student Federation who was arrested and sent to a concentration camp on the eve of the 1945 visit to Asunción by Argentina's President Farrell. The incident was a further development in the growing hostility toward the regime of President Higinio Morínigo.

BARBERO, ANDRES, 1877-1949. Doctor and philanthropist, noted for his sponsorship of numerous organizations and societies related to science, health and public welfare. One of the founders of the "Sociedad Científica del Paraguay."

BARCO CENTENERA, FATHER MARTIN DEL, 1536-1605. Member of the Juan Ortiz de Zárate expedition to Paraguay. Colonial era poet and one of the first to use Paraguay and La Plata as a setting. His La Argentina was published at Lisbon in 1602.

BAREIRO, CANDIDO. Originally a student selected for the overseas study program during the administration of President Carlos Antonio López, Bareiro remained in France during the Triple Alliance War where he acted as Paraguay's diplomatic representative. Elected as Paraguay's third post-war president, he died in office in 1880.

BARING BROS., LONDON. London financial firm which negotiated two notorious loans for Paraguay, backed by
bond issues, in 1871-1872. Of the expected two million
pounds stirling expected from the loans, high interest
and huge commissions cut the proceeds for Paraguay
to less than half the amount. This post Triple Alliance
War disaster was compounded later when the government was forced to sell public lands in order to meet
its debt obligations.

BARREIRO, JOSE LUIS. Briefly president of the Comunero
Junta at Asunción in 1731. For his involvement in the
arrest of Comunero leader Fernando Mompox y Zayas,
Barreiro was forced to flee to the Misiones Jesuit
stronghold.

BARRERO GRANDE see EUSEBIO AYALA. Original name
for the interior city of Eusebio Ayala near which the
battle of Acosta Ñú was fought in 1869.

BARRET, RAFAEL, 1874-1910. Spanish national of uncertain
origin, probably Catalonia, who traveled to Paraguay
in the early twentieth century to become the republic's
foremost author of the social protest school. Famed
for his essays and novelistic treatment of life in Paraguay's yerba maté plantations. His works rank with
those of Peru's Matto de Turner, Ecuador's Ycaza,
Peru's Ciro Alegría, and Bolivia's Alcides Argüedas.
Left Paraguay to return to his native Spain shortly before his death in 1910.

BARRETO, MENA. General Joâo Propicio Mena Barreto.
Brazilian army officer who commanded the original invasion force in December, 1864, which crossed the
Uruguayan border and laid siege to the Uruguay River
port of Paysandú. The city's fall in early January,
1865, and the execution of its Uruguayan commander,
were major events leading to the outbreak of the Triple
Alliance War.

BARRETT, WILLIAM E. American author of the popular
and romanticized version of the life of Mme. Elisa
Alicia Lynch entitled Woman on Horseback.

BARRIOS, AGUSTIN, 1885-1944. Musicologist noted for his
success in the 1920's in promoting international interest
in Paraguayan music. Famed as an artist with the

guitar. Died in San Salvador, El Salvador, where he was professor of the guitar in the National Music Conservatory.

BARRIOS, INOCENCIA DE see LOPEZ, CARILLO DE BARRIOS, INOCENCIA.

BARRIOS, FATHER JUAN DE. First bishop to be named for Paraguay following approval for the establishment of a bishopric in 1547. Never arrived at his post.

BARRIOS BEDOYA, GENERAL VICENTE, 1825-1868. One of Paraguay's ranking generals at the outbreak of the Triple Alliance War. Executed in 1868 for suspected treason during the conspiracy episode. Married to Inocencia López Carillo, daughter of President Carlos Antonio López.

BARRIOS DE GILL, ESCOLASTICA. A prominent Asunción society figure who on January 10, 1867, promoted a meeting of women for the purpose of donating jewels and other valuables to Marshal President López to meet expenses in the Triple Alliance War.

BARROS, VICE-ADMIRAL JOAQUIM JOSE IGNACIO DE. Succeeded the Barão de Tamandaré in command of Brazil's Triple Alliance War naval squadron on December 21, 1866.

BARSENA, FATHER ALFONSO. Jesuit missionary in the late 1500's noted for his evangelizing efforts among Indian tribes north of Asunción.

BARSONELLI, FATHER JOSE. Recorded as an expert architect employed by the Jesuits in the construction of their larger reduction edifices, and in teaching sculpture and woodwork to the Indians.

BARTHE, DOMINGO. French immigrant in the late nineteenth century who purchased land in eastern Paraguay along the Paraná River, and soon amassed a fortune from yerba maté and timber production.

BARTHE, OBDULIO, 1907-   . Next to Oscar Creydt the most prominent leader of Paraguay's Communist Party. Split with Creydt in 1960 to form his own faction in exile. Known for his vitriolic demagoguery.

BARUA, MARTIN DE. Briefly governor of Paraguay at the
    height of the Comunero movement in 1730. Resigned
    his office from apprehension over his Comunero connec-
    tions and sympathies.

BEDOYA, JOSE DIAZ DE   see   DIAZ DE BEDOYA, JOSE.

BEDOYA, RAFAELA DE   see   LOPEZ, RAFAELA and
    LOPEZ DE BEDOYA, RAFAELA. Sister of Marshal
    President Francisco Solano López. Originally married
    to Saturnino de Bedoya, who died a victim of the 1868
    arrests and executions of persons suspected of treason
    against President López. Following the Triple Alliance
    War, Rafaela married a Brazilian, Milcíades Augusto
    Acevedo Pedra.

BEDOYA, SATURNINO   see   DIAZ DE BEDOYA Y VALDO-
    VINOS, SATURNINO.

BEDOYA DE GILL, CONCEPCION DE. Wife of President
    Juan Bautista Gill who was assassinated in 1877. Fol-
    lowing Gill's death, she re-married to General Bernardi-
    no Caballero, thus acquiring the unique honor of being
    the wife of two presidents.

BELAIFF, GENERAL JUAN, 1874-1957   see also   MAKKA
    INDIANS. One of the most engaging foreign technicians
    to make Paraguay their new home, General Belaiff
    reached Asunción in 1924, a former Czarist officer and
    refugee from the Russian Revolution. Named professor
    of Paraguay's Escuela Militar and later a director of
    the army's cartographic section, he was credited with
    the first complete surveys of the isolated Chaco terri-
    tory. Following the Chaco War, he dedicated himself
    to study of Chaco indigenous tribes and in particular,
    to betterment of the lot of the Makkás, a tribe living
    near Asunción. His efforts and success on their behalf
    led after his death to his burial in a special "hallowed"
    hut in their new "tolderóa" across the Paraguay River
    from Asunción. Belaiff was also a founder of the "So-
    ciedad Indigenista del Paraguay."

BELEN MISSION. Founded in 1760, one of the last of the
    Jesuit reduction missions.

BELGRANO, GENERAL MANUEL. Prominent military and
    political figure in Argentina's early independence era

who commanded an expedition to Paraguay in 1811 in order to secure the adhesion of the Province of Paraguay to the Argentine provinces comprising the former Viceroyalty of La Plata. Defeated by Paraguayan troops at the battles of Cerro Porteño (Paraguarí) and Tacuarí, two military actions which immediately preceded the May, 1811, Paraguayan movement for independence from Spanish rule.

BELGRANO EXPEDITION see also BELGRANO, MANUEL; CERRO PORTEÑO, BATTLE OF; and TACUARI, BATTLE OF. The Argentine expedition sent in 1810 to persuade Paraguay, by force if necessary, to remain under the hegemony of the Buenos Aires Junta administering the area of the former Viceroyalty of La Plata. The expedition was defeated and forced to retreat; Paraguay subsequently overthrew its Spanish administration in the movement of May 14, 1811.

BELLA VISTA, ARGENTINA. Argentine riverport on the lower Paraná River, and high-point reached by the right wing or western invasion force of Paraguay's 1865 offensive of the Triple Alliance War. The force was stopped and required to retreat northward across the Upper Paraná by the naval defeat of Riachuelo and the surrender of the left wing force at Uruguayana.

BENITEZ, GREGORIO, 1834-1910. Diplomat, author and statesman. Paraguayan charge d'affaires at London and Paris during the Triple Alliance War period. Negotiator of the Benítez-Ichazo Treaty with Bolivia in 1894.

BENITEZ, GUMESINDO, 1835-1868. Foreign Minister in the wartime cabinet of Marshal President Francisco Solano López who, like his predecessor José Berges, was arrested and executed during the conspiracy episode of 1868. Previously private secretary of Carlos Antonio López and director of the newspaper El Semanario.

BENITEZ, LUIS G., 1925-   . University professor and historian. Specialist in Paraguayan history, history of the Americas, and of Greece and the Orient. Author of several works on the history of the Americas and of ancient civilizations.

BENITEZ, MANUEL, 1870-1939. Jurist, cabinet minister and educator during the early twentieth century.

BENÍTEZ-ICHAZO TREATY.   Bolivian-Paraguayan agreement
of 1894, not ratified by Paraguay, which contemplated
equal division of the Chaco region as a formula for
settlement of the growing dispute between the two nations.

BENÍTEZ VERA, COLONEL VICTORIANO see FRENTE
DE GUERRA.   Army chief of staff in 1946, and chief
of the Frente de Guerra, a group of Fascist sympathizers who are alleged to have strongly influenced
President Higinio Morínigo during the World War II
era.

BERGES-PARANHOS TREATY.   Agreement negotiated by
Paraguayan Foreign Minister José Berges in Rio de
Janeiro in 1856 which postponed solution of boundary
problems between the two nations for six years.

BERGES VILLALTA, JOSE DE LA PAZ.   One of the most
prominent Paraguayan intellectuals of his era, minister
to Brazil and to the United States, and minister of
foreign relations in the administration of President
Francisco Solano López.   Suspected of treason in 1868
and executed in December at the end of the conspiracy
episode during the Triple Alliance War.

BERGTHAL COLONY.   One of the more recent Mennonite
colonization projects, located about 180 miles east of
Asunción on the highway to Puerto Presidente Stroessner
and begun in 1948.

BERMEJO, ILDEFONSO ANTONIO, 1820-1892.   Spanish-born
professor and author whose services were contracted
for by President Carlos Antonio López.   Following arrival in Paraguay in 1855, he initiated numerous cultural projects which served to revitalize Paraguay's
educational facilities after the vacuum of the Dr.
Francia era.

BERMEJO RIVER.   Argentine Chaco drainage stream which
enters the Paraguay River across from the Paraguayan
riverport of Pilar about 160 miles south of Asunción.
Site of an unsuccessful colonization attempt during
Paraguay's colonial era.   Paraguayan claims to the
Chaco, originally extending north from this point, were
altered to the Pilcomayo River line by the Hayes arbital award of 1878.

BERREIRO, JOSE LUIS. Briefly "president" of Paraguay
appointed by rebels during the late stages of the Comunero Revolt. Noted for his treachery to the Comunero
cause through his arrest of Fernando Mompox y Zayas,
the movement's last important leader.

BERRO, BERNARDO P. Uruguayan Blanco president in 1863
during the crucial pre-Triple Alliance War period. His
efforts to elicit Paraguayan support against alleged
Argentine backing of the Uruguayan Colorados under
Venancio Flores was one of the factors which trans-
formed Uruguay into the Powder Keg of La Plata.

BERTONI, GUILLERMO TELL, 1889-   . Specialist in
studies of the Guaraní language. Founder in 1949 of
the Academia de la Lengua y Cultura Guaraní at Asunción, and author of numerous studies of Paraguayan
demography, economics and geography.

BERTONI, MOISES S., 1857-1929. Swiss-born naturalist
who traveled to Paraguay in 1887 to become the republic's foremost recognized authority in local flora and
fauna. His works, especially in the field of Paraguayan
botany, are regarded as definitive. Established a sci-
entific research station along the Upper Paraná River
named Puerto Bertoni, and was one of the first formal
explorers of the Guairá Falls Region in 1893.

BESO, CRISTOBAL DE. Noted in historical records as a
Spanish cooper employed in shipbuilding at Asunción
during the early colonial era.

BESTARD, JAIME, 1892-   . Noted painter of the modern
era.

BIBLIOTECA AMERICANA Y MUSEO HISTORICO Y DE
BELLAS ARTES see MUSEO HISTORICO Y DE
BELLAS ARTES DE JUAN-SILVANO GODOI.

BIBLIOTECA NACIONAL. Formerly the Biblioteca Municipal
founded in 1869 and organized by Jaime Sosa Escalada.

BIBOLINI, BENIGNO CASACCIA, 1907-   . Author of the
modern school whose Hombres, mujeres y fantoches,
published in 1930, is regarded as having initiated the
modern novel in Paraguay.

BLANCO RIVER   see also   APA RIVER.   River which flows
    due west to enter into the Paraguay River north of the
    riverport of Concepción and the Apa River.   Prior to
    the Triple Alliance War, Paraguay claimed the Blanco
    as its northern frontier boundary, while the Brazilian
    Empire claimed the frontier with its Mato Grosso
    province to be the Apa River to the south of the Blanco.
    Post war treaty agreements set the modern frontier at
    the Apa.

BLASQUEZ DE VALVERDE, JUAN   see also   ARECAYA
    PUEBLO.   Governor of Paraguay during 1656-1659
    whose weak policies led to an uprising of Guaraní In-
    dians of the Arecayá pueblo and the rebellion of 1659.

BLISS, PORTER CORNELIUS   see also   WASHBURN,
    CHARLES AMES.   American citizen, unofficial secre-
    tary to Minister Charles Ames Washburn, and one of
    the more curious figures in the record of United States
    relationships with Paraguay during the Triple Alliance
    War era.   An enterprising historical researcher, Bliss
    came to Paraguay in 1865 on his own account, eventual-
    ly became employed by Washburn, and with him was
    embroiled in the Conspiracy episode of 1868.   As a
    prisoner of Francisco Solano López at the San Fernando
    detention camp, he was forced to write a biography of
    Washburn which implied the minister's involvement in
    a plot against López.   Finally released when an Amer-
    ican naval squadron reached Paraguay, Bliss quickly
    recanted his biography and confession, and subsequently
    presented testimony at a congressional inquiry into
    Paraguayan affairs which supported former Minister
    Washburn.

BLOQUE DE DEFENSA DE LA REVOLUCION   see also
    FEBRERISTA PARTY.   Ultra-radical wing of the Febre-
    rista Party in the late 1940's which openly espoused its
    sympathies with the Soviet bloc.   Expelled from the
    Febrerista Party in 1951.

BLYTH, J. and A.   English business firm utilized during
    the administration of Carlos Antonio López for the
    acquisition of ships, equipment, and foreign technicians
    for employment in Paraguay.

BOETTNER, JUAN MAX, 1899-1958.   Medical doctor, novel-
    ist and music composer.   Noted equally for his publica-

tions on medical topics and of musical scores. An accomplished pianist, he is also regarded as Paraguay's foremost composer of the modern era.

BOETTNER, VICTOR. Member of the so-called "Democratic" branch of the Colorado Party in the late 1940's.

BOGARDO, DEAN EUGENIO. One of the most intellectual and cultured Paraguayan priests of the pre-Triple Alliance War era. Rector of Asunción's Seminario Conciliar, and in 1867 a member of the council of state of the vice-presidency. Implicated in the alleged conspiracy plot against Marshal President Francisco Solano López, he was executed on December 21, 1868, along with several other prominent Paraguayans.

BOGARDO, COLONEL JOSE FELIX,   -1830. Prominent member of a group of Paraguayans among the liberation army of General José de San Martín in the Chilean and Peruvian independence campaigns.

BOGARIN, FRANCISCO JAVIER, 1763- ? . Member of the Superior Governing Board (Junta Superior Gubernativa) appointed by the first National Congress of June 17, 1811. No further record of his career and ultimate death.

BOGARIN, JUAN. Involved in the Conspiracy of 1820 against Dr. José Gaspar Rodríguez de Francia, Bogarín reportedly revealed the nature and composition of the plot to El Supremo.

BOGARIN, MONSEÑOR JUAN SINFORIANO, 1863-1949. Consecrated Catholic bishop of Paraguay in 1895 and subsequently in 1930 designated first Archbishop of Asunción. Known for his eloquent oratory and outstanding ability in delivering sermons in the Guaraní language.

BOGGIANO, GUIDO, 1861-1900. Italian painter, musician and poet who traveled to Paraguay to become a recognized expert in the ethnography of the Chaco Indian tribes. Author of several basic ethnographic studies. Conducted several extended Chaco expeditions on the last of which in 1900 he was presumed killed by hostile natives.

BOGGINO, DR. JUAN. Rector of Asunción's National Uni-

versity who, in December, 1944, headed a petition to
President Higinio Morínigo calling for a return to a
more democratic atmosphere in Paraguay's government.
He was subsequently removed in the mass arrests of
early 1945.

BOLAÑOS, FATHER LUIS DE, 1549-1629. Celebrated
    Franciscan missionary and regarded as the first to
    have learned Guaraní under instruction of Father Gabriel
    de la Anunciación. Arrived originally in Paraguay in
    1575 with the expedition of Adelantedo Ortiz de Zárate.
    Noted especially for a translation of the Holy Catechism
    into Guaraní which was approved by a Provincial Coun-
    cil at Lima in 1583 and by a Synod at Asunción in
    1603. Also credited with the recording of the alleged
    miracles of the formation of Lake Ypacaray, and of the
    discovery of the famed Blue Virgin of Caacupé. Died
    at Buenos Aires in October, 1629.

BOMBILLA. The metal straw/spoon used in drinking maté.

BONEO, MARTIN. Commander of a 1790 expedition sent
    from Asunción northward along the Paraguay River in
    an unsuccessful attempt to dislodge Portuguese forces
    and settlers at the new settlements of Nova Coimbra
    and Albuquerque.

BONPLAND, AIME JACQUES ALEXANDRE, 1773-1858.
    French scientist-botanist and friend of Alexander von
    Humboldt, whose experiences in Paraguay under the
    regime of Dr. José Gaspar Rodríguez de Francia rival
    those of the Scottish Robertson brothers. Coming to
    the Candelaria region of the Upper Paraná River zone
    about 1819 to study yerba maté cultivation, Bonpland
    was arrested on El Supremo's orders two years later
    and forced to become an involuntary Paraguayan resi-
    dent for nine years. Eventually released by El Supre-
    mo, he returned to Argentina's Corrientes province
    where he resided until his death in May, 1858.

BOQUERON, BATTLE OF. One of the first major battles
    of the Chaco War. An outnumbered Bolivian force
    finally surrendered on September 29, 1932, as a result
    of brilliant tactics by the then Colonel José Félix
    Estigarribia, Paraguay's foremost Chaco War hero.
    The date is still honored in Paraguay as the "Día de
    la Victoria"--Day of Victory.

BOQUERON, FORTIN see BOQUERON, BATTLE OF.

BORBON, PRINCESS CARLOTA JOAQUINA DE. Spanish
"Infanta" and sister of King Fernando VII of Spain, and
married to João VI of Portugal who moved the Portuguese court to Brazil in 1807 during the Napoleonic
era. Considering herself the successor of the captive
Fernando, Carlota Joaquina allegedly intrigued to secure sovereignty over the Spanish colonies, including
Paraguay. Such efforts are considered by several
historians as the basis for Governor Velasco's reported
negotiations with the Governor of Brazil's Rio Grande
do Sul Province in 1811 just prior to the May, 1811,
independence movement.

BORBON, FUERTE DE (FORT BORBON). Spanish Chaco
military post established in 1792 by Colonel José Antonio de Zavala y Delgadillo during the administration of
Governor Joaquín Alós y Brú. Located north of Asunción below the confluence of the Paraguay and Blanco
Rivers and known today as Fuerte Olimpo. Its purpose
was to bar further southward advance by Portuguese
from Brazil, and to facilitate expansion into the Chaco
toward Peru.

BORCHE, CARLOS. Uruguayan newsman whose reports of
alleged brutalities against civilians under the regime
of President Higinio Morínigo were given wide credence
in 1945. Borche, himself, was permitted to conduct
a personal observation of Chaco detention camps.

BORI BORI. A typical and succulent Paraguayan native soup
which includes chicken and small corn dumplings as
principal ingredients.

BORJA, CAYETANO DE. Franciscan priest who accompanied
Fernando de Mompox y Zayas to Paraguay from Lima
in 1729 at the climax of the Comunero movement.

BOURGADE LA DARDYE, E. DE, 1854-   . French investigator who visited Paraguay prior to the Triple
Alliance War. His Le Paraguay, published at Paris
in 1889, is a useful source record of the era.

BOWEN, GEORGE. One of the more singular figures in
Paraguayan history, and the only Black American so
far to be recorded therein. Bowen was apparently a

a crewman aboard one of the two Argentine vessels
captured at Corrientes by Paraguayan forces in April,
1865. Subsequently released, he came to live with
Minister Charles Ames Washburn's official family at
Asunción. His behavior irritated the minister who
sent him away. No record remains of George Bowen's
ultimate fate.

BOWLIN, JAMES B. see BOWLIN MISSION. Special Commissioner appointed in 1858 by President Buchanan
and approved by Congress to proceed with a U.S. naval
squadron to Paraguay. His mission was to settle
claims arising from the Water Witch and Rhode Island
Company affairs, and to negotiate a treaty of friendship, commerce and navigation. In Asunción in late
1858 and early 1859, Bowlin successfully accomplished
his mission, although Paraguay ultimately received a
favorable decision in arbitration to settle the Rhode
Island Company's claims.

BOWLIN MISSION. Urged by President Buchanan and authorized by Congress on June 2, 1858, for the purpose of
resolving unsettled problems with Paraguay: the Water
Witch affair, the status of the 1853 treaty, and the
Rhode Island Company claim. Special Commissioner
James B. Bowlin was appointed on September 9, 1858,
to proceed to Paraguay, using force if necessary, to
achieve his objectives. His mission included 19 American naval vessels and some 2,500 men; until then,
the largest foreign expedition to be sent against Paraguay. Following discussions with Argentine provincial
caudillo chieftain Justo José de Urquiza, Bowlin opted
to continue to Asunción with only one vessel. Contrary to expectations, he was well received in 1858 by
Carlos Antonio López who agreed to pay indemnity for
the Water Witch affair and to conclude new treaties
with the United States. Agreement was also reached
to settle the Hopkins-Rhode Island Company affair by
subsequent arbitration. In all, the Bowlin Mission
represented the most delicate crisis involving foreign
powers for Carlos Antonio López, and an early major
instance of United States intervention in Latin America.

BOX, PELHAM HORTON, 1898-1937. British historian who
prepared the definitive work entitled Origins of the
Paraguayan War, published in 1927.

BRANCO RIVER see also BLANCO RIVER. Northern fron-
tier limit formerly claimed by Paraguay prior to the
Triple Alliance War. A post-war treaty established
Brazil's claim to the Apa River, to the south of the
Branco, as the permanent frontier with Paraguay.

BRASANELLI, JOSE, 1659-1728 see also ITAPUA and
BARSONELLI, FATHER JOSE. Born in Milan and arrived in Paraguay in 1691. Noted architect and sculptor during the Jesuit mission era. Constructed, mod-
eled and decorated the old early eighteenth century
church at Itapúa, now Encarnación.

BRAY, ARTURO, 1898-   . Soldier, diplomat and author,
noted for his studies of the Triple Alliance War era
and President Francisco Solano López. As a major
he commanded Paraguay's forces, in which Alfredo
Stroessner was an officer, at the early Chaco War
battle of Boquerón. Earlier in World War I, he served
as an infantry lieutenant in the British army in France,
and was wounded in action. Noted for his Hombres y
épocas del Paraguay (1943 and 1957) and Solano López,
soldado de la gloria y del infortunio (1946).

BRIZUELA, COLONEL FRANCISCO, 1879-1947. Chaco War
hero noted for his defense of the Paraguayan positions
at the battle of Nanawa, former Asunción chief of police, and rebel participant in the 1947 Revolution.
Died in an airplane accident in 1947 while attempting
to return to Paraguay from exile at Montevideo.

BRIZUELA, JUAN JOSE, 1820-1889. Poet, novelist, statesman and diplomat. Paraguayan minister to Uruguay
whose efforts resulted in the return of trophies taken
by Uruguay in the Triple Alliance War and cancellation
by Uruguay of its war debt claims against Paraguay.

BRUGADA, ARTURO, 1895-1940. Journalist, politician and
historian. Collaborator for La Prensa, La Tribuna,
Los Principios and La Patria Asunción papers. Author
of several monographs on post Triple Alliance War
history.

BRUGUEZ RIOS, GENERAL JOSE MARIA. Regarded as
Paraguay's most competent artillery expert during the
Triple Alliance War. Executed in 1868 for suspected

treason against President López during the conspiracy
episode.

BUCARELI, FRANCISCO. Spanish intendant at Buenos
    Aires who, in July, 1767, issued orders to carry out
    the mandate of Charles III for the expulsion of the Jes-
    uits from the Paraguayan-Argentine missions region.
    The swift departure of the Jesuits brought a near-im-
    mediate and wholescale end to the once powerful and
    extensive reduction system.

BUENA ESPERANZA, FORT (NUEVA SEÑORA DE BUENA
    ESPERANZA). Small outpost built by the Pedro de
    Mendoza expedition on the lower Paraná River in 1536.
    Located near the site of the earlier Sancti Spíritu fort
    built during the expedition of Sebastián Cabot. A de-
    tachment of the Mendoza expedition under command of
    Juan de Ayolas sailed upstream from Buena Esperanza
    past the site of modern Asunción to the headwaters of
    the Paraguay River.

BUENAVENTURA, FATHER ALONSO DE. Arrived at Asun-
    ción in 1575 with the expedition of Governor Juan Ortiz
    de Zárate. A Franciscan, Father Buenaventura is
    credited together with Father Luis de Bolaños as having
    founded numerous towns and villages in the vicinity of
    Asunción.

BUENOS AIRES CHACO CONFERENCE see also ALVEAR,
    MARCELO T. DE. Unsuccessful conference at Buenos
    Aires convened by Argentina's President Alvear between
    September, 1927, and July, 1928, to settle the Para-
    guayan-Bolivian Chaco dispute. No formula for fruitful
    mediation could be agreed upon.

BURREL, VALPY AND THOMPSON see also FERROCAR-
    RIL CENTRAL DEL PARAGUAY and PARAGUAY
    CENTRAL RAILROAD. English engineering company
    credited with construction of the Paraguay Central Rail-
    way, the first government-owned railway in La Plata
    and one of the first in Latin America. Constructed
    during the administration of President Carlos Antonio
    López, and one of the major achievements of his re-
    gime. Plans for its construction were ready in 1853,
    and line work commenced in 1856. The first six loco-
    motives, all British-built, were received in 1858.
    They were the Sapucay, La Paraguaya, Asunción, 14

de Mayo, Lambaré, and Cerro León. The first stretch
of line to the suburb of Trinidad was inaugurated on
September 21, 1861, by Brigadier General Francisco
Solano López. By 1864, at the outbreak of the Triple
Alliance War, the line was operational to the Cerro
León military camp and beyond to the city of Paraguarí.
One of the early locomotives, the Sapucay, is preserved
as an historic relic at Asunción's railway station. The
line itself still operates to Encarnación for connection
with Argentina's rail system, and is one of the continent's last lines using wood-burning steam locomotives.

BURTON, SIR RICHARD FRANCIS, 1821-1890. Noted British
explorer and author who visited the Triple Alliance
War zone in 1869. His Letters from the Battlefields
of Paraguay is an excellent prime source of information
on existing conditions and personalities.

BUZO, FELIPE.   -1868. Uruguayan national who reached
Paraguay in the early independence period and remained
until his death in 1868 during the Triple Alliance War.
Recorded as the probable author of the "Himno de la
Independencia," the first national hymn of Paraguay.
Also wrote popular wartime songs honoring Francisco
Solano López and General José Díaz.

BUZZARD, H. M. S. British naval vessel which along with
its companion, H. M. S. Grappler, pursued and menaced
the Paraguayan naval ship Tacuarí near Buenos Aires
in December, 1859. The incident, probably stimulated
by the "Canstatt Affair," served further to exacerbate
Paraguayan-British relations. On board Tacuarí was
Brigadier Francisco Solano López, seeking to return
to Asunción following his successful mediation in the
Pact of San José de Flores. The incident, together
with the Canstatt problem, was discussed in Britain by
the Calvo mission.

- C -

CAACUPE see also CAACUPE, BLUE VIRGIN OF. Lo-
cated about 35 miles (54 kms) east of Asunción on
Route 2, the city was founded in 1770 by Carlos Morphi.
Famed for its Sanctuary of the Virgin of the Miracles
(Virgencita Azul de Caacupé), and as Paraguay's last
arsenal for the production of armaments during the
Paraguayan War.

CAACUPE, BLUE VIRGIN OF see also CAACUPE. Known
   also as the Virgin of the Miracles and "Virgencita
   Azul de Caacupé," this religious saint of the Catholic
   faith is Paraguay's most widely respected and visited
   image. The shrine is located in the city of Caacupé,
   about 35 miles east of Asunción.

CAAGUAZU, CITY OF. Located about 105 miles east of
   Asunción along Highway Route Two running to Puerto
   Presidente Stroessner and the Brazilian border in the
   Yguazú Falls area. Immediately east of Caaguazú are
   situated the newer Mennonite colonies and Japanese
   immigrant colonies promoted in the 1950-1960 period
   as part of the government's colonization program.

CAA-YBATE, BATTLE OF. Portuguese victory in 1756 over
   a Guaraní Indian army in the area of the Seven Missions of the Upper Uruguay River. Terminated the so-
   called "Guaraní War."

CAAZAPA GUAZU, BATTLE OF. Fought in 1639 and a significant victory by a mixed-Paraguayan-mission Indian
   army over a Brazilian mameluke slave raiding force
   in eastern Paraguay.

CABALLERISTAS. Splinter faction of the Colorado Party in
   the late 1890's which supported General Caballero. Its
   opponents, also Colorados, were the "Egusquicistas,"
   or partisans of Juan B. Egusquiza.

CABALLERO, GENERAL BERNARDINO, 1839-1912. Remembered popularly as the "Centauro de Ybicuí"--
   Centaur of Ybicuí (his birthplace) for his cavalry exploits during the Paraguayan War, General Caballero
   is remembered also as the founder in 1887 of the
   Asociación Nacional Republicana, today the Colorado
   Party. President of Paraguay 1880-1884. His remains are entombed along with others of the principal
   national heroes in Asunción's Panteón Nacional.

CABALLERO, FATHER FERNANDO. Uncle of Dr. José
   Rodríguez de Francia who materially aided El Supre-
   mo's candidacy as a member of the first Triumvirate.
   Ordained in the Franciscan Order at the University of
   Córdoba.

CABALLERO, PEDRO JUAN, 1786-1821. Military hero of

the battles against Belgrano's Argentine forces at Paraguarí and Tacuarí. Early leader of the May 14, 1811, revolutionary movement, and member of the first Superior Governing Board (Junta Superior Gubernativa). Accused of complicity in the 1820 conspiracy plot, he committed suicide in his cell. The northeastern border city of Pedro Juan Caballero is named after him.

CABALLERO, COLONEL PEDRO PABLO. Commander of the Paraguayan garrison at Piribebuy on August 12, 1869, who was captured and allegedly brutally executed by Brazilian troops. His stubborn defense of the city is included among Paraguay's Triple Alliance wartime deeds of valor.

CABALLERO, RIGOBERTO. Member of the "Democrático" branch of the Colorado Party in the late 1940's.

CABALLERO DE AÑASCO, JUAN. Asunción councilman who in some historical accounts is reported to have opposed nomination of José de Antequera y Castro as governor in the early phase of the Comunero movement.

CABALLERO DE BEDOYA, RAMON, 1881-   Noted philologist and specialist in the Guaraní language.

CABALLERO IRALA, COLONEL BASILIANO. Appointed director of the Departmento Nacional de Trabajo in 1944 by President Higinio Morínigo, but shortly ousted and forced into exile for his sponsorship of proposed mild labor legislation.

CABAÑAS, COLONEL MANUEL ATANASIO see CAVAÑAS, COLONEL MANUEL ATANASIO. Variant in the name spelling of one of the army's generals against the 1811 Argentine invasion of Manuel Belgrano.

CABEZA DE VACA, ALVAR NÚÑEZ, Circa 1490-1564. Perhaps the most durable of all Spanish conquistadors. Performed remarkable long-distance walking exploration ventures in North America's southwest, and in 1542 from the Brazilian coast to Asunción. Brought with him the first herd of horses for Paraguay. Acted as the second "Adelantado de la Plata," but was disliked by the Spanish colonists at Asunción. He was deposed and returned by them to Spain in 1544.

CABEZA DE VACA, PERO ESTOPIÑAN. Cousin of Alvar
Núñez Cabeza de Vaca who took the 1541 expedition's
ships by water route to Asunción, while Alvar Núñez
performed his overland march from the Brazilian
coast.

CABICHUI. The third of Paraguay's 1864-1870 wartime
newspapers, this three-column four-page work was
published at army headquarters from May, 1867, to
September, 1868. By means of caricature and satire
in both Spanish, Portuguese and Guaraní, it sought to
ridicule the enemy and to extol the virtues of the Paraguayan troops.

CABILDO. Also known as "Ayuntamiento"--the city hall or
city government in urban areas. Members of the
Cabildo included such officials as the "regidores,"
"alcaldes," "alferez real," and "escribano."

CABILDO DE ASUNCION see CONGRESO NACIONAL.

CABOT, SEBASTIAN, Circa 1469-1549. Sailing in Spanish
service, an early Venetian discoverer who in 1527-
1528 ascended the Paraná River and reportedly reached
Paraguayan territory in a fruitless search for the
"riches of the Indies." Recorded as the first European
to reach Paraguay by water route. He resumed service for England following his return to Spain in 1530.

CABRERA, ALONSO. Originally sent from Spain in 1537
as an official court inspector to inquire into rumored
disputes among the early Spanish conquistador arrivals.
Recommended the abandonment of Buenos Aires in
1541, and subsequently became a regidor of the Asunción government. A foe of Alvar Núñez Cabeza de
Vaca, he accompanied the deposed governor back to
Spain in 1545.

CABRERA, COLONEL FELIX. Paraguayan officer involved
in the original plan for the construction of fortified
outposts (fortines) in the central Chaco, and commander at Fortín Corrales when attacked by Bolivian forces
in December, 1932, at the beginning of the Chaco War.

CABRITA, JOÃO CARLOS DE VILAGRAN. Engineer expert
in the Brazilian army sent to Paraguay on a special
mission in 1851-1852 to assist in the planning and con-

struction of the Humaitá fortifications above the confluence of the Paraguay and Paraná Rivers. A hero
in the early phases of the Triple Alliance War, Colonel Cabrita was killed while on a patrol in 1867.

CABRIZA, COLONEL FRANCISCO LINO. Paraguayan War
hero, member of the escort regiment of Marshal López
and one of his closest personal adjutants. Witnessed
the death of Paraguay's president at Cerro Corá on
March 1, 1870, and helped dig the grave in which he
was temporarily buried.

CACERES, FELIPE DE. A member of the 1541 Alvar
Núñez Cabeza de Vaca expedition, Cáceres was an
able conquistador who contributed much to Paraguay's
early development until his forced return to Spain in
1570 following disputes with Bishop Pedro Fernández
de la Torre. Particularly noted for his introduction
into Paraguay in 1569 of a large cattle and sheep herd.

CACIQUE LAMBARE. The fourth of Paraguay's 1864-1870
wartime newspapers, this was a bi-weekly published
at Asunción by the government press between July,
1867, and September, 1868. Its last editions were
printed at nearby Luque, to which the government was
moved after the Brazilian fleet's bombardment of
Asunción. Lambaré, as the paper was known, was
the first one published entirely in Guaraní.

CACIQUE LAMBARE. Indian chieftain residing in Asunción's
area who originally fought the first Spanish conquistador arrivals, but who later became their ally against
other native tribes.

CADOGAN, LEON, 1899-   . Paraguay's foremost ethnographic expert noted for his research on the origins
and customs of native Guaraní Indian tribes. Currently curator of Guayakí Indian affairs of the Government's Ministry of Culture and Education.

CALDERON, MENCIA DE see also SANABRIA, MARIA
DE. Mother of Juan and Diego Sanabria, ill-fated
"Adelantados" who never reached Paraguay; intrepid
woman adventurer who, though shipwrecked in 1551
near the Atlantic Coast Brazilian island of Santa Ca-
talina, proceeded with her expedition on foot to Asunción, taking with her the first cattle herd to reach
Paraguay.

CALLEJON HISTORICO   see also   CASA DE LA INDEPEN-
DENCIA.   This small but well-preserved lane alongside
the Casa de la Independencia in downtown Asunción was
reputedly used by the Paraguayan conspirators in the
independence movement from Spain, May 14, 1811.

CALVO MISSION   see also   CANSTATT, SANTIAGO.   Special
Paraguayan mission headed by Carlos Calvo.   Sent to
Great Britain to argue Paraguay's position in the
"Canstatt Affair" of 1859.   Britain's court of inquiry
refused to accept Paraguay's claims and the matter
was finally settled by President Carlos Antonio López'
action in freeing the imprisoned Canstatt.

CAMACHO, FORTIN.   Original name for Fortín Mariscal
Estigarribia, one of Paraguay's most important Chaco
military posts.

CAMALOTES.   Floating patches or "islands" of hyacinths on
the Paraguay River.   Utilized successfully as camoflage
by Paraguayan soldiers in the Triple Alliance War in
attacks upon Brazil's naval vessels.

CAMARGO, JUAN DE.   Spanish conquistador, probably a
member of the Ñufrio de Chaves expedition from Peru,
who was executed at Asunción for treason by Domingo
Martínez de Irala.

CAMBA   see   VOLUNTARIOS DE PATRIA.   A nickname
bordering on an epithet used by Paraguayans during the
Triple Alliance War, referring to Brazil's Negro soldiers.

CAMBYRETA.   Fertile dairy zone located to the east of the
southern riverport of Encarnación, and locale for the
settlement after World War II of a modestly prosperous
German refugee colony project.

CAMINO DE ANTAS.   Guaraní Indian expression referring
to the Milky Way.

CAMINO REAL.   The approximate 700-mile long old colonial
trail leading from Sao Vicente on Brazil's Atlantic
Coast near Santos across the interior to Paraguay.
Another variant of the Camino Real led from Asunción
south to Pilar and the Humaitá area.

CAMINOS, LUIS. Last minister of war in the government
of Francisco Solano López, serving between 1868-1870.
Killed with López at Cerro Corá, March 1, 1870.

CAMIRE, CHIEF. Chief of a Xarayes Indian tribe in the
headwaters area of the Paraguay River who proved
friendly to an exploring expedition sent to the north by
Alvar Núñez Cabeza de Vaca in 1543.

CAMISÃO, COLONEL CARLOS DE MORAIS. Commander of
the ill-fated Brazilian army expedition which in early
1867 sought to invade Paraguay from the north during
the Triple Alliance War. Camisão and many of his
troops died on the epic retreat which became the theme
of one of Brazil's Visconde de Taunay's famous literary
works, the Retreat from Laguna.

CAMPAMENTO CERRO LEON. "Training Camp of Cerro
León." Probably the most popular Paraguayan martial
tune and march, and today the theme song of the national radio station. The precise authors are unknown,
but were possibly popular guitarists among soldiers
stationed at Humaitá during the Triple Alliance War.
According to one music source, the appearance in 1865
of "Campamento Cerro León" represented the birth of
the Paraguayan polka.

CAMPICHUELO, ACTION AT see also THOMPSON, MAJOR
PABLO. Skirmish in extreme northern Argentina near
the Paraná River won by Manuel Belgrano's Argentine
invasion force on December 19, 1810, over a Paraguay
force commanded by Major Pablo Thompson. A prelude to the later battles of Cerro Porteño and Tacuarí
in 1811.

CAMPO. Name universally used in Paraguay to denote interior rural areas in contrast to urban areas.

CAMPO GRANDE, BATTLE OF see ACOSTA ÑU, BATTLE
OF. Name used in some historical accounts, particularly those of Brazilian authorship, for the battle of
Acosta Ñú, fought August 16, 1869, and the last major
action of the Triple Alliance War prior to final action
at Cerro Corá, March 1, 1870.

CAMPO JORDAN see KILOMETER SEVEN, CONTEST FOR.

CAMPO VIA, BATTLE OF   see also   ALIGUATA-ZENTENO,
    BATTLE OF.   Major Paraguayan Chaco War victory
    at the close of 1933, capping the Aliguatá-Zenteno
    campaign.   A brilliant encircling movement directed
    by General Jóse Félix Estigarribia resulted in the sur-
    render at Campo Vía of more than 8,000 Bolivian
    troops and the capture of immense supplies of war
    equipment.   The debacle forced the retirement of Ger-
    man General Hans Kundt as Bolivia's field commander.

CAMPOS, AUGUSTIN DE.   Spanish conquistador in the early
    discovery and conquest era who figured in the expedi-
    tion of Alvar Núñez Cabeza de Vaca.

CAMPOS, BERNARDO.   Prominent member of the Colorado
    Party hierarchy in the period following the 1947 Revolu-
    tion at the close of the Morínigo era.

CAMPOS, COLONEL FEDERICO CARNEIRO DE.   Newly ap-
    pointed governor of Brazil's Mato Grosso Province and
    captured by Paraguayan forces while a passenger
    aboard the steamer Marquês de Olinda in November,
    1864.   Seizure of the vessel represented the beginning
    of the long Triple Alliance or Paraguayan War.   Car-
    neiro de Campos died in a Paraguayan prison camp
    in 1867.

CAMPOS CERVERA, ANDRES   see also   HERRERIA, JU-
    LIAN DE LA.   Paraguay's major contribution to inter-
    nationally known art, who preferred to use the adopted
    name of Julián de la Herrería.

CAMPOS CERVERA, HERIB, 1908-1953.   Major figure in
    the post-Chaco War era of Paraguayan poetry.   His
    principal work is Ceniza redimida, published in 1950.
    Died at Buenos Aires.

CAMPOS CERVERA, JULIAN   see also   CAMPOS CERVERA,
    ANDRES.   Variant in the name spelling of Andrés
    Campos Cervera.   Modern Paraguayan painter special-
    izing in Indian motifs.   Known also as Julián de la
    Herrería.

CAÑA.   Next to non-alcoholic yerba maté, the Paraguayan
    national drink.   A sugar cane distillate, it is similar
    to rum, aguardiente, puro, and cachaça found in others
    of the Latin American republics.   Use of caña is al-

leged to have been a strong contributing factor to the dissolution of the nineteenth century Nueva Australia colonization project, while American Minister Martin T. McMahon at Piribebuy in 1869 noted that it was a welcome addition to his domestic surroundings.

CAÑADA ESPERANZA see CAÑADA-STRONGEST, BATTLE OF.

CAÑADA-STRONGEST, BATTLE OF. One of Paraguay's few Chaco War defeats, this action occurred in May, 1934, and involved the surrender of a portion of a Paraguayan division which had been surrounded. The defeat, however, failed to halt Paraguay's westward advance toward the Bolivian Andean foothills.

CANDELARIA. Originally the name of an area in extreme northern Paraguay near Bahía Negra used as a point of departure for early Spanish expeditions toward Alto Perú (Bolivia). It was never a significant inhabited point. In the Jesuit Mission era of the seventeenth and eighteenth centuries, Candelaria was a name given to a zone occupied by the Jesuit reduction or mission system across the Paraná River at Encarnación in northern Argentina. The area still contains some of the largest and most important mission ruins.

CANDEVILLA, PEDRO VICENTE. Conspirator who, with Pedro Somellera, led an unsuccessful coup against the new Junta government of Paraguay in September, 1811.

CAÑETE, AUGUSTO. One of the principal leaders of the Communist Party in the 1940-1950 period.

CAÑETE, PEDRO VICENTE, 1754-1816. Regarded by some as the most brilliant mind appearing in colonial Paraguay, Cañete became a royalist sympathizer who held high positions in Spain's colonial government at Buenos Aires and in Upper Peru.

CANSTATT, JAMES see CANSTATT, SANTIAGO.

CANSTATT, SANTIAGO (OR JAMES). Uruguayan national claiming British citizenship through his father who in 1859 became embroiled as a suspect in a conspiracy plot in Asunción. His arrest and the rejection by President Carlos Antonio López of the British consul's

demands for his release, produced a rupture in Paraguayan-British relations.   A British court of inquiry
declined to accept Paraguay's claims, and the affair
was only settled upon the release by López of Canstatt.
Coincident with this event, relationships with Great
Britain were further strained when HM ships Buzzard
and Grappler harrassed the Paraguayan vessel Tacuari
off Buenos Aires and carrying Brigadier Francisco
Solano López aboard.

CAPIATA.   Located about 12 miles (22 kms) east of Asunción
on Route 2, this village was founded in 1640 by Governor Martín de Ledesma Balderrama.   Known principally for its pre-independence era church constructed
by native Indians under supervision of Franciscan missionaries.

CAPITULACION.   Royal license contracted between the Spanish crown and a conquistador, usually specifying that
in return for the privately assumed expenses of conquest the conquistador would receive title to a specified
amount of land and the profits to be derived therefrom.

CAPTAIN GENERAL.   Spanish colonial administrative position about equal to that of viceroy but on a provincial
basis.   Directly responsible to the Council of the
Indies unless the province was formally included within a viceroyalty.

CARAGUATA see also TREUENFELDT, R. FISCHER VON.
A species of Agave plant from which, during the Triple
Alliance War, Paraguayans under the supervision of
German engineer von Treuenfeldt were able to produce
a substitute for newsprint.   One of the more ingenious
innovations of the many developed by Paraguay during
the war.

CARAGUATAY.   Founded in 1770, this interior city is located about 60 miles (95 kms) to the northeast of
Asunción in the valley of the Yhaguy River.   Noted
today for its small industries engaged in the production
of petit grain oil.   Near it is situated Vapor Cué, site
of the scuttling of the remaining ships of the Paraguayan navy, the rusted hulks of which are still visible.

CARDENAS, FATHER BERNARDINO DE.   Bishop of Asun-

ción during 1642-1651 and one of the most controversial figures in Paraguayan church history. A Franciscan and an enemy of the Jesuits, he continuously
sought to undermine their position and strength in Paraguay. Such excesses and his disputes with the governor were factors which finally forced his departure
for his native Bolivia in 1651.

CARDOZO, EFRAIM, 1906-   . One of modern Paraguay's
most prominent and internationally known historians.
Specializes in the general history and historiography
of Paraguay, and the Triple Alliance War. President
in 1971 of Paraguay's Liberal Radical political party.

CARDOZO, RAMON INDALECIO, 1876-1943. Prominent
historian and educator responsible for major reforms
introduced in 1924 into Paraguay's primary instruction
system. The changes involved abandonment of the
former so-called encyclopedic method and the introduction of courses in the trades. Also noted for his
published research on his native city of Villarrica.
One of the founders of the Instituto Paraguayo de Investigaciones Históricas, the nation's foremost historical association.

CARILLO, JUANA PABLA see CARILLO DE LOPEZ,
JUANA PABLA. Wife of Carlos Antonio López and
mother of Francisco Solano López.

CARILLO, COLONEL LUCAS. Paraguayan officer and relative of Francisco Solano López who surrendered with
Colonel George Thompson at Angostura, December 30,
1868, at the end of the Pikysyry campaign of the
Triple Alliance War.

CARILLO DE LOPEZ, JUANA PABLA. Wife of President
Carlos Antonio López and mother of Marshal President
Francisco Solano López. Survived the last action of
the Triple Alliance War at Cerro Corá, March 1, 1870.

CARIO INDIANS. Branch of the Guaraní Indian family, said
to have possessed a superior culture, who lived in the
Asunción area at the time of the Spanish discovery
and conquest.

CARISIMO, JOSE. The central figure of an unauthenticated
tale of Dr. Francia's era who allegedly failed to obey

El Supremo's order to repair a street fault which had inconvenienced the dictator. He was forced to wear leg irons ordered by his own wife until friends rescued him by paying El Supremo's stipulated fine.

CARLISLE, J. MANDEILLE. Attorney who defended Paraguay's position in the 1860 arbitration proceedings at Washington stemming from the Hopkins-United States and Paraguay Navigation Company case.

CARLOS ANTONIO LOPEZ, FORTIN see also PITIANTUTA, LAKE. Located on the east bank of Lake Pitiantuta in the central Chaco. Attacked by Bolivian troops on June 15, 1932, in an incident which marked the beginning of the Chaco War.

CARLYLE, THOMAS, 1795-1881. Famed early nineteenth century British essayist and author noted for his studies of contemporary leaders. His 1843 essay on Paraguay's Dr. Francia was a particularly illuminating and favorable portrait arousing early European attention to South American affairs.

CARMELITA. Central figure of a tale regarding amorous adventures of the adolescent Francisco Solano López. Carmelita, a pretty Asunceña, attracted young López' attention. She reportedly resisted his advances, however, as the betrothed of Carlos Decoud. López is alleged to have had treason charges pressed which resulted in Decoud's execution.

CARMEN (EL), BATTLE OF. Major Paraguayan Chaco War victory occurring on November 16, 1934, and involving the capture of some 7,000 Bolivian prisoners.

CARMEN (EL), FORTIN see CARMEN (EL), BATTLE OF.

CARRERA, CARLOS. Asunción intellectual who was discharged from his teaching position and exiled during the early 1945 repressive measures of the Higinio Morínigo regime.

CARRERAS, ANTONIO DE LAS. Uruguayan diplomat sent to Asunción by the Blanco government in 1864 in an unsuccessful effort to solicit aid from Francisco Solano López before growing Brazilian and Argentine pressure. One of several incidents preluding the Triple Alliance War.

CARRETAS.   Form of transport utilized in rural areas or
the "campo," usually consisting of two-wheeled carts
drawn by oxen or mules.   In some zones, particularly
in the Alto Paraná region, such "carretas" are strongly
reminiscent of the covered wagons of America's Far
West.

CARVALLO, HECTOR.   Provisional president of Paraguay
in 1902 following the revolt which overthrew President
Emilio Aceval on January 9.

CASA DE CONTRATACION.   Spain's Board of Trade located
in Seville, responsible for the administration of all
economic matters between Spain and her New World
colonies.

CASA DE LA INDEPENDENCIA.   Situated on Calle 14 de
Mayo between Calle Palma and Calle Presidente Franco
in downtown Asunción, this remarkably well-preserved
historic site marks the point at which Paraguay's independence movement from Spain began the night of
May 14, 1811, the national independence anniversary
date.   Now a national historical site, the old colonial-
style residence contains an interesting collection of
contemporary relics.

CASADO, CARLOS see also PUERTO CASADO. Argentine
financier and for many years "Quebracho King" of
Paraguay's Chaco.   Purchased enormous holdings in
the 1880's, and constructed Puerto Casado, which became the Chaco's most important port for cattle and
quebracho shipments on the Paraguay River above
Asunción.   The availability of his financial empire was
reportedly an asset to several Paraguayan government
administrations.

CASAL, JOSE MAURICIO.   Once wealthy Paraguayan, resident near Asunción, who figures in history as an early
personal friend and confidant of Charles Ames Washburn, first American Minister to Paraguay in the
1860's.

CASTEL FUERTE, MARQUES DE see also ARMENDARIZ,
JOSE DE.   Viceroy of Peru at Lima and foe of José
de Antequera y Castro during the Comunero episode of
the 1720's.   Ordered Antequera expelled from Paraguay, and eventually imprisoned him at Lima where he
was executed on July 5, 1731.

CASTRO, GENERAL ENRIQUE. Commander-in-chief of the
remaining Uruguayan units in the allied army after
1866 in the Triple Alliance War.

CATALDINO, FATHER JOSE. Early Jesuit missionary who
reached Paraguay in 1604 and subsequently was responsible for the foundings of several missions or reductions at Villa Rica del Espíritu Santo and the Guairá
region.

CATEDRAL DE LA CIUDAD DE NUESTRA SEÑORA DE LA
ASUNCION. Another of Asunción's ancient historical
sites, the Cathedral was constructed in 1850. Located
near the old Cabildo, today the National Congress.
Considered Paraguay's fifth cathedral in terms of age.

CATHOLIC UNIVERSITY see UNIVERSIDAD CATOLICA.

CAUDILLO. Term frequently used in referring to the local
political chief or leader in rural areas.

CAVALLERO, PEDRO JUAN see CABALLERO, PEDRO
JUAN. Variant in the name spelling of one of the
principal 1811 independence movement heroes.

CAVAÑAS, COLONEL MANUEL ATANASIO, ? -1828. One
of Paraguay's most wealthy and influential men of the
early independence period. Took command of Paraguay's army after the flight of Spanish Governor Velasco at the battle of Paraguarí, and commander-in-
chief at the subsequent battle of Tacuarí, 1811. Never
prominent in the early independence governments possibly because of poor relationships with Dr. José
Gaspar Rodríguez de Francia.

CAXIAS, DUQUE DE see also LIMA E SILVA, LUIS
ALVES DE. Brazil's greatest soldier, commander-
in-chief of the allied army during the later stages of
the Triple Alliance War, and the only Brazilian to be
named Duque (Duke) in Dom Pedro II's empire.

CEDULA REAL OF SEPTEMBER 12, 1537. Royal order
from the Spanish Government authorizing the newly
established Province of Paraguay to elect its own high
officials. The right was abolished after 1735 as a
penalty against Paraguay for the Comunero Revolt.

CEDULAS REALES.   Royal orders and instructions issued
     by Spain's centralized government applying to adminis-
     trative affairs in the New World possessions.

CELSO PUSINIERI Y HIJOS.   Italian company credited with
     establishing the first shoe factory in Paraguay.   Rep-
     resentative of the spill-over of Italian immigrants enter-
     ing La Plata in the late nineteenth century who reached
     Paraguay.

CENSO, MARCO.   Mentioned in historical records as a
     Spanish shipwright at Asunción in the early colonial
     era.

CENTAURO DE YBICUI--CENTAUR OF YBICUI see CA-
     BALLERO, GENERAL BERNARDINO.   Popular name
     for General Bernardino Caballero, Triple Alliance War
     hero and founder of the Colorado Party, who was born
     in the interior village of Ybicuí.

CENTENO, DIEGO.   Governor of Charcas (Upper Peru) in
     the late 1540's who was appointed as Governor of Para-
     guay by Viceroy Pedro de la Gasca, but whose death
     in 1549 nullified the possibility of his assuming the
     post.

CENTINELA (EL).   A semi-official wartime weekly newspa-
     per published between April, 1867, and July, 1868.   A
     complement to El Seminario, it had as its purpose that
     of providing amusing reading matter by inclusion of a
     permanent column in Guaraní to promote the confidence
     and morale of the troops.

CENTRAL PARAGUAYAN RAILWAY see PARAGUAY CEN-
     TRAL RAILWAY, and FERROCARRIL PRESIDENTE
     CARLOS ANTONIO LOPEZ--FPCAL.

CENTRO DEMOCRATICO see also LIBERAL PARTY.
     Original name for the Liberal Party.   Founded on July
     2, 1887, as a result of protests against the proposed
     Aceval-Tamayo Treaty of that year which contemplated
     acceptance of Bolivian Chaco claims.   Founded about
     a month before the Asociación Nacional Republicana,
     the Colorado Party.   Principal organizers were Anto-
     nio Taboada, José de la Cruz Ayala and Cecilio Báez.

CENTURION, CARLOS R., 1902-1969.   Noted twentieth cen-

tury Paraguayan intellectual historian and author whose
work Historia de las letras paraguayas, published at
Asunción in two editions in 1946 and 1961, is a definitive one covering the evolution of a national culture.
A monumental research achievement, this work encom-
passes all facets of Paraguay's historical development.

CENTURION, MAJOR GASPAR, 1843-1898. Triple Alliance
War veteran who fought throughout the entire war.
His Recuerdos de la Guerra del Paraguay, published
in 1931 and edited by his son Juan Bautista Centurión,
is a valuable source record of the era. Public official
in the postwar period, and several times president of
the Chamber of Deputies.

CENTURION, JUAN BAUTISTA, 1878-1953. Prolific Asunción journalist in the early twentieth century. Co-
founder and editor of the Revista Histórica in 1899,
and an editor of El Cívico, organ of a splinter group
of the Liberal Party. Also director of the Revista del
Touring Club paraguayo, and author of several manuscripts on Paraguay's highway system.

CENTURION Y MARTINEZ, JUAN CRISOSTOMO, 1840-1903.
Diplomat, journalist and author. Secretary and trusted
aide to Marshal President Francisco Solano López, and
a survivor of Cerro Corá, the last action of the Triple
Alliance War. Appointed to several cabinet positions.
Author of Memorias o reminiscencias históricas sobre
la guerra del Paraguay, published at Buenos Aires,
1894-1897, one of the more complete and useful war
memoirs from the Paraguayan side.

CEPO URUGUAYANA. A particularly painful form of torture
similar to "bucking" as practiced in the Union Army
in the American Civil War. Employed in La Plata
republics to force confessions from prisoners. Suspects during Paraguay's 1868 conspiracy period frequently underwent this torment.

CERDA, GREGORIO DE LA. Junta member in the early
independence era. Reportedly resigned his post because of suspicion possibly instigated by Dr. José
Gaspar Rodríguez de Francia, of undue friendship with
Buenos Aires contacts.

CERRO CORA. Undoubtedly the historic site of most emotional impact in Paraguay. Located about 80 miles northeast of the riverport of Concepción near the highway to the border city of Pedro Juan Caballero, and near the small Aquidabán-Nigüí River. At this point on March 1, 1870, pursuing Brazilian army units attacked the Paraguayan army's last camp and killed or captured all defenders. Among those killed fighting to the last were Marshal President López, his teenage son, and Vice President Sánchez. Marshal López' last words before he was killed remain a proud Paraguayan national heritage: "Muero con mi patria!"--I die with my nation! He was buried in a shallow grave by his Irish consort, Mme. Elisa Alicia Lynch, who accompanied him on the long 1869-1870 retreat from Piribebuy. His remains were later exhumed in 1937 and deposited in Asunción's Pantheon of the Heroes.

CERRO LAMBARE. A curious conical-shaped high wooded hill about four miles south of Asunción on the east bank of the Paraguay River. A landmark indicating the nearby vicinity of Asunción, and named after an Indian chieftain who lived in the area at the time of the Spanish arrival.

CERRO LEON. Located about 38 miles (62 kms) east of Asunción near the village of Pirayú and along the railway facing the Cordillera de los Altos. Part of a level grass plain stretching 100 kms long and about six kms wide from Lake Ypacaray to the city of Villarrica. Probably originating after the inauguration of President Francisco Solano López in 1862, Cerro León became the Paraguayan army's general headquarters and training site. It was from there that López sent instructions to halt and seize the Brazilian river steamer, Marqués de Olinda, a move which officially began the Triple Alliance War. Nothing remains of the Cerro León site today except the brick and stone residences and headquarters buildings, both of which are preserved as national historic sites. A basin of a water stream in the nearby Cordillera is reputed to be the bathing pool of Mme. Elisa Alicia Lynch.

CERRO PELADO. Rocky hill near the east central city of Villarrica on which strange and as yet undeciphered hieroglyphics are found. Possibly of pre-Colombian origin.

CERRO PORTEÑO. Near the city of Paraguarí, this small
tree-covered hill marks the site of the battle between
Argentine and Paraguayan forces on January 19, 1811.
Stopped by the Paraguayans, the Argentine commander,
General Manuel Belgrano was forced to retreat south
to Tacuarí where he was again defeated. The two actions halted Argentine efforts to retain hegemony over
the Spanish Province of Paraguay, and were significant
to the subsequent revolutionary movement in May, 1811,
at Asunción.

CESAR, FRANCISCO. Member of the 1527-28 Sebastián
Cabot expedition to La Plata who performed an exploration of the area northwest of the Paraná River. His
reports of an "El Dorado" golden city, heard from Indians, stimulated further Spanish exploration of the
Paraná-Paraguay Rivers.

CESPEDES, LIEUTENANT. Mentioned in records as a Paraguayan exile, possibly a member of the Legión Paraguaya, who acted as a guide for the Argentine and
Brazilian armies during the Triple Alliance War. Accompanied the American Allen brothers on their balloon ascents during the Humaitá siege.

CESPEDES JERAY (XERIA), LUIS DE. Appointed governor
of Paraguay in 1634. His regime was noted principally for his alleged inability or unwillingness to cope
with the growing frequency and extent of Brazilian
mameluke slaving raids in the Jesuit mission region.

CHACO. The huge, near desolate region west of the Paraguay River stretching to Bolivia's Andean foothills and
composing about two-thirds of modern Paraguay's land
area. It is both a "Green Hill" and an arid desert,
depending upon location and climatic factors. A vast
alluvial plain, it forms the northern portion of the
Chaco Boreal stemming from Argentina. Though its
potential economic value is still to be proven, the
Chaco has historically represented an unknown region
possessing both capacity as a ranching zone and probably as the site of petroleum discoveries. Additionally,
since the 1920's, it is the location of Mennonite colonization projects. Traditionally an area of contention
between Paraguay and Bolivia, its importance was
magnified in the late nineteenth century by the War of
the Pacific which resulted in elimination of Bolivia's

access to the Pacific. Bolivia's search for an eastern
outlet, and the possibilities of significant petroleum
discoveries, engendered the Chaco War of the 1930's,
Latin America's bloodiest and longest war after the
Triple Alliance War of the nineteenth century. Paraguay's victory gave it nearly the maximum of its territorial claims while Bolivia's pretensions were re-
stricted to a zone along the Andean foothills. In the
1960's prospects for future development of the Chaco
were brightened with completion of the Trans Chaco
Highway, a segment of the Pan American Highway from
Asunción to the Bolivian border.

CHACO COMMISSION, LEAGUE OF NATIONS. Ineffective
special commission appointed by the League to seek a
formula for ending the Chaco War. Its one achievement was the securing of a temporary peace in late
1933 which was soon terminated by renewal of hostili-
ties in January, 1934.

CHACO MEDIATION COMMISSION. Special inter-American
commission composed of representatives of Argentina,
Chile, Uruguay, Brazil, and the United States which
arranged a lasting truce to end the Chaco War on June
12, 1935.

CHACO NEUTRAL MILITARY COMMISSION. Special commission formed after the June, 1935, truce ending the
Chaco War for the purpose of establishing fixed lines
to which each of the former combatants would be required to withdraw.

CHACO PEACE CONFERENCE. Provided for by the Protocol of June 12, 1935, which brought the Chaco War
to a halt. After many vicissitudes, a definitive Chaco
peace was achieved on July 21, 1938, due largely to
the participation of Paraguay's Chaco War hero General
Jóse Félix Estigarribia.

CHACO VETERANS ASSOCIATION see NATIONAL VETER-
ANS ASSOCIATION. Association of Chaco War veterans which became a powerful political factor particularly in the period immediately following the end of the
war and prior to the Febrerista Revolt of 1936.

CHACO WAR. Most serious, prolonged and bloodiest conflict in twentieth century Latin America, as well as

the second most sanguinary in the area's entire history,
ranking after the Triple Alliance War of 1864-1870.
Fought between June, 1932, and June, 1935, between
Paraguay and Bolivia, the war concerned sovereignty
over the Chaco.   Perhaps the two most important factors sparking its outbreak were a) rivalry over the
still unknown economic potential of the Chaco, especially petroleum deposits, and b) Bolivia's search for an
outlet to the sea following amputation of its coastal
zone as the result of the War of the Pacific with Chile.
Although Paraguay had never pursued an active colonization policy in the Chaco, it had historically pressed
its claims to the area since the discovery period.
Full-scale war broke out in 1932 after a number of
border incidents and international efforts to arrange
mediation of the sovereignty dispute.   It lasted three
years and involved about 80,000 killed, of which an
estimated two-thirds were Bolivian.   In many respects
it was a forerunner of World War II like the Spanish
Civil War.   The fighting took place in one of the most
unlikely regions for a war in the world--an alternating
parched desert and a jungle Green Hell.   Paraguay
ultimately won due to superior leadership in the person
of General Jóse Félix Estigarribia, and the ability of
the Paraguayan soldier to adjust swifter to the Chaco
environment than his Bolivian counterpart accustomed
to an Andes mountain habitat.   At the war's close,
Paraguay received nearly the maximum of its Chaco
territorial claims.   The conflict engendered a period
of unrest in Paraguay which led to the Febrerista Revolt in 1936, while Bolivia's defeat produced a surge
of nationalism and inward searching which eventually
resulted in the movement of the MNR--Movimiento
Nacionalista Revolucionario.   In all, the war gave the
world the sad spectacle of two largely Indian populated
republics desperately striving to liquidate one another.

CHACRA.   Name applied to the small farms, usually about
one or two acres in size, of interior Paraguay's peasant population.

CHAMBER OF TRUTH.   An alleged secret torture chamber
used by El Supremo, Dr. Francia, to extort confessions from political prisoners.   The reported existence
of the chamber was an additional factor in cooling con-
spiratorial activities during El Supremo's administration.

CHAMORRO, DELFIN, 1863-1931. Together with Ramón
    Indalecio Cardozo, a personal friend, one of Paraguay's
    most accomplished and honored educators. Though
    without formal academic degrees, Chamorro became an
    acknowledged expert in Spanish language grammar and
    construction. Appointed secretary of the National Uni-
    versity in 1911, and awarded the honorary title of pro-
    fessor in 1923.

CHANEY, SAMUEL. Quartermaster of the USS Water Witch
    killed in the February, 1855, exchange of gunfire with
    Paraguay's Fort Itapirú on the Paraná River. The
    government of Carlos Antonio López subsequently agreed
    to a $10,000 indemnity for Chaney's death during the
    1859 visit at Asunción of the Bowlin Mission.

CHARCAS, AUDIENCIA OF. Administrative district of the
    Viceroyalty of Peru under Spain's colonial system.
    From 1542 to 1776, when the Viceroyalty of La Plata
    was established, the Province of Paraguay was admin-
    istratively subject to the Viceroyalty of Peru and the
    Audiencia of Charcas. Charcas, modern-day Bolivia,
    was also known as Upper Peru.

CHATAS. Low-lying wooden barges usually mounting one
    artillery piece used by the Paraguayan army in forays
    against the Brazilian fleet during the Humaitá campaign
    of the Triple Alliance War.

CHAVES, ALVARO DE. Spanish conquistador in Paraguay's
    early conquest period, and a follower of Martínez de
    Irala in expeditions across the Chaco toward Bolivia.

CHAVES, FEDERICO, 1882?-   . Prominent Colorado Par-
    ty leader in the late 1940's during the administration of
    Higinio Morínigo, and president during the period 1949-
    1954. Removed from office by a military coup in 1954.
    His regime was followed by that of General Alfredo
    Stroessner.

CHAVES, FRANCISCO C., 1875-1961. Educator and states-
    man. Professor of civil law, rector of the National
    University, holder of numerous government cabinet
    posts, president of the Supreme Court, and president
    of the Banco de la República. Special envoy to sev-
    eral international conferences.

CHAVES, JUAN RAMON   see also   COLORADO PARTY,
     1902-   . Asunción lawyer and president of the Junta
     Gubernativa del Partido Colorado (Governing Board of
     the Colorado Party).

CHAVES, JULIO CESAR, 1907-   . One of modern Para-
     guay's most prominent historians, known international-
     ly for his well-researched works on the periods of
     Dr. Francia, President Carlos Antonio López and the
     Triple Alliance War.

CHAVES, COLONEL MANUEL WENCESLAO, 1912-   .
     Director of the Historical and Military Institute and
     the Historical and Military Museum of the Ministry of
     National Defense in Asunción. A Chaco War veteran,
     Colonel Chaves is a specialist in both the Triple Al-
     liance and Chaco Wars.

CHAVES, MARIA CONCEPCION DE LOURDES   see CHAVES,
     MARIA CONCEPCION LEYES DE.

CHAVES, MARIA CONCEPCION LEYES DE, 1889-   .
     One of Paraguay's leading feminine authors, Mrs.
     Chaves has produced several significant works includ-
     ing a study of the life of Mme. Elisa Alicia Lynch,
     consort of Marshal President Francisco Solano López.
     Member, director and representative on numerous na-
     tional and international cultural organizations including
     the UN, OAS and UNESCO.

CHAVES, ÑUFRIO DE, 1518-1568. Explorer of the area
     known as Alto Perú (Bolivia) in the late 1550's, and
     founder of the city of Santa Cruz in 1561. His claims
     for independence of the region from La Plata were ap-
     proved by the Viceroy of Peru, thus resulting in the
     first reduction or "desmembración" in the size of the
     Province of Paraguay. Friend and confidante of Do-
     mingo Martínez de Irala, and recorded as the first
     conqueror of the Chaco.

CHAVEZ, OSVALDO, 1918-   . Contemporary author,
     diplomat and philosopher; one of the founders of Para-
     guay's first school of philosophy. Formerly president
     of the Banco Central del Paraguay, ambassador to the
     United States and to the Organization of American
     States. Regarded as one of modern Paraguay's most
     brilliant intellectuals.

CHIPA. A Paraguayan delicacy of various styles and forms, usually made with mandioca flour and cheese. Similar to buns or cakes and taken with maté.

CHIPA-ABATI. Small Paraguayan bread-like cake made of corn flour.

CHIPA-PIRU. Small drier type of chipá, made especially in the village of Barrero Grande, or Eusebio Ayala, east of Asunción.

CHIPA-SOO. A Paraguayan delicacy, similar to chipá-abatí, but filled with ground meat.

CHIQUITOS, DESMEMBRACION DE see also DESMEMBRA-CION DE CHIQUITOS. First formal separation in 1560 of land area from the original region designated as Paraguay.

CHIRIFE, COLONEL ADOLFO. Minister of war in the 1921 administration of President Manuel Gondra. Led a revolt against the subsequent provisional government of Dr. Eusebio Ayala which eventually forced the latter's resignation in favor of Eligio Ayala.

CHIRIGUANO INDIANS. A fierce and adept Chaco tribe, possibly a member of the Guaycurú group, which resided in the general area west of Asunción and bordering the Pilcomayo River. Noted in historical accounts for their resistance to the Spanish conquest.

CHIRIGUELO, PICADA DE see also CERRO CORA. Small valley and clearing at Cerro Corá in extreme northeastern Paraguay, where on March 1, 1870, the final action of the Triple Alliance War occurred.

CHIRIPAS. Form of leather breeches in skirt style drawn up between the legs. In common use in eighteenth and nineteenth century rural Paraguay and neighboring Uruguay and Argentina. Ranch hands and gauchos commonly wore this item.

CHODASIEWICZ, MAJOR ROBERT A. Polish-born special engineer attached to the Argentine army in Paraguay during the Triple Alliance War. Accompanied the American Allen brothers on their balloon ascents at the Humaitá siege. Regretably, he left no known memoirs of his wartime experiences.

CHRISTIAN DEMOCRATIC PARTY see also PARTIDO
    DEMOCRATA CRISTIANO and MOVIMIENTO SOCIAL-
    DEMOCRATA CRISTIANO. The youngest of Paraguay's
    modern political parties, espousing principles similar
    to the Christian Democrat parties in Chile, Brazil and
    Venezuela. Founded at Asunción May 15, 1960.

CHRISTIE, WILLIAM D. Special envoy sent by Great Brit-
    ain to Asunción in June, 1858, to negotiate a friend-
    ship, commerce and navigation treaty with the Carlos
    Antonio López government. After waiting vainly for
    20 days for negotiations to commence, Christie be-
    lieved himself diplomatically slighted and abruptly de-
    parted Asunción without formally taking his leave. His
    pique over the incident is held as a motive for the
    subsequent Buzzard-Grappler affair at Buenos Aires in
    which the two British vessels prevented Paraguay's
    Tacuarí, carrying Francisco Solano López, from pro-
    ceeding up the Paraná River. Minister Christie
    achieved greater notoriety subsequently in Brazil for
    his handling of a British seaman's incident known as
    the "Christie Affair."

CIUDAD REAL, IN GUAYRA (GUAIRA). Early Spanish set-
    tlement near the Yguazú Falls area in a region known
    as Guairá, founded by Captain Rui Díaz de Melgarejo
    in 1556. Abandoned and never re-settled as a result
    of large-scale Brazilian mameluke slave raids in the
    early seventeenth century.

CIUDADANO (EL) see also LOPEZ, CARLOS ANTONIO.
    "The Citizen." Title used occasionally in reference
    to President Carlos Antonio López, the second of Para-
    guay's triumvirate of early autocratic leaders.

CIVICOS see also RADICALES. Name given to one of the
    groups resulting from the 1895 division of the Liberal
    Party, their opponents being the "Radicales." The
    Cívicos were headed by the Benigno Ferreira, and
    published a paper called El Cívico. The two groups
    resolved their differences in a 1902 convention pre-
    ceeding the 1904 Revolution which brought the Liberal
    Party to power.

CIVILS, MANUEL J. Author of a valuable interpretive
    study published in 1957 entitled Anarquía y revolución
    en el Paraguay.

CLORINDA. Argentine border city located about three miles southwest of Asunción, across the Paraguay River and facing the Pilcomayo River and the Paraguayan Chaco. Noted for its continuous traffic in contraband small merchandise with Asunción, and as a convenient locale for Paraguayans exiled for political reasons.

CLOSS, WILHELM see also COLONIA HOHENAU. German national from Brazil's Rio Grande do Sul State. Credited with the founding in March, 1900, of Colonia Hohenau, about 35 miles north of the Paraná River port city of Encarnación.

CLUB DE AMIGOS DE ALEMANIA. Pro-German civic association permitted to function in Paraguay during the World War II administration of President Higinio Morínigo.

CLUB DEL PUEBLO see also CLUB OF THE PEOPLE and CLUB UNION. Early forerunner in the post-Triple Alliance War period of the Asociación Nacional Republicana, today's Colorado Party. Originally established as the "Club Unión" in 1869 by Cándido Bareiro, the organization took the name of the former members of the "Club del Pueblo," united to form the "Club Libertad," which in turn again became the "Club del Pueblo" in 1886. Members of the group formed the Asociación Nacional Republicana in August, 1887, under leadership of General Bernardino Caballero.

CLUB LIBERTAD see also CLUB UNION and COLORADO PARTY. Organized in 1878 and the forerunner of the Asociación Nacional Republicana; formed in 1887 -- today's Colorado Party.

CLUB OF THE PEOPLE see CLUB DEL PUEBLO, CLUB UNION, and ASOCIACION NACIONAL REPUBLICANA. Early forerunner in the post-Triple Alliance War era of the modern-day Colorado Party.

CLUB UNION. Also known as the "Club Unión Republicana." Early political organization in the post-Triple Alliance War period formed by Cándido Bareiro at Asunción in 1869. Its name was subsequently changed to "Club del Pueblo" in opposition to the newly developed rival political group known as the "Gran Club del Pueblo," formed in 1870 by Juan José Decoud. In 1878 many

of the former members of the "Club del Pueblo" re-
united to form the "Club Libertad," and subsequently in
1886 the former "Club del Pueblo" reappeared. Eventually in August, 1887, the members of these organizations, under the leadership of General Bernardino Caballero, formed the "Asociación Nacional Republicana,"
the Colorado Party of modern Paraguay.

CODAS, DANIEL, 1869-1941. Journalist and politician.
Especially noted for his militant articles on behalf of
the Liberal Party published while he was editor of
several Asunción newspapers.

CODAS PAPULUCA, ALCIDES, 1900-   . Author of
Cuestiones rurales del Paraguay, 1942, an interpretive study of the nation's rural problems.

COIMBRA, BRAZIL. Important Brazilian Paraguay river
port north of Asunción in Mato Grosso state. An early
commerce entrepot accepted by Dr. Francia during the
early independence era. Captured by Paraguay's north
invasion army in December, 1864, in the first and
only successful Paraguayan offensive of the Triple Alliance War.

COLEGIO ALEMAN, ASUNCION. German school operating
at Asunción during the World War II administration of
Higinio Morínigo, and an example of German influence
in Paraguay during the war period.

COLEGIO CAROLINO, ASUNCION see also REAL COLEGIO
Y SEMINARIO DE SAN CARLOS. Name variant for
one of Paraguay's oldest educational institutions, originally authorized in 1776.

COLEGIO DE NUESTRA SENORA DE MONSERRAT. Founded
April 9, 1695, at Córdoba, Tucumán, Argentina. Early
institution of higher learning in La Plata, and famed
in the first half of the nineteenth century for its preparation of future independence era leaders, including
Paraguay's Dr. José Gaspar Rodríguez de Francia.

COLEGIO DE SAN JOSE. Catholic private college of sec-
ondary education and one of the largest and most popular in Asunción. Founded June 30, 1904, by the
Congregation of the Sacred Heart, known as the "Pad-
res Bayoneros."

COLEGIO INTERNACIONAL, ASUNCION. Paraguay's best
     private institution of learning, founded in 1920 by the
     United Christian Missionary Society.

COLEGIO MILITAR. Paraguay's national Military College.
     The original building, constructed during the era of
     President Carlos Antonio López, still stands near the
     Palacio de Gobierno. In 1970 the Military College
     was transferred to a new modern complex near the
     village of Capiatá, about 12 miles east of Asunción.
     The college is Paraguay's West Point.

COLEGIO MILITAR MARISCAL FRANCISCO SOLANO LOPEZ
     see also COLEGIO MILITAR. Founded in 1916 and
     Paraguay's West Point. Originally located in Asunción
     and named the Escuela Militar de la Asunción. Name
     changed to its present one in 1948. Its new location
     is near the city of Capiatá, about 12 miles east of
     Asunción along Highway Route Two. Cadets of the
     Colegio received their baptism of fire at the Chaco
     War battle of Boquerón September, 1932.

COLEGIO NACIONAL see COLEGIO NACIONAL DE LA
     CAPITAL. One of Paraguay's best secondary public
     schools originally established in 1872.

COLEGIO NACIONAL DE LA CAPITAL see also ACEVAL,
     BENJAMIN. Colegio Nacional de la Asunción, founded
     in 1877 under the terms of a law of August 28. First
     director was a Mexican national, Dr. José Agustín de
     Escudero. Its principal sponsor was Benjamín Aceval,
     then secretary of state for Justice, Culture and Public
     Instruction.

COLMAN, NARCISO, 1880-1954. Twentieth century poet
     who specialized in verse in Guaraní. Wrote under the
     pseudonym "Rosicrán."

COLMENA (LA) see COLONIA LA COLMENA.

COLONIA ALTO PARANA. Japanese agricultural coloniza-
     tion project established in 1961 in the Itapúa region of
     southeastern Paraguay.

COLONIA BERGTHAL see BERGTHAL COLONY.

COLONIA COSME. Splinter branch of the Nueva Australia

colonization experiment founded by William Lane in 1894 after the failure of the Australian Cooperative Society.

COLONIA FERNHEIM see also MENNONITES. One of the three Mennonite colonies clustered around Filadelfia, the project's urban center, located at the geographic center of the Chaco about 250 miles from Asunción. Founded in 1930 by immigrants from Russia, Fernheim has been moderately successful.

COLONIA FRAY BARTOLOME DE LAS CASAS, 1474-1566 see also MAKKA INDIANS. Official name for the government-protected Makká Indian "toldería" or camp located on the Chaco bank of the Paraguay River across from the Jardín Botánico slightly north of Asunción. Fray Bartolomé de las Casas, also known as the Apostle of the Indies, was an early Spanish priest and missionary in the Caribbean area noted for his humane efforts to improve the lot of conquered Indian tribes under Spanish rule.

COLONIA FRIESLAND see also MENNONITES. Mennonite colony formed in 1937 by some 740 members of the Chaco Fernheim colony who wished to live in closer proximity to Asunción. Located east of the Paraguay River port of Rosario and about 70 miles north of Asunción.

COLONIA GABOTO. Colonization experiment founded by German, Spanish and Argentine immigrants southeast of Asunción in the area near the Tebicuary River.

COLONIA HOHENAU. Located shortly to the north of the Paraná River port city of Encarnación in southern Paraguay, and settled by German immigrants from Brazil's Rio Grande do Sul state in 1900. The largest and most prosperous colony experiment until the Mennonite Chaco project of the 1920's.

COLONIA INDEPENDENCIA. Rich farming immigrant colonization site located near the city of Villarrica, east of Asunción. Settlers are mostly Austrian.

COLONIA LA COLMENA. Most important Japanese colonization project in Paraguay. Founded in 1936 in the Department of Paraguarí, southeast of Asunción. A Paraguayo-Japanese agreement of 1959 provided for the im-

migration of 85,000 Japanese farmers over a 30-year
period, but the only modest success of colonization
projects has not stimulated activity on any such large-
scale level.

COLONIA MENNO see also MENNONITES. Original Mennonite colony at the Filadelfia site approximately at the
geographic center of the Chaco. Established in 1927
on land purchased from the Casado quebracho company,
and with approval of the Paraguayan government which
guaranteed colonists exemption from military service.
The majority, originally of Dutch origin, reached the
Chaco from Russia by way of an unsuccessful effort in
Canada. Menno Colony, with its sister colonies of
Fernheim and Neuland, have thrived moderately through
a dairy industry which has developed a good market at
Asunción.

COLONIA NEULAND see also MENNONITES. Most recent
of the Chaco Mennonite colonies founded in 1947 by
Mennonites who fled from Russia between 1941-1943.

COLONIA NUEVA AUSTRALIA see NUEVA AUSTRALIA.

COLONIA NUEVA BURDEOS see NUEVA BURDEOS and
VILLA HAYES.

COLONIA NUEVA GERMANIA. Located about 130 miles
northeast of Asunción, and originally settled in 1887
by German immigrants under a socialistic scheme
similar to William Lane's Nueva Australia plan. The
leader, Dr. Bernard Foerster, was married to Elizabeth Nietzsche, sister of the German philosopher-his-
torian Wilhelm Nietzsche. Foerster was soon in debt
over the project's failure, and he committed suicide
in 1889. His wife sought to continue the colony, but
most of the settlers returned to Germany. Only a few
of the descendants of the remaining settlers reportedly
still reside in the area.

COLONIA NUEVA ITALIA. Founded in 1906 south of Asunción between Lambaré and Angostura by Italian immigrants. The colony prospered, but the settlers have
since dispersed and no longer form a homogeneous
group.

COLONIA PRIMAVERA see HUTTERITES. Hutterite col-

ony of German-English composition established in 1941
near the Friesland Mennonite colony about 70 miles
north of Asunción.   Most of the colonists departed during the 1960's to search for less isolated areas.

COLONIA SAN BERNARDINO   see also   SAN BERNARDINO.
First permanent foreign colony established on the
shores of Lake Ypacaray about 35 miles east of Asunción.   Founded by German immigrants in 1881 under
its organizer Jacob Schaerer and with the support of
General Bernardino Caballero.   Several colony members became prominent business and professional leaders in Asunción, and one descendant, Eduardo Schaerer,
was elected president of the republic.

COLONIA SOMMERFELD   see   SOMMERFELD COLONY.

COLONIA TRINACRIA.   Founded by Italian immigrants in
1898 at a site about 60 miles north of Asunción.   Like
the settlers of the Nueva Italia project, most of the
survivors and descendants of the Trinacría project
moved to Asunción.

COLONIA YGUAZU.   Japanese agricultural colony project
established in 1960 east from Asunción along the highway near Puerto Presidente Stroessner on the upper
Paraná River.   A cooperative, it has only been moderately successful due to the difficulties in clearing
land in the heavily forested eastern Paraná region.

COLORADO PARTY   see   ASOCIACION NACIONAL REPUBLI-
CANA.

COMANDANCIA GENERAL DE ARMAS OF 1841   see also
JUNTA PROVISORIA OF 1840 and TRIUMVIRATE OF
1840.   The successor to the Triumvirate of 1840,
organized in February 1841, following the death of Dr.
Francia.   Composed of Commander Mariano Roque
Alonso and as secretary, Carlos Antonio López.

COMENTARIOS.   Memoirs and recollections of Adelantado/
Governor Alvar Núñez Cabeza de Vaca, published in
Valladolid, Spain, in 1555 and considered one of the
earliest accounts of the foundings and early years of
the Asunción colony.

COMISARIO   see also   ALCALDE.   Term referring to the

chief of police in Paraguay's urban centers. Appointed
by the Ministry of the Interior.

COMITE REVOLUCIONARIO. Forerunner of the Asociación
Paraguaya and Legión Paraguaya, the major Paraguayan
exile organization organized at Buenos Aires in the
1860's to oppose Francisco Solano López.

COMMISSION OF INQUIRY, BOLIVIA AND PARAGUAY.
Special commission stemming from the 1928-1929 Washington Conference on Conciliation and Arbitration appointed to seek a formula for resolution of the Chaco
dispute. The nine member commission included representatives from Paraguay, Bolivia, Mexico, Cuba,
Colombia, Uruguay, Chile, and the United States. Its
efforts bogged down when Paraguay and Bolivia failed
to agree on what points should be submitted for arbitration.

COMMUNIST PARTY   see   PARTIDO COMUNISTA.

COMPAÑIA PARAGUAYA DE NAVEGACION Y COMERCIO
MARCELINO CAMIHORT, S. A. River navigation com-
pany which operated a small fleet of steamers on the
Paraguay River for a brief period commencing in 1925.

COMPAÑIA PRO-FOMENTO DE MIGRACION JAPONESA,
S. A. Semi-official corporation in Japan established
in 1955 to promote, facilitate and finance Japanese
emigration projects including those in Paraguay.

COMUNERO REVOLT see also COMUNEROS, and ANTE-
QUERA Y CASTRO, Dr. José de. Occurring between
1717-1735 in Paraguay, the event is regarded historically as the first major and largest uprising against Spanish authority in the New World prior to the early nineteenth century independence movements. Angered by
the poor and abusive administration of Governor Reyes
Balmaceda, the criollo population at Asunción supported
Dr. José de Antequera y Castro who deposed the governor and assumed the post himself. Under pressure
from royalist forces from Buenos Aires, Antequera was
forced to return to Lima where he and a Paraguayan
companion, Juan de Mena, were subsequently tried for
treason and executed in 1731. Fernando de Mompox,
last important Comunero leader, fled to Brazil. The
movement collapsed totally in 1735 when Comunero

forces were defeated by royalist troops from Buenos
Aires. As a penalty for the actions of Asunción's
creoles, the Spanish government rescinded the Royal
Order of 1537, which had provided for local election
of provincial officials, and required that all export
trade from Paraguay be landed at the Paraná River
port of Santa Fe for onward land transport to Buenos
Aires. These actions were factors in the subsequent
growth of Paraguayan sentiment toward independence
from Spain.

COMUNEROS see COMUNERO REVOLT. Term originating
in Spain meaning "those who defend the rights of the
people." Its first usage occurred in 1520 in Spain
when areas of Castille rose in revolt against Emperor
Charles V because of his abuse of privileges traditionally enjoyed by village governments. Many survivors
of the Spanish "Comunero revolt" subsequently emigrated to the new world. Paraguayan "Comuneros"
were the followers of Dr. José de Antequera y Castro
in his Comunero Revolt.

COMUNIDAD. Catholic weekly published at Asunción which
in recent years has tended to support church-oriented
organizations such as the Confederación Cristiana de
Trabajadores while criticizing rival government organizations.

CONCEPCION. Founded in 1773 by Colonel Agustín Fernando
de Pinedo, this river port is located north of Asunción
on the left bank of the Paraguay River. It is the most
important commercial center in the northern half of the
republic by virtue of its road transport connections
with the northeast city of Pedro Juan Caballero and its
status as a free port for Brazilian commerce. It was
the point at which the major revolution of 1947 originally commenced.

CONCEPCION DEL BERMEJO see also BERMEJO RIVER.
Spanish colony site which existed briefly during the
early colonial period near the mouth of the Bermejo
River across the Paraguay River from the modern city
of Pilar.

CONCILIATION AND ARBITRATION CONFERENCE OF 1929.
Inter-American conference convened at Washington
which recommended fruitlessly that both Paraguay and

Bolivia adopt a formula for the peaceful solution of
their Chaco problems.

CONDE D'EU   see   ORLEANS, GASTON DE.

CONFEDERACION CRISTIANA DE TRABAJADORES (CCT).
Young Christian Worker's Confederation, church-sup-
ported, and organized in the 1960's with its activities
centered mainly in rural areas.

CONFEDERACION DE TRABAJADORES DEL PARAGUAY.
Original major Paraguayan labor organization in the
twentieth century. Suppressed after the January, 1941,
general strike by the Higinio Morínigo administration.
Its role as the nation's largest labor organization was
later assumed by the Confederación Paraguaya de Trabajadores (CPT) formed in 1951 with the assistance of
the ICFTU.

CONFEDERACION NACIONAL DE TRABAJADORES DEL
PARAGUAY (CNTP)   see also   CONFEDERACION
PARAGUAYA DE TRABAJADORES (CPT).   First significant Paraguayan labor organization established in
1936.   Reorganized in 1939 under the name Confederación de Trabajadores del Paraguay, but dissolved by
the government following the 1944 general strike.   Subsequently in 1955 Paraguay's second labor Congress
voted for the establishment of the Confederación Paraguaya de Trabajadores (CPT).

CONFEDERACION PARAGUAYA DE TRABAJADORES (CPT).
Modern Paraguay's labor organization, formed in
1951 with the assistance of the ICFTU.   Its one and
only effort to call a general strike, in 1959, failed
when the government called the effort illegal.   It has
since been under official control.

CONFERENCE OF BUENOS AIRES, 1927-1928.   Unsuccessful negotiations held at Buenos Aires between Paraguayan and Bolivian delegates in an effort to arrive
at a means for settlement of the growing Chaco dispute.

CONFERENCE OF CONCILIATION AND ARBITRATION OF
1929   see   CONCILIATION AND ARBITRATION CON-
FERENCE OF 1929.

CONFERENCE OF MENDOZA, 1933. Held at Mendoza,
Argentina, between the foreign ministers of Chile and
Argentina in an effort to solve the Chaco War problem.
Their arbitration proposal of February 2, 1933, was
accepted by Paraguay but rejected by Bolivia.

CONGRESO NACIONAL. Paraguay's National Congress building. Located near the National Palace, it is another
of Asunción's major historical sites having been originally constructed in 1847-1857.

CONGRESS OF JULY 24, 1810. Convened by Paraguay's
Spanish Governor Bernardo de Velasco following the
mission to Asunción of Colonel José de Espínola y
Peña seeking Paraguay's adherence to the new Buenos
Aires government. The Congress resolved to recog-
nize the Spanish Regency acting in the absence of King
Fernando VII, but not to recognize the authority of the
Junta of the new Buenos Aires government. This ac-
tion stimulated the Junta to dispatch the Manuel Belgra-
no army expedition to Paraguay.

CONGRESS OF 1811, FIRST NATIONAL. Approved separation of Spanish Governor Velasco from the new revolutionary government, dissolved the composition of
Asunción's city government, and designated a new government called the Superior Governing Board (Junta
Superior Gubernativa).

CONGRESS OF 1813. Paraguay's second National Congress,
convened on October 12, 1813. Provided for the adoption of the name "Republic" instead of Province of
Paraguay, and for a consular form of government.
The two consuls elected were Fulgencio Yegros and
Dr. José Gaspar Rodríguez de Francia. Considered
as Paraguay's first effort at evolving a constitutional
document.

CONGRESS OF 1814. Paraguay's third National Congress
was convened on October 3, 1814. Provided for a one-
person executive with the provisional title of Supreme
Dictator of the Republic of Paraguay. Dr. José
Gaspar Rodríguez de Francia was elected to occupy
the position. He held it for less than two years of
the contemplated five-year term.

CONGRESS OF 1816.   Paraguay's fourth National Congress
    was convened on May 30, 1816.   Its achievement was
    the election of Dr. José Gaspar Rodríguez de Francia
    as Dictador Perpétuo de la República--Perpetual Dic-
    tator of the Republic.   He ruled Paraguay as El Supre-
    mo from then until his death on September 20, 1840.

CONGRESS OF 1841.   Convoked March 12, 1841, Paraguay's
    Fifth National Congress provided for the Second Con-
    sulate to be effective for a three-year period.   The
    two consuls elected were Carlos Antonio López and
    Mariano Roque Alonso.   Principal achievements of the
    Second Consulate were the re-establishment of friendly
    relations with neighboring countries, the re-opening of
    ports and foreign commerce, the establishment of an
    Academia Literaria, and a decree providing that all
    children born of slaves henceforth would be free.

CONGRESS OF NOVEMBER, 1842.   An extraordinary con-
    gress convoked by the Second Consulate on November
    15, 1842, for the purpose of declaring formally Para-
    guay's independence.   Also approved the national colors
    and escudo, still in current usage.

CONGRESS OF 1844.   Convoked March 13, 1844, to estab-
    lish a new form of government following termination
    of the Second Consulate.   Approved a constitution
    drafted by Carlos Antonio López which provided for the
    executive, legislative, and judicial branches.   By unan-
    imous vote, the congress elected Carlos Antonio López
    as president for a ten-year term.   Regarded as the
    second of Paraguay's constitutional documents.

CONGRESS OF 1849.   Convened May 30, 1849, by President
    Carlos Antonio López to present a review of interna-
    tional affairs and of the nation's development since his
    assumption of office in 1844.

CONGRESS OF 1854.   Convened March 14, 1854, on expira-
    tion of the first ten-year administration of President
    Carlos Antonio López.   The Congress re-elected him
    to an additional ten-year period, but he reduced his
    new mandate to a three-year term for health reasons.

CONGRESS OF 1857.   Re-elected President Carlos Antonio
    López to a third ten-year term in office.

CONGRESS OF MARCH, 1865.   Convoked by President
Francisco Solano López to consider the state of inter-
national relations on the eve of the Triple Alliance
War.   Conferred the title of Marshal on President
López, and on March 18 authorized declaration of war
against Argentina.

CONQUISTA ESPIRITUAL   see   MONTOYA, FATHER RUIZ
DE.   First history of the evangelizing efforts of the
Jesuits in Paraguay, written by the Peruvian Father
Antonio Ruíz de Montoya, published circa 1632.

CONSEJO DE ESTADO.   A supreme Council of State provided for in the Constitution of 1967 which acts in an
advisory capacity to Paraguay's chief executive.

CONSEJO DE INDIAS.   Council of the Indies.   The prime
governing board under the Spanish king for the administration of New World affairs.   Responsible for all legislation affecting the Spanish Colonies, and for the issuance of directives concerning colonial administration.
The principal administrative unit of Spain's centralized
form of government.

CONSEJO DE MUJERES DEL PARAGUAY.   Prominent femi-
nist organization noted for activity in cultural and
literary projects.

CONSEJO NACIONAL DE COMERCIO EXTERIOR.   Paraguay's National Foreign Trade Council, created in
1962 to replace the former National Free Trade Zone
Council.   Composed of representatives of the principal
government ministries, the Central and National Development Banks, and of FEPRINCO, the major industrial and business organization, and of the Paraguayan
Industrial Union.   Responsible for advice to the government on commercial policy and participation in LAFTA,
the Latin American Free Trade Association.

CONSEJO OBRERO.   Paraguayan labor organization active
in the late 1930's and affiliated in the 1940's with the
Confederation of Latin American Workers, the extreme
left Latin American labor movement directed by Mexico's Vicente Lombardo Toledano.

CONSPIRACY OF 1820.   Plot against the life of Dr. Francia
organized by a group of prominent Asunción citizens

and scheduled to occur on Good Friday, 1820. Reported by an informant, the plot failed with the subsequent execution and jailing of many of Paraguay's
early independence era heroes, including Fulgencio
Yegros, Pedro Juan Caballero and José Fernández
Montiel. No other plot occurred during the remainder
of El Supremo's reign to his death in 1840.

CONSPIRACY PERIOD see also TRIBUNALES DE SANGRE.
The period during February to December, 1868, when
numerous Paraguayan and foreign nationals were suspected of a plot against Marshal President Francisco
Solano López. Many were arrested or executed following trials by the "tribunales de sangre," the special
military courts convened by the marshal president.
No definitive proof of the existence of such a conspiracy plot has yet been authenticated.

CONSTANT, BENJAMIN. Leader of Brazil's post Triple
Alliance War "positivista" group espousing the philosophy of France's August Comte, and one of the organizers of the coup which toppled the imperial government of Dom Pedro II. In the early years of the Paraguayan War he served with the army before Humaitá
as an editor of the official record, Diário do Exército.

CONSTITUTION OF 1813 see also CONGRESS OF 1813.
Paraguay's first basic government document. It provided for the name "Republic" instead of "Provincia,"
and established a consular form of government to be
exercised by two persons.

CONSTITUTION OF 1844 see also CONGRESS OF 1844.
Paraguay's second basic government document. It provided for a government comprised of the executive,
legislative and judicial powers, and for the election of
Carlos Antonio López as president for a ten-year period.

CONSTITUTION OF 1870. Third of Paraguay's basic constitutional documents of government, and the first of
the water-shed post-Triple Alliance War period.
Drawn and approved by a Constitutional Convention
which was convened August 15, 1870. Democratic and
liberal in its provisions and based largely on the Argentine model, although unitary and not federal in nature. Remained effective until the new constitution

promoted by President José Félix Estigarribia in July, 1940.

CONSTITUTION OF 1940. Proclaimed by Marshal President José Félix Estigarribia in 1940 and promulgated without public consent through a national referendum. Included amendments to the 1870 document providing for expanded and more vigorous presidential power.

CONSTITUTION OF 1967. The fifth and most recent of Paraguay's basic constitutional documents, promulgated in August, 1967, following approval by a national constitutional assembly. Basically a document aimed at promoting a more liberal and democratic base for Paraguay's unitary and centralized form of government, it provided for expansion of the National Congress to include an elected Senate as well as the existing Chamber of Deputies. Both houses, however, remain still subservient to the executive branch which continues to administer by decree when the Congress is not in session. The three-branch form of government is retained--executive, legislative and judicial. A "Consejo de Estado" or Council of State is provided for to advise the chief executive. A Supreme Court composed of a president and four members attends cases stemming from the lower appelate and circuit courts. The franchise to vote is extended to all persons 18 years or older of both sexes. Voting is compulsory. The constitution formally provides that the chief executive must be at least 40 years of age and a Catholic. He may be re-elected to a second five-year term. President and Commander-in-Chief of the Army, General Alfredo Stroessner is the first president to be elected under the 1967 constitution.

CONSTITUTIONS OF PARAGUAY see CONSTITUTIONS OF 1813, 1844, 1870, 1940, and 1967.

CONSULATE, FIRST see also CONGRESS OF 1813. Established by the second National Congress of 1813. The two consuls were Fulgencio Yegros and Dr. José Gaspar Rodríguez de Francia. Remained in effect until 1814.

CONSULATE, SECOND. In effect from March, 1841, to March, 1844. Authorized by the Congress of 1841 and composed of Carlos Antonio López and Mariano

Roque Alonso. Its principal achievement was the reorganization of Paraguay following the death in 1840 of
El Supremo, Dr. José Gaspar Rodríguez de Francia,
the formal ratification of national independence, and a
relaxation in El Supremo's former strict isolationist
policies. The Congress of 1844 ended the Second Consulate and provided for the unipersonal government of
Carlos Antonio López as president for ten years.

CONTRABANDOS, PARTY. Splinter faction of the Comunero
movement at Asunción in 1730 at the height of its efforts to resist royalist domination.

CONTRERAS, ROSITA. Illegitimate daughter of Marshal
President Francisco Solano López who accompanied
Mme. Elisa Alicia Lynch to Europe following the death
of López at Cerro Corá, March 1, 1870.

CONVICTORIO DE ASUNCION   see also   SEVERINO, DR.
BLAS. Early eighteenth century project for the establishment of an institution of higher learning at Asunción.

COPACAR   see   CORPORACION PARAGUAYA DE CARNES.

CORDILLERA DE AZCURRA. Portion of the Cordillera de
los Altos range east of Asunción and facing the village
of Pirayú. Its Paso de Azcurra was the central point
of the Paraguayan army's defenses until forced by the
Brazilian envelopment movement of August, 1869.

CORDILLERA DE LOS ALTOS. The long range of hills,
running northwest/southeast about 30 miles east of
Asunción, marking the western escarpment of the Paraná plateau. Lake Ypacaray lies before it in the
plain in which the former military encampment of
Cerro León is located slightly to the south. Its obvious military defensive position thwarted the Brazilian
army in the last stages of the Triple Alliance War until an enveloping attack succeeded at Piribebuy.

CORO MASCULINO, ALEMAN. German Male Chorus--pro-
Nazi propaganda device functioning in Asunción during
the World War II era.

CORONEL OVIEDO. One of modern Paraguay's newer cities
located about 90 miles east of Asunción on major high-

way Route Two leading to Puerto Presidente Stroessner
and the Friendship Bridge over the Paraná River. The
city developed swiftly with completion of the highway
and is today an important transport center. Named
after Florentino Oviedo, a Triple Alliance War hero.

CORPORACION DE OBRAS SANITARIAS DE ASUNCION
(CORPOSANA). Established by Law No. 244 of October 26, 1954, the Asunción Sanitary Works Corporation supplies the capital with its fresh water and main-
tains the sewage system. The corporation's water
plant, inaugurated in 1959, is one of the most modern
and impressive of its type in Latin America.

CORPORACION PARAGUAYA DE CARNES (COPACAR).
Established by Decree Law No. 3810 of March 6, 1944,
and reorganized under Law. No. 710 of July 25, 1961,
COPACAR is now the government controlled authority
which supervises the movement, sale and pricing of
livestock within Paraguay.

CORPOSANA   see   Corporación de Obras Sanitarias de
Asunción.

CORRALES, ACTION AT.   An early action of the Humaitá
campaign occurring on the Corrientes or Argentine side
of the Paraná River across from Paso de Patria, Paraguay, on January 31, 1866.   A Paraguayan success,
it proved a diversionary tactic to disrupt allied plans
for crossing the Paraná.

CORRALES, FORTIN.   Paraguayan fortified position in the
central Chaco abandoned in January, 1933, on the eve
of the Chaco War Bolivian attack on the Toledo position.

CORREA, ANTONIO.   Spanish conquistador and member of
the 1543 Cabeza de Vaca exploration expedition which
reached the Lake Xarayes region of the headwaters of
the Paraguay River.

CORREA, JULIO, 1890-1953.   One of the most popular
authors and dramatic actors in Paraguay's post-Chaco
War theater.   Known especially for his use of the
Guaraní language, for which he is recorded as the
initiator of the use of the vernacular in the national
theater.

CORREA DA CAMARA, ANTONIO MANOEL. Sent by Emperor Pedro I as Brazilian consul to Paraguay in 1824 during the regime of Dr. José Gaspar Rodríguez de Francia. Sought to return in 1827 as charge d'affaires but El Supremo refused to allow him to reach Asunción. Both missions were early attempts to secure formal Brazilian-Paraguayan relationships.

CORREA DA CAMARA, GENERAL JOSE ANTONIO. Commander of Brazilian forces at Cerro Corá, March, 1870, the last engagement of the Triple Alliance War. Personally witnessed the death of Marshal President Francisco Solano López.

CORRIENTES, ARGENTINA. Paraná River port city located shortly below the confluence with the Paraguay which was attacked and taken by a Paraguayan invasion force on April 13, 1865. Coming shortly after Paraguay's declaration of war on March 19, the event stimulated formal signature of the Triple Alliance Treaty and aroused patriotic fervor at Buenos Aires. Totally underestimating Paraguay's stamina, Bartolomé Mitre announced his nation's goals as "To the barracks in 24 hours; on campaign in three weeks; in Asunción in three months!"

CORRIENTES PROVINCE, ARGENTINA. Adjacent to extreme southern Paraguay and separated therefrom by the Paraná River. The scene in 1846 of a Paraguayan expedition under then Brigadier Francisco Solano López to aid General José María Paz against Buenos Aires dictator Juan Manuel de Rosas, and in 1865 of Paraguay's capture of the river port of Corrientes.

CORUMBA, BRAZIL. Brazilian riverport and modern-day rail head located on the upper reaches of the Paraguay River. A Mato Grosso base at the opening of the Triple Alliance War, it was captured by Paraguay's northern invasion army in December, 1864. Supplies taken here and at other nearby river ports aided Paraguay's defense during most of the war.

CORVALAN, FRANCISCO REYE see CORVALAN, REGE.

CORVALAN, REGE. Governor of Paraguay credited with having constructed a fort on the Chaco side of the Paraguay River opposite Asunción in 1675. The event is mentioned in Paraguayan claims to their nation's long-standing interest and rights in the Chaco as against Bolivian claims.

COSTA. The edge of the "Monte" or forested area bordering on a plain or prairie zone.

COSTA LOBO, DR. MANOEL CARDOSO DA. Brazilian physician attached to the forces of General Corrêa da Câmara at Cerro Corá, March 1, 1870, the last engagement of the Triple Alliance War. Performed an official autopsy on the corpse of Paraguay's Marshal President López, attesting to the manner of his death.

COTEGIPE, BARÃO DE see WANDERLEY, JOÃO MAURICIO DE.

COTEGIPE-LOIZAGA TREATY see LOIZAGA-COTEGIPE TREATY. Boundary limits treaty between Brazil and Paraguay.

COTY GUAZU. Building reserved for orphans, widows and the aged located near but outside the perimeter of Jesuit-built Indian missions or reductions during the Jesuit era.

CREYDT, OSCAR ADALBERTO FEDERICO, 1907-   . Asunción intellectual and perennial head of Paraguay's exiled Communist Party. Scion of a wealthy family, he spent a considerable inherited fortune in the Party's cause. His political views have forced him to live in permanent exile.

CRIOLLO. Term applied to those of pure Spanish stock living in the Spanish colonies but born in them rather than Spanish-born. The latter were known in Paraguay either as Gachupines or Peninsulares. The term criollo is not to be confused with creole, used elsewhere and meaning offspring of mixed racial origin.

CRISTIANO, JUAN. Spanish armament-maker noted in historical accounts as having succeeded in making gunpowder from local Paraguayan salt peter deposits in the early discovery and conquest period.

CROSBY, CAPTAIN PIERCE. Commander of the USS

Shamokin which returned American Minister Charles
Ames Washburn to Paraguay in 1866 during the Triple
Alliance War.

CUADRILATERO see HUMAITA. The commonly-used
name referring to the four-sided shaped Paraguayan
defenses around the Humaitá area in extreme southwestern Paraguay during the Triple Alliance War.

CUARTELAZO. Barracks revolt aimed at military take-over
of the government. A frequent phenomenon in Paraguay
prior to the advent of the Stroessner government in
1954. Usually accompanied by a "pronunciamiento"--
a combined call-to-arms and political manifesto by the
military leader involved.

CUATI, SERGEANT. A native Payaguá Indian and personal
servant of General José E. Díaz. Sergeant Cuati is
remembered among Paraguayan War deeds of valor for
having rescued Díaz after his wounding during a river
reconnaissance in early 1867.

CUERPO DE BOGABANTES. Canoe paddlers corps. Special
units organized by Marshal President Francisco Solano
López in 1868 during the Triple Alliance War. Conceived as an ingenious means of attacking Brazilian
naval vessels by using canoes and Paraguay River hya-
cinth camoflage, the "cuerpo" men actually succeeded
in boarding one vessel. Fear of the possibility of
their attacks served to restrict allied naval river pa-
trols during the Humaitá campaign.

CUNHA MATTOS, MAJOR ERNESTO AUGUSTO DA. Brazilian army officer who served throughout the Triple Alliance War, was a Paraguayan prisoner, and who was
present at Cerro Corá, the war's concluding action.
Noted for his colorful and illuminating recollections.
A prominent participant in Brazil's postwar "Questão
Militar"--military question, a prelude to the downfall
of Dom Pedro II's empire.

CUNNINGHAM-GRAHAM, R. B., 1852-1936. British author
noted for his specialization in the River Plata republics.
Wrote Portrait of a Dictator, a derogatory account of
the life of Francisco Solano López.

CURUGUATI see CURUGUATY and SAN ISIDRO DE CURU-
GUATY.

CURUGUATY see also SAN ISIDRO DE CURUGUATY. Interior village in northeastern Paraguay located about
150 miles from Asunción. Noted as the residence in
exile of Uruguay's founding father, José de Artigas,
and as a last capital for Paraguay in the Triple Alliance War.

CURUPAITY, BATTLE OF. Fought September 22, 1866,
Curupaity was Paraguay's most resounding and decisive
victory of the Triple Alliance War. Like the battle of
New Orleans, the outcome was wholly one-sided; under
the command of General José E. Díaz, entrenched
Paraguayan troops suffered losses of less than 100 in
comparison to an estimated 9,000 allied casualties.
The action caused a temporary halt in operations at
Humaitá.

CURUZU, BATTLE OF. Prelude to the Paraguayan victory
at the major battle of Curupaity in the Triple Alliance
War, this action on September 3, 1866, proved an Allied success. Allied troops overran the Curuzú ad-
vanced redoubt below Humaitá, and were thus enheart-
ened to continue their advance to the Curupaity disaster.

CURUZU CUARENTA. Literally translated as "40 crosses."
A curious and largely unknown memorial of the 1868
Triple Alliance War battle of Itá Ybaté near Asunción,
which comprises a mass grave reportedly containing
the remains of hundreds of Paraguayan soldiers.

CURUZU INFANTE. Translated as "Cross of the Child,"
this term refers to the grave-site, in Eusebio Ayala,
45 miles from Asunción, of a mortally wounded unknown Paraguayan boy soldier who died there after the
battle of Acosta Ñú on August 16, 1869.

CUYABA, BRAZIL. Capital of Mato Grosso province and a
Brazilian base during the Triple Alliance War. One of
Brazil's earliest settlements in the era of expansion
westward.

- D -

DAVIS, REAR ADMIRAL C.H. Commander of the American
South Atlantic naval squadron in 1868-69 who proceeded
through the allied blockade of the Paraná-Paraguay Riv-

ers on several occasions to take aboard retiring Minister Charles Ames Washburn and new Minister Martin
T. McMahon.   His record survived a subsequent post-
war congressional committee of inquiry into American
relationships with Paraguay.

DECIDEE (LA).   French gunboat which reached Paraguay in
1868 to remove French nationals.   Allegedly took a
number of cases of bullion consigned to the Paraguayan
legation in Paris on its departure from Paraguay.

DECLARATION OF AUGUST 3, 1932.   Doctrine enunciated
at a special Inter-American Congress at Washington to
the effect that the American republics henceforth would
not recognize any territorial acquisitions won by force
of arms.

DECLARATION OF INDEPENDENCE.   Paraguay's first formal declaration of independence occurred during a special congress convened June 17, 1811, following the
May 14 movement against Spanish Governor Velasco.
The congress adopted a resolution declaring that all relations with Spain were severed, but did not define its
relationships with Buenos Aires.

DECLARATION OF LIMA, 1960 see also FEBRERISTA
PARTY.   Declaration issued at Lima in August, 1960,
following a general assembly of Latin America's major
liberal/popular political parties: Peru's APRA, Venezuela's AD, the Partido de la Liberación Nacional of
Costa Rica, Bolivia's MNR, and Paraguay's Febrerista
Party.   The declaration affirmed their agreement on
nationalistic, anti-imperialistic and democratic-socialist
orientation, and accused the United States of supporting
tyrannies and dictatorships.

DECOUD, ADOLFO, 1852-1929.   Attorney and journalist.
Co-founder with his brothers and editor of the post
Triple Alliance War newspaper La Regeneración.
Spent most of his adult life at Buenos Aires in his pro-
fession as an attorney.   Co-founder of the Junta de
Historia y Numismática, later to become the Academia
de la Historia Argentina.   Died at Buenos Aires.

DECOUD, CARLOS see also CARMELITA.   Allegedly a
victim of the passions of the young Francisco Solano
López because he was the fiancé of Carmelita, an

Asunción beauty to whom López had reportedly become
attracted. The story is related in several accounts.

DECOUD, HECTOR FRANCISCO, 1855-1930. Journalist and
author-historian. Brother of Juan José, José Segundo,
Adolfo and Diógenes Decoud. Imprisoned with his
mother in Paraguay during the Triple Alliance War.
Worked with his brothers on La Regeneración newspaper after the war, and in 1890 became editor of La
República. Author of numerous studies of the 1865-
1870 war era which, though useful as contemporary accounts, are impaired by the author's obvious bias
against Francisco Solano López.

DECOUD, JOSE SEGUNDO, 1848-1909. Prominent statesman, journalist and diplomat whose activities were of
constant importance in Paraguay's evolution from the
post-Triple Alliance War era until the Liberal Revolution of 1904. Co-founder of the anti-López exiled
Paraguayan organization, the Asociación Paraguaya, in
the pre-Triple Alliance War era, and a noted political
figure in the early post-war reconstruction era. Editor
of La Regeneración, La Opinión Pública and La Re-
forma newspapers, and one of the founders and principal directors of the Asociación Nacional Republicana,
the modern-day Colorado Party.

DECOUD, COLONEL JUAN FRANCISCO. Exiled Paraguayan
national resident at Buenos Aires prior to the Triple
Alliance War. One of the founders of the Legión Paraguaya, an association of exiles opposing President
Francisco Solano López which joined the allied forces
in the 1870 war.

DECOUD, JUAN JOSE see also DECOUD, JOSE SEGUNDO,
1847-1871. Brother of José Segundo Decoud, and with
him, a co-author of the Constitution of 1870. Also
co-founder and editor of the post-1870 war Asunción
newspaper La Regeneración. Accompanied his father,
Colonel Juan Francisco Decoud, in organizing the Legión Paraguaya, a militant group of Paraguayan exiles
opposed to Francisco Solano López, but left the Legión
when the terms of the Triple Alliance Treaty were
made public.

DECOUD-KLUBY TREATY. Signed with Uruguay in April,
1883, and providing that Uruguay would renounce its

indemnity claims stemming from the Triple Alliance
War.

DECOUD-QUIJARRO TREATY. Signed with Bolivia in 1879
but never ratified. Provided for renunciation by Paraguay to Bolivia of considerable northern and western
Chaco territory.

DECREE LAW 152 OF MARCH 10, 1936. Possibly the most
notorious legislative act of the short-lived Febrerista
government. Drafted by noted author Gómez Freire
Esteves, it linked the Febrerista movement to the contemporary totalitarian European social movements, and
abolished all labor unions, political parties and political
activity except when stemming directly from the government. Stimulated widespread resentment and antago-
nism toward the Febreristas.

DELEGADOS. Delegates appointed by Dr. Francia after the
National Congress of 1816 to represent him and to inform him of events at strategic points in Paraguay including Itapúa, Misiones, Concepción, and Villarrica.
Delegado de Gobierno is a title used in modern Paraguay for the appointed chief administrative officials in
each of the republic's administrative departments.

DELGADO, FRANCISCO. Soldier and blacksmith who accompanied the 1542 Cabeza de Vaca expedition overland
to Paraguay.

DELGADO, GENERAL NICOLAS, 1892-1947. Professional
soldier, Chaco War veteran, commander-in-chief of
the armed forces, and minister of war and marine.
Noted as author of one of the first complete memoirs
of the Chaco War, entitled Historia de la guerra del
Chaco--Mis recuerdos personales, published in 1939.

DELGADO RODAS, MODESTO. Painter of the modern era
who specializes in Paraguayan landscapes.

DEMERSAY, L. ALFRED. French physician who reached
Paraguay from Mato Grosso in 1845. Securing friendly relations with Carlos Antonio López and his family,
he was permitted to travel widely throughout the republic. His several works published on the basis of
his research, including a general history and a study
of Dr. Francia, are useful source records of the era.

DEMOCRACIA (LA) see also IBARRA, IGNACIO. Post
Triple Alliance War Asunción newspaper first published
on March 1, 1881. Co-founder and first editor was
Ignacio Ibarra, political figure who also exercised a
major role in the evolution of Paraguayan journalism.

DEMOCRACIA SOLIDARISTA. Democratic solidarity. Term
denoting the philosophy which grew up among a number
of Paraguayan intellectuals during the post-Chaco War
period and which formed the ideological basis of Colonel Rafael Franco's Febrerista Revolt in 1936. Its
chief spokesman was Dr. Juan Stefanich, foreign minister of the Febrerista government. A long-time specialist in Paraguayan affairs and one with first-hand
knowledge of the era, Dr. Harris Gaylord Warren,
describes Democracia solidarista as a philosophy that
"seeks to extract all that is good from individualistic
democracy, fascism, nazism, and communism and to
weld them together to form a political philosophy valid
for American realities and capable of answering needs
created by complex modern societies."

DEMOCRATICOS see also GUION ROJO. Name given to
a faction of the Colorado Party in 1947 which opposed
the "Guión Rojo" faction and supported the candidacy
for president of Federico Chaves.

DENAPRO see DEPARTMENTO NACIONAL DE PROPA-
GANDA.

DENIS, COLONEL BERNARDINO. Considered one of the
oldest Paraguayan army officers on record at the on-
set of the Triple Alliance War, having entered the
army in 1840. One of the principal organizers of the
Cerro León military encampment.

DEODORO DA FONSECA, COLONEL MANOEL. One of
Brazil's most prominent national heroes, the general
who overthrew the empire of Dom Pedro II and became first president of the republic. Deodoro da
Fonseca, a professional, fought through the entire Triple Alliance War in Paraguay as an infantry commander. Promoted three times for bravery, severely
wounded at the battle of Ytororó, and had three of his
eight brothers killed in the war.

DEPARTAMENTO NACIONAL DE PROPAGANDA see also

DENAPRO. National Propaganda Department, known
as Denapro, established by decree of December, 1944,
during the regime of Higinio Morínigo. Denapro was
charged with the supervision and censorship of all
phases of Paraguayan literary and social life, assuring
that nothing detrimental to the government occurred or
was printed.

DEPARTAMENTO NACIONAL DE TRABAJO. Paraguay's
National Labor Department, responsible for the supervision and direction of labor affairs. Traditionally
has exercised strong control over all union movements
to assure that their activities are compatible with official policies.

DEPARTMENTS - DEPARTAMENTOS: ADMINISTRATIVE
ORGANIZATION OF PARAGUAY. The republic is
divided into 16 departments and the capital city of
Asunción. Of the 16, three are located in the Chaco
west of the Paraguay River: Presidente Hayes, Boquerón and Olimpo. Thirteen are located in eastern
Paraguay: Concepción, San Pedro, La Cordillera,
Guairá, Caaguazú, Caazapá, Itapúa, Misiones, Paraguarí, Alto Paraná, Central, Ñeembucú, and Amambay.

DERQUI, MANUEL. Argentine diplomatic representative
sent to Asunción in 1875 to settle post-Triple Alliance
War problems with Paraguay. His mission resulted
in the final mutually acceptable treaty of 1875.

DERQUI, DR. SANTIAGO. Emissary of Entre Ríos Argentine caudillo chieftain Justo José de Urquiza, sent to
Paraguay in 1852 to negotiate a boundary treaty also
recognizing Paraguay's independence. Its frontier
terms were rejected by Argentina's congress.

DESMEMBRACION DE CHIQUITOS. Occurring in 1560, and
the first formal separation of land area from the original region designated as Paraguay. Chiquitos, roughly the area now eastern Bolivia, was declared the
"Gobernación de Santa Cruz de la Sierra" by the Viceroy of Peru, Andrés Hurtado de Mendoza, following
the foundation of settlements in the area by Ñuflo de
Chaves.

DESTINADAS. Term applied to those women who for various reasons were forced to accompany Marshal Presi-

dent López on his long 1869-1870 retreat to Cerro
Corá, and for whom residence points in extreme northeastern Paraguay had been selected.

DEUTSCHE, WINTERHILFE. Pro-German organization in
Paraguay during World War II which allegedly carried
on a large contribution assessment campaign among
resident German nationals and descendants of German
immigrants.

DIA DE LA VICTORIA see BOQUERON, BATTLE OF.
Day of Victory. The date September 29, 1932, marking the Bolivian surrender at the battle of Boquerón,
is celebrated in Paraguay as the "Dia de la Victoria."

DIABO, CORPORAL CHICO see LACERDA, CORPORAL
JOSE FRANCISCO. Brazilian cavalry corporal who
hurled the lance which mortally wounded Paraguay's
Francisco Solano López at Cerro Corá, March 1, 1870,
terminating the Triple Alliance War.

DIABO, JOSE see DIABO, CHICO and LACERDA, CORPO-
RAL JOSE FRANCISCO. Variant used by some his-
torians for the name of Corporal José Francisco La-
cerda, the Brazilian alleged to have mortally wounded
Paraguay's Francisco Solano López at Cerro Corá,
March 1, 1870, the last action of the Triple Alliance
War.

DIAGUITES INDIANS. Guaraní tribe living in the area between the Paraná and Tebicuary Rivers who were
Christianized and induced to live in reductions during
the Jesuit mission era.

DIARIO (EL). Asunción daily newspaper published in 1936
as the voice of the ex-Chaco War Veterans Association. Reappeared in 1937.

DIAZ, ISIDORA. Sister of Paraguayan Triple Alliance War
hero General José E. Díaz, and companion-servant of
Mme. Elisa Alicia Lynch, Irish consort of Marshal
President López. Isidora accompanied Mrs. Lynch to
Europe after the debacle at Cerro Corá in March,
1870.

DIAZ, GENERAL JOSE EDUVIGIS, 1833-1867. A major
hero of the Triple Alliance War, Díaz is remembered

popularly as the "Vencedor de Curupaity"--the Victor
of the battle of Curupaity, Paraguay's most significant
wartime victory. Popular with his troops and highly
regarded by Marshal President López, his death in a
river reconnaissance in 1867 proved as harsh a blow
to López and the Paraguayan army as that of Stonewall
Jackson to General Lee in the American Civil War.

DIAZ, PEDRO. Lumberman-carpenter recorded as having
accompanied the 1542 Cabeza de Vaca overland expedition to Paraguay.

DIAZ DE BEDOYA, JOSE see also TRIUMVIRATE OF
1869. Member of the Legión Paraguaya, an organization of Paraguayan exiles at Buenos Aires opposed to
President Francisco Solano López. Also member of
the Triumvirate of 1869, the provisional Paraguayan
government prior to the promulgation of the Constitution of 1870. Retired to Buenos Aires following the
end of the Triple Alliance War, reportedly with much
wealth illegally obtained during his brief Asunción
sojourn.

DIAZ DE BEDOYA Y VALDOVINOS, SATURNINO, 1812-1868.
Minister of the Treasury during the administration of
Francisco Solano López. Suspected of political activi-
ties against the president, he was arrested and exe-
cuted during the 1868 conspiracy episode of the Triple
Alliance War.

DIAZ DE GUZMAN, RUY, 1560-1629. Born at Asunción
the son of Captain Alonso Riquelme and the mestizo
girl Ursula, daughter of Domingo Martínez de Irala,
prominent early governor of Paraguay. One of the
colony's most prominent "mancebos de la tierra," or
native-born of mixed parentage, Díaz de Guzmán was
the leader of numerous expeditions which explored the
region of Paraguay and founded new cities and fortified
points. His major contribution was the writing of La
Argentina, the first published history of the Río de la
Plata area. Recorded as the first native-born historian
of Paraguay and La Plata.

DIAZ DE MELGAREJO, RUY, 1520-1595. Spanish explorer
and conquistador who founded the cities of Ciudad Real
(now extinct) and Villarrica del Espíritu Santo in the
Guairá region of extreme northeast Paraguay.

DIAZ DEL VALLE, PERO. Spanish conquistador named by
Martínez de Irala as alcalde (mayor) of the newly established municipality of Asunción in 1541.

DIAZ LEON - GUTIERREZ PROTOCOL. Signed April 22,
1927, by Paraguayan and Bolivian representatives at
Buenos Aires, and provided for acceptance of Argentina's good offices in organizing a conference to settle
the Chaco dispute. The subsequent 1927-1928 conference at Buenos Aires foundered on the growing intran-
sigence of both republics.

DIAZ PEREZ, VIRIATO, 1875-1958. Spanish-born historian,
literary critic and bibliophile who emigrated to Paraguay in 1906 where he resided until his death. Regarded as one of the most prominent Asunción intellectuals in the first half of the twentieth century.
Member of numerous international organizations, and
founder and editor of several Paraguayan scholarly
publications including Revista del Instituto Paraguayo
and Revista del Paraguay.

DICTADOR PERPETUO DE LA REPUBLICA   see FRANCIA,
DR. JOSE GASPAR RODRIGUEZ DE.   Title of Per-
petual Dictator bestowed upon Dr. Francia by the
Fourth National Congress of 1816.

DIEZ DE ANDINO, JUAN. Commander of an Asunción army
sent in 1676 against mameluke and Bandeirante raiders
attacking missions in the eastern Guairá region. Governor in 1663 and 1681.

DIEZ DE MEDINA, EDUARDO. Bolivia's diplomatic representative in Washington during the unsuccessful efforts
of the 1928-1929 meetings of the Conference on Conciliation and Arbitration called to resolve the Chaco
problem.

DIFUNTO (EL) see also FRANCIA, DR. JOSE GASPAR
RODRIGUEZ DE, and EL SUPREMO.

DIRECTORIO REVOLUCIONARIO DEL PARTIDO LIBERAL
see also LIBERAL PARTY. Formed in October,
1962, as a splinter group of the traditional Liberal
Party, and for the purpose of supplying formal, authorized opposition in the 1963 general elections. Its
leader, Dr. Ernesto Gavilán, reportedly received

45,000 votes compared to the government's 470,000 in an election which for the first time in Paraguay's history featured the participation of women.

DIVISION OF 1617. Occurring during the administration of Governor Hernandarias, proposed by the Viceroy of Peru and approved by the Spanish court, this act formally separated the developing region of Buenos Aires from the Province of Paraguay. Deprivation of its free access to the sea as of this date represented for Paraguay an international problem which plagued it for more than two centuries.

DOM PEDRO II see PEDRO II, EMPEROR OF BRAZIL, 1825-1891. Dom Pedro de Alcântara João Carlos Leopoldo Salvador Bebiano Francisco Xavier de Paula Leocádio Miguel Gabriel Rafael Gonzaga, Second Emperor of Brazil. Famed in his nation's history as the "First Brazilian," and a peaceful man by nature who listed school-teaching as a second profession were he forced to abdicate, Dom Pedro, nevertheless, viewed the Triple Alliance War as a personal contest with Paraguay's Francisco Solano López. Determined to redeem what he believed to be a blight on his nation's honor, he pursued the war to ultimate victory and the disappearance of López.

DOMINGUEZ, MANUEL, 1866-1935. Prominent author, educator, orator, historian, and statesman. Director of the Colegio Nacional and Universidad Nacional. Known for his expert researching of Paraguay's Chaco claims. Regarded by many as one of the greatest intellects appearing in Paraguay.

DOMINGUEZ DE LA COSTA, JUAN. One of the first recorded teachers in colonial Paraguay, reported to have taught classes in 1630.

DOMINGUEZ DE OBELAR, CRISTOBAL. Provisional governor of Paraguay during the 1733-1735 interlude in the Comunero movement between the departure of Juan de Aguerri and the March, 1735, battle of Tabapy at which the Comuneros were defeated by Bruno Mauricio de Zavala.

DOMINICANS. Catholic religious order established early in Paraguay's colonial period. The Dominicans were not as zealous or as determined in their missionary projects as the more widely known Jesuits and Franciscans.

DORADO (EL)--"THE GOLDEN ONE." As in most Latin
American areas, notably in Colombia, Spaniards in the
discovery and conquest era in Paraguay were obsessed
with visions of discovering fabulous lodes of precious
minerals. El Dorado was a particularly enticing legend. By the mid-seventeenth century, however, count-
less expeditions had proved that the true wealth of
Paraguay lay in its fertile land and not in the form of
gold and silver mines or fabulously rich Indian tribes.

DORANTES, PEDRO, ? -1579. Spanish conquistador who accompanied the 1541-1542 Alvar Núñez Cabeza de Vaca
overland expedition from the Brazilian Atlantic coast to
Paraguay. Subsequently a prominent official in the
Asunción colonial government known for his loyalty and
probity.

D'ORBIGNY, ALCIDES. French naturalist and early explorer of the Amazon Basin, including Paraguay, who
prepared one of the first complete and reliable ethnographic studies of the region.

DORREGO, MANUEL. Governor of Buenos Aires in 1828
who entertained a plan, never carried to fruition, of
having one of his generals, Fructuoso Rivera, attempt
to invade Paraguay.

DUARTE, MANUEL J. Naval officer and Liberal Party
politician. One of the architects of the Liberal Revolution of August, 1904, temporarily appointed as Minister
of War and Marine.

DUARTE, GENERAL PEDRO, 1829-1903. Commander of the
right arm of Colonel Estigarribia's invasion force proceeding down the banks of the Uruguay River in the
1865 phase of the Triple Alliance War. His force was
annihilated by the allies at the battle of Yatay, August,
1865. Appointed to numerous postwar government posts
including that of Minister of War and Marine. Died at
Asunción.

DU GRATY, ALFRED M. Belgian scientist-investigator in
Paraguay during the Carlos Antonio López administration. Noted for his La République du Paraguay, published at Brussels in 1860, and containing a thorough
report on minerals found in Paraguay.

DUPUY, PEDRO, 1816-1886. French national resident at
    Buenos Aires who was invited by Carlos Antonio López
    to come to Asunción as director of the new Escuela de
    Matemáticas. Following the 1864-1870 war, he returned
    to Asunción where in 1875 President Juan B. Gill made
    him rector of the Colegio Nacional. Died at Buenos
    Aires.

DUVALL, MARIUS. Physician with the U.S. naval squadron
    in 1868 who examined Cornelius Porter Bliss and George
    F. Masterman, associates of American Minister Charles
    A. Washburn, and found no evidence of alleged torture
    by the conspiracy tribunals of Francisco Solano López.

                                - E -

ECHAGUE, PASCUAL. Argentine national and resident of
    Asunción who, in the early years of Dr. Francia's re-
    gime, is alleged in historical records to have run afoul
    of El Supremo's wishes and to have died in prison as
    a result.

ECHAURI, CAPTAIN MARTIN JOSE DE. Commander of a
    loyal army of Guaraní mission Indians which defeated
    the last Comunero army at the Tebicuary River in
    1735, thus ending the Comunero Revolt era. Echauri
    as governor later used mission Indians to repel an at-
    tack upon Asunción by Chaco Indians.

ECHEVERRIA, DR. VICENTE ANASTASIO. Argentine emis-
    sary who accompanied General Manuel Belgrano on a
    special mission to Asunción in October, 1811, for the
    purpose of establishing formal Buenos Aires/Paraguayan
    relationships. The resulting Treaty of October 12, 1811,
    though it proved premature in establishing Paraguay's
    independence, remains as Paraguay's first international
    convention.

ECHEVERRIA Y GALLO, DR. GABINO DE see also REAL
    SEMINARIO CONCILIAR DE SAN CARLOS. First rec-
    tor of the Real Seminario Conciliar de San Carlos on
    its founding in 1783 during the governorship of Pedro
    Melo de Portugal.

ECO DEL PARAGUAY (EL). Early and short-lived independ-
    ent Asunción newspaper noted for having proposed

in 1857 the candidacy for the presidency of Francisco
Solano López.   Its 108 issues were published between
April, 1855, and 1857, when the official paper El Se-
manario resumed publication.   Director of El Eco was
the Spanish literateur and educator, Ildefonso Antonio
Bermejo.

EGUSQUICISTAS.   Splinter faction of the Colorado Party in
the late 1890's which supported Juan B. Egusquiza.
Its opponents were the "Caballeristas," or partisans of
General Bernardino Caballero.

EGUSQUIZA, FELIX.   Paraguayan confidential agent at Buenos Aires during the period immediately preceding the
Triple Alliance War.

EGUSQUIZA, JUAN BAUTISTA, ? -1902.   President, 1894-
1898, whose administration is remembered principally
for the splitting into rival factions of both the Liberal
and Colorado parties.

EL.   Phrases and place names beginning with an article,
with few necessary exceptions, are found under the
word following the article.

ELIO, DR. TOMAS MANUEL.   Bolivian foreign minister
representing his nation in the 1935-1938 negotiations
ending the Chaco War.

ELIZALDE, RUFINO DE.   Argentine foreign minister in the
Bartolomé Mitre government on the eve of the Triple
Alliance War.   Involved in the negotiations with Uruguay
over Blanco-Colorado Party problems which made that
nation the powder keg of La Plata.

EMBOSCADA.   Small inhabited point about 20 miles north of
Asunción along the Paraguay River known historically as
one of the two points in Paraguay at which persons of
Negro descent settled, the other being Laurel-ty also
near Asunción.   The Emboscada site was probably settled by persons moving westward from Brazil in the
early seventeenth century, who were permitted to remain there to form a buffer against Indian attacks on
Asunción.

ENCARNACION.   Founded in 1614 by Roque González de
Santa Cruz, this port city is the most important in

southern Paraguay. It is located about 230 miles (370 kms) south of Asunción on the right bank of the Paraná River facing Argentina. Known originally as Itapúa, it served as Paraguay's principal import/export point for the limited trade during the Jesuit and early independence eras. Today it is the southern terminus of the Presidente Carlos Antonio López Railway, which links with the Argentina system across the Paraná at Posadas.

ENCARNACION CHURCH. Formerly existent in the area now occupied by Asunción's Estadio Comuneros. Dr. Francia was entombed in its atrium after his death on September 20, 1840. In 1870, his remains were allegedly disinterred by Carlos Loizaga and others of his enemies and thrown into the Paraguay River.

ENCISO VELLOSA, GUILLERMO, 1899-   . Contemporary essayist, journalist and former ambassador specializing in political topics. Director on several occasions of Colorado Party publications.

ENCOMENDERO see also ENCOMIENDA. Proprietor of the Encomienda. The encomienda system in Paraguay was far less widespread and severe as practiced in other republics. It was, however, of the "Yanacona" type, involving perpetual service by the Indians on the large plantations or "estancias."

ENCOMIENDA. The division or "repartimiento" of land and Indians among Spanish conquistadors as the fruits of conquest.

ENGREN, FRED. Advance representative of the Mennonite Chaco project of the 1920's who is credited with having resolved most of the initial settlement problems faced by the arriving immigrants.

ENTRADA. Arrival, entrance or penetration into a newly discovered land. Commanders of such expeditions were usually commissioned as Adelantados.

ENTRE RIOS PROVINCE, ARGENTINA. Argentine province located between the Uruguay and Paraná Rivers below the northernmost province of Corrientes. Strategically important during the Triple Alliance War for the possibility that it might adhere to Paraguay's side. Its caudillo chieftain, General Justo José de Urquiza,

though a friend of Carlos Antonio and Francisco Solano
López, was neutralized as a possible opponent to Buenos Aires by the diplomacy of Bartolomé Mitre.

EPOCA, LA.   One of Paraguay's earliest independent newspapers at mid-nineteenth century.   Succeeded El Eco
del Paraguay.

ESCALADA, ASUNCION, 1850-1894.   Remembered as Paraguay's first female teacher.   Accompanied her grandfather, Juan Pedro Escalada, as a "residenta" during
the tragic 1869-1870 retreat to Cerro Corá.   On returning to Asunción in 1869, she assisted him in founding on November 7, 1869, the city's first municipal
school for women, the Escuela Central de Niñas.   Acted
as the school's first director and instructor until 1875
when she accompanied her husband, Jaime Sosa, on his
diplomatic mission to Brazil.   Died at Buenos Aires.

ESCALADA, JUAN PEDRO, 1777-1869.   Argentine educator
noted for his efforts toward developing primary schools
during the Carlos Antonio López administration.   Officially commended for his efforts by a government
decree of December 22, 1862.   Remained in Paraguay
during the Triple Alliance War, and died at Asunción
in 1869.   Recorded also as the probable teacher of the
Carlos Antonio López family, including Francisco Solano.

ESCOBAR, ALONSO DE.   Spanish tailor mentioned in records
as having reached Asunción in the mid-sixteenth century
as a member of the Ñufrio de Chaves expedition from
Peru.

ESCOBAR, GENERAL PATRICIO, ? -1912.   Triple Alliance
War hero and president of Paraguay, 1886-1890.   With
General Bernardino Caballero, one of the early stal-
warts of the Colorado Party.   Both of Paraguay's principal political parties, Colorados and Liberals, were
formed during his administration.

ESCOBAR DE OSORIO, DIEGO.   Governor of Paraguay in
1647-1649 who succeeded Governor Gregorio de Hinestrosa during the troubles with Bishop Bernardino de
Cárdenas.   Escobar permitted Cárdenas to return from
exile, and Cárdenas himself became governor on the
former's death in 1649.

ESCUELA DE DERECHO CIVIL Y POLITICO. Founded
    through the initiative of President Carlos Antonio López
    under the terms of a decree of March 15, 1850. A
    modest civil and political law school recognized as an
    early step toward the establishment of a future national
    university.

ESCUELA GRADUADA DE PERCEPTORES. Inaugurated at
    Asunción in 1890 under the direction of Adela Speratti
    for the training of teachers. Subsequently evolved into
    the Escuela Normal in 1896.

ESCUELA MILITAR see COLEGIO MILITAR MARISCAL
    FRANCISCO SOLANO LOPEZ.

ESCUELA NORMAL. Paraguay's first teacher training in-
    stitution founded at Asunción in 1855 under the direc-
    tion of the Spanish intellectual Ildefonso Antonio Berme-
    jo.

ESCUELA NORMAL DE MAESTRAS see also SPERATTI,
    ADELA. Founded at Asunción in 1896 under govern-
    ment auspices provided by a decree of March 7, 1896.
    Its first director was Adela Speratti, also director of
    the Escuela Graduada de Niñas and a foremost expo-
    nent for the need to improve educational opportunities
    for women.

ESCURRA, COLONEL JUAN A. Leader of a Colorado Party
    faction which overthrew President Emilio Aceval in
    January, 1902. Escurra became president in Novem-
    ber, 1902, but was deposed and forced into exile in
    December, 1904, following the Liberal Party revolt in
    August.

ESPINOLA Y PEÑA, COLONEL JOSE DE. Paraguayan-born
    representative of the Buenos Aires Junta who in 1810
    failed in a mission to Asunción for the purpose of se-
    curing Paraguay's adhesion to the new Buenos Aires
    government.

ESTABELECIMIENTO REDOUBT. Fortified Paraguayan posi-
    tion on extreme left of the Humaitá entrenchments.
    Captured by Brazilian troops in a closing action of the
    Humaitá campaign of the Triple Alliance War.

ESTADO DE SITIO. The principal device employed continu-

ously by Paraguay's government, especially since 1947,
to prevent serious disturbances of a political nature.
Totally dissimilar to the harsher methods of the Perón,
Trujillo, Duvalier, and Castro regimes. Involves only
a minimum of official control. Authorized by constitutional provision and a prerogative of the executive
branch which seeks order through peaceful evolution.
Currently in effect only at Asunción and border zones
adjacent to Brazil and Argentina.

ESTANCIA. The most frequently used name in Paraguay for
large ranches at which cattle growing is the major industry. Prevalent especially in the Chaco area.

ESTANCIERO. Name used in Paraguay and the other La
Plata republics for large ranch or "estancia" owners.

ESTERO BELLACO, BATTLE OF. Fought May 2, 1866,
in the early stages of the Humaitá campaign of the
Triple Alliance War. A forerunner of the more important battle of Tuyuty on May 24. Estero Bellaco
was a Paraguayan probing action which proved incon-
clusive for both sides.

ESTERO DE ÑEEMBUCU. Sluggish drainage stream in extreme southern Paraguay in the Humaitá area. Formed
roughly an eastern boundary of the 1865-1868 Humaitá
zone of the Triple Alliance War. Enters the Paraguay
River at the riverport of Pilar.

ESTERO ROJAS see ESTERO BELLACO, BATTLE OF.
Also known as the Estero Bellaco del Norte. The
right flank of the allied positions at the 1866 battle of
Estero Bellaco of the Triple Alliance War.

ESTEVEZ, GOMEZ FREIRE see FREIRE ESTEVEZ, GO-
MEZ.

ESTIGARRIBIA, COLONEL ANTONIO DE LA CRUZ see also
URUGUAYANA, SIEGE OF. Commander of the left
prong of Paraguay's invasion of La Plata in 1865. Far
from his base of supply and cut off from reinforce-
ment, he surrendered his army to allied forces at
Uruguayana, September 18, 1865. The defeat was a major blow to the plans of Marshal President López to
achieve a quick victory in the Triple Alliance War.

ESTIGARRIBIA, EULOGIO.   Member of the Guión Rojo faction of the Colorado Party in the 1940's and 1950's,
   and former minister of education.

ESTIGARRIBIA, MARSHAL JOSE FELIX, 1888-1940.   One of
   Paraguay's foremost national heroes and the only other
   besides Francisco Solano López to be honored with the
   title of Marshal.   Outstanding commander of Paraguay's
   army in the Chaco War whose strategy and tactics are
   regarded as forerunners of those of Germany's Field
   Marshal Rommel in World War II.   Made president in
   1939, he promulgated the Constitution of 1940, a document contemplating a new era for Paraguay under
   stronger chief executive powers.   His promising career
   was cut short by his death in an airplane accident near
   Asunción in 1940.   His remains are entombed in Asunción's Pantheon of the Heroes.

ESTIGARRIBIA, DR. JUAN VICENTE, 1788-1862.   Ancestor
   of Chaco War hero Marshal José Félix Estigarribia,
   and physician friend of Dr. José Gaspar Rodríguez de
   Francia.

ESTIGARRIBIA, MATEO.   Father of Chaco War hero Marshal José Félix Estigarribia.

ESTRELLA (LA).   The fifth and last of Paraguay's wartime
   newspapers, published at Piribebuy from February,
   1869, until the assault on the city by allied forces on
   August 12, 1869.

EU, COMTE D' see ORLEANS, GASTON DE.

EUSEBIO AYALA, CITY OF see also BARRERO GRANDE.
   Known also by its original name of Barrero Grande,
   this interior city is located approximately 45 miles
   (72 kms) to the east of Asunción on Route 2.   Founded
   in 1770 by Carlos Morphi, it is historically important
   for the battle of Acosta Ñú, one of the last major actions of the Paraguayan War, fought nearby on August
   16, 1869.

- F -

FALCON, JOSE, 1810-1883.   Historian, archivist and
   prominent government official during the administra-

tions of Carlos Antonio and Francisco Solano López.
Director of Paraguay's National Archives in 1854 and
1871. Responsible for their reorganization after the
Triple Alliance War.

FARIÑA, LIEUTENANT JOSE MARIA, 1836-1917. Famed
as a prominent hero for his Triple Alliance War exploits as a commander of Paraguayan armed launches
and barges against Brazilian naval vessels in 1865-
1866. His successes in such exploits delayed the allied army's crossing of the Paraná River in the early
Humaitá siege operations. Served throughout the remainder of the war as an artillery commander.

FARIÑA NUÑEZ, ELOY, 1885-1929. Foremost Paraguayan
literary figure of the first quarter of the twentieth century, and the first to win a prize abroad. His Buclos
de oro was awarded first prize in a 1912 literary ex-
position sponsored by the Buenos Aires La Prensa.
Philosopher, anthropologist and economist, he is also
known for his Canto secular, published in 1911 in com-
memoration of the first century of Paraguay's independence.

FASSARDI, JOSE. Italian immigrant who began a sawmill
business in the late nineteenth century which prospered
to become one of Paraguay's most important business
establishments.

FEBRERISMO see also FRANCO, GENERAL RAFAEL,
and FEBRERISTAS. The ideology espoused by the
Febrerista Party and generally similar to that of such
other extreme liberal Latin American political parties
as Peru's APRA, Venezuela's AD and Bolivia's MNR.
Originally socialistic in nature and patterned after European movements of the 1930's. Sought a larger participation by the state in the management of Paraguay's
affairs through directed cooperation of all socio-economic interests.

FEBRERISTAS see also FRANCO, COLONEL RAFAEL.
Name applied to the supporters of Colonel Rafael
Franco and the Febrerista Party.

FEDERACION DE ESTUDIANTES DEL PARAGUAY. University Students Federation. Progressive and politically
active student organization at Asunción which, like its

counterparts in other republics, has frequently figured
in politically inspired riots and demonstrations in Paraguay's history. Such episodes have been infrequent
during the Colorado regime since 1954 due to the State
of Siege precautionary orders maintained by the government.

FEDERACION DE LA PRODUCCION, LA INDUSTRIA Y EL
COMERCIO (FEPRINCO). Paraguay's largest and most
active business organization established as a legal en-
tity by Decree No. 15, 332 of December 26, 1952.
Originally organized to defend private business interests
against state intervention, FEPRINCO in recent years
has evolved into a more progressive organization which
is a dynamic and effective force looking to expand
Paraguayan industrial development.

FEPRINCO see FEDERACION DE LA PRODUCCION, LA
INDUSTRIA Y EL COMERCIO.

FERDINAND VII. Spanish monarch in the early nineteenth
century whose weak and vacillating policies, and his
capitulation to Napoleon's wishes, were major factors
in the swift spread of 1810 independence movements in
La Plata and all Spanish Latin America.

FERMIN, MASTER see LOPEZ, MESTRE FERMIN. Near-
legendary Triple Alliance War hero, a school-teacher
who reportedly led his pupils in the trenches at the
bloody 1869 battle of Piribebuy.

FERNANDEZ, ANDRES. Mentioned in colonial records
as treasurer of Asunción present at the ceremonies
confirming Martínez de Irala as governor in 1555.

FERNANDEZ, FRANCISCO F. Post-Triple Alliance War
Paraguayan government official. Involved in an unsuccessful scheme with President Salvador Jovellanos to
negotiate an early post-war peace treaty with Argentina.

FERNHEIM COLONY see MENNONITES.

FERREIRA, GENERAL BENIGNO, 1846-1920. With Dr.
Cecilio Báez an architect of the Liberal Revolution of
1904, and president for a brief period during November, 1906 - July, 1908. An officer in the Argentine
army during the Triple Alliance War, he nevertheless

opposed Argentine claims to the Chaco during the post-
war Reconstruction era.

FERREIRA DE OLIVEIRA, ADMIRAL PEDRO   see   OLIVEI-
RA, ADMIRAL PEDRO FERREIRA DE.

FERROCARRIL CENTRAL DEL PARAGUAY   see   PARA-
GUAY CENTRAL RAILWAY.

FERROCARRIL PRESIDENTE CARLOS ANTONIO LOPEZ
(FPCAL) see also   PARAGUAY CENTRAL RAILWAY.
Paraguay's only major common rail route known formerly as the Paraguay Central Railroad.   Purchased
by the government from British interests in 1961.   A
true historical anachronism of the past, its services
are vividly reminiscent of those of the Union Pacific
in the pageant of America's Far West.   Its traffic
volume is now minimal due to expanding highway truck
transport.   Provides the only rail link with the Argentine system at Encarnación-Posadas.

FIELDS, FATHER THOMAS.   Either an Irishman or a Scot,
and one of the first Jesuit missionaries to arrive in
Paraguay in 1588.   Credited with the establishment of
missions in the Guairá region of eastern Paraguay.

FILADELFIA   see also   MENNONITES.   Capital and largest
urban center of the Chaco Mennonite colonies of Menno,
Neuland and Fernheim.   Located at the geographic center of the Paraguayan Chaco about 250 miles from
Asunción.   Since 1961, when completion of the Trans
Chaco Highway finally permitted road connections with
Asunción, Filadelfia has become increasingly more
important as a cattle and dairy products center.   Its
many European features, including its largely German-
speaking population and German street names--Hinden-
burg Avenue, for example--make it a curious enclave
within Paraguay.

FISCHER-TREUENFELDT, R. VON   see   TREUENFELDT,
R. FISCHER VON.   Variant in the spelling of the name
of the German engineer who constructed the telegraph
line from Asunción to Humaitá, one of the first to be
operated in South America.

FLEITAS, LIEUTENANT BLAS.   Paraguayan officer attached
to the garrison at the Angostura river battery com-

manded by Colonel George Thompson in December, 1868, during the Pikysyry Campaign. The only officer who refused to agree to surrender to the allies, Fleitas succeeded in breaking through the allied lines and reaching the main Paraguayan positions.

FLEITAS, EPIFANIO MENDEZ see MENDEZ FLEITAS, EPIFANIO.

FLOMERE see FLOTA MERCANTE DEL ESTADO.

FLORES, JOSE ASUNCION, 1902-   . Paraguay's most famed music composer noted particularly for his introduction of the popular "Guarania" rhythm. Regarded as a Communist, he resides in exile at Buenos Aires.

FLORES, VENANCIO. Caudillo or chieftain of Uruguay's Colorado Party prior to the Triple Alliance War. Defeated the ruling Blanco Party and allied Uruguay with Brazil and Argentina against Paraguay. Commanded Uruguay's wartime contingent until 1866 when he returned to Montevideo as president. Assassinated in 1868.

FLOTA MERCANTE DEL ESTADO (FLOMERE). Paraguay's State Merchant Fleet was established as an autonomous government agency by Decree Law No. 9, 351 of June 27, 1945. Its major purposes are to assure Paraguay adequate national flag transport facilities along the vital Paraná-Paraguay River waterway to the Río de la Plata, and to compete with traditional Argentine and other foreign-flag shipping interests. By 1965 the fleet composed 30 cargo vessels with a cargo capacity of 18, 800 metric tons, and was hauling close to half of the nation's foreign trade. FLOMERE has since acquired several modern and efficient Spanish-built passenger cargo vessels designed expressly for service between Asunción and downstream ports including Corrientes, Argentina. Expansion and capability of the fleet still remain subject to restrictions imposed by the draught and shifting sand bars of the Paraguay River north of its confluence with the Paraná.

FOERSTER, DR. BERNARD see also COLONIA NUEVA GERMANIA. Leader of the 1887 German immigrant colony project of Nueva Germania, about 130 miles northeast of Asunción. His wife, Elizabeth, was the

99   Foerster, Mrs. Elizabeth

sister of Friedrich Wilhelm Nietzsche, famed German
philosopher. After study of the earlier Colonia San
Bernardino project, Foerster gathered a group to settle
Nueva Germania along socialistic lines similar to William Lane's Nueva Australia. The project foundered,
and unable to obtain help, Foerster committed suicide
in June, 1889. His wife sought unsuccessfully to keep
the project alive, but returned to Germany in 1893.

FOERSTER, MRS. ELIZABETH see also FOERSTER, DR.
BERNARD. Wife of the ill-fated Dr. Bernard Foerster
and sister of famed German philosopher Friedrich Wilhelm Nietzsche. After her husband's suicide in 1889,
Elizabeth sought to revive the Nueva Germania colony
project but was unsuccessful and returned to Germany
in 1893. She later achieved much more fame as the
custodian and possible editor of her brother's studies
and essays.

FONSECA, COLONEL MANOEL DEODORO DA see DEO-
DORO DA FONSECA, COLONEL MANOEL.

FORTIN. Military outposts in the Chaco prior to the 1932-
1935 war, both Paraguayan and Bolivian, were known
as "fortines." Made generally of logs and adobe, they
were small and isolated posts which usually were held
by only a squad. Most of the war's major battles were
fought in their vicinity and bear their names.

FPCAL see FERROCARRIL PRESIDENTE CARLOS ANTO-
NIO LOPEZ, and PARAGUAY CENTRAL RAILWAY.

FRANCIA, GARCIA RODRIGUEZ see RODRIGUEZ DE
FRANCIA, GARCIA. Reputed father of José Gaspar
Rodríguez de Francia, Paraguay's father of independ-
ence and famed El Supremo.

FRANCIA, DR. JOSE GASPAR RODRIGUEZ DE see also
FRANCIA, GARCIA RODRIGUEZ DE, 1766-1840. Paraguay's famed El Supremo and the Founding Father of
the nation's formative independence era. Still largely
an enigma--he never married nor amassed a fortune,
Dr. Francia made Paraguay an "Inland Japan" nearly
in total isolation from the outside world. A member
of the early revolutionary juntas, he swiftly rose to
sole power by his firm demands of Paraguayan freedom
from both Spanish and Argentine hegemony, and by his

superior education as Paraguay's only confirmed schol-
ar--he received his doctorate in theology from the University of Córdoba, Argentina. His long rule and
stern policies made his nation a homogeneous nation set
firmly in the mold of an autocratically directed republic.
In his memory Paraguay's people continued to remem-
ber him as "El Difunto"--The Deceased One. His singular role encouraged both France's Voltaire to mention Paraguay in his Candide, and Britain's Thomas
Carlyle to include him in his catalog of great men.

FRANCIA, PEDRO. Brother of Dr. José Gaspar Rodríguez
de Francia, but otherwise undistinguished in Paraguay's
history.

FRANCIA, PETRONA. Sister of Dr. José Gaspar Rodríguez
de Francia, and possibly the only close relative for
whom he showed esteem.

FRANCISCANS see also YAGUARON. The Franciscans
were the first to arrive in Paraguay, reaching Asunción
shortly after its founding. Unlike the Jesuits, they dedicated themselves solely to the conversion of Indians
and not to the establishment of jurisdictions separated
totally from political and civil control. Responsible for
the founding of numerous cities in the Asunción area
including Yaguarón, Ypacaray, Villarrica, Caaguazú,
Itá, and Ypané. The old church at Yaguarón remains
an especially well-preserved monument to their efforts.

FRANCO, DR. MANUEL, 1871-1919. President, 1916-1919;
died in office. A university professor and able administrator, he is principally remembered as having introduced the secret ballot into Paraguay's electoral system.
Puerto Presidente Franco, on the Upper Paraná River
near Puerto Presidente Stroessner, is named after him.
Senator, Supreme Court Justice, Minister of Justice
and president of the Liberal Party.

FRANCO, COLONEL RAFAEL see also FEBRERISTA PAR-
TY and FEBRERISMO, 1897-   . Perennial leader
of the Febrerista Party and popular Chaco War veteran.
Headed the 1936 movement of discontented war veterans
and other social factions which gave rise to the Febrerista Party. President from February, 1936, to August, 1937, when his regime was overthrown. Exiled
for several long periods at Montevideo. Now residing
in semi-retirement at Asunción.

FRANK, EUGENE. German consul at Encarnación during
the World War II era. Allegedly distributed pro-Nazi
propaganda in southern Paraguay.

FREIRE ESTEVEZ, GOMEZ, 1886-   . Poet, journalist,
historian, and politician. One of Paraguay's outstanding intellectuals in the first decades of the twentieth
century. Minister of the interior in the Febrerista
government of Colonel Rafael Franco. Best known for
his Historia contemporánea del Paraguay, published at
Buenos Aires in 1921.

FRENTE DE GUERRA. Allegedly pro-Fascist group of army
officers during the World War II period who are held
to have strongly influenced the Higinio Morínigo government. Leaders were Chief of Staff Colonel Victoriano
Benítez Vera, and Colonels Bernardo Aranda and Pablo
Stagni.

FRENTE NACIONAL SOCIALISTA DEL TRABAJO. Pro-Nazi
labor union reportedly composed of German laborers in
Paraguay during the World War II period.

FRENTE UNIDO DE LIBERACION NACIONAL (FULNA).
Organized in 1959-1960 as a parallel group to the Movimiento 14 de Mayo. Paraguay's Communist Party.
Inactive since several unsuccessful invasion attempts
into Paraguay of 1960.

FRIAS, MANUEL DE. Governor of Paraguay in the early
seventeenth century, and noted for his successful campaigns against hostile Payaguá Indians.

FRIENDSHIP BRIDGE see PUENTE DE LA AMISTAD.

FRUTOS, JUAN MANUEL. President of Paraguay's Supreme
Court who served briefly as president of the republic
from the removal from office of Higinio Morínigo in
June, 1948, to the inauguration in August of Juan Natalicio González.

FUENTE, PEDRO DE LA. Married Isabel, one of the nine
mestizo children of Martínez de Irala. A son from
this marriage, Pedro Hurtado, became a prominent
colonial official in La Plata.

FUEROS. Special rights or privileges granted to or inherited by municipalities in both Spain and its colonies, usually involving choice of their own officials and the maintenance of their own civil and criminal courts. Usurpation of such rights by the crown occasionally stimulated local revolts such as the famed Comunero movements in both Spain and Paraguay.

FUERTE OLIMPO. Base and riverport located on the Chaco side of the Paraguay River about 300 miles north of Asunción. Probably occupies the site of the notorious Tevegó prison of El Supremo's era.

FULNA see FRENTE UNIDO DE LIBERACION NACIONAL.

FUSTER, MARCOS. Chief of the secret police in the Higinio Morínigo regime, and reportedly pro-Axis in sympathies during the World War II period.

FUSTES, JUAN DE. Spanish conquistador and follower of Domingo Martínez de Irala during the early discovery and conquest era.

- G -

GACHUPINES. Sobriquet used in early Paraguay referring to native-born Spaniards. Also known as "Peninsulares."

GALAN, FRANCISCO RUIZ see RUIZ GALAN, FRANCISCO.

GALEANO, COLONEL ALFREDO see REVOLUTION OF 1947. Former commander of the army's First Cavalry Division, and commander of the revolutionary forces in the early stages of the 1947 Revolution against the Higinio Morínigo government.

GALPON, FORTIN. Minor riverport along the Chaco side of the Paraguay River above Bahía Negra in extreme northern Paraguay. A military base during the Chaco War.

GALVAN, LARIOS. Prominent Asunción citizen arrested and executed during the 1820 conspiracy plot episode of El Supremo's regime.

GALVEZ, MANUEL. Prolific Argentine novelist. His tril-
ogy--Caminos de la muerte, Humaitá and Jornadas de
agonía, with the Triple Alliance War as a background,
rank in Latin America's literature as prominently as
Gone With the Wind in that of North America.

GAMARRA, JUAN MANUEL. Paraguayan commander who
with Manuel Atanasio Cavañas and Fulgencio Yegros
led Paraguayan forces to victories over Belgrano's
Argentine expedition at the 1811 battles of Cerro Porteño and Tacuarí. The actions were preludes to Paraguay's independence movement.

GAMBOA, SARMIENTO DE. Leader of a sixteenth-century
Spanish exploration expedition wrecked in the Straits of
Magellan, but whose survivors were rumored still alive
south of Buenos Aires. Paraguay's famed early creole
governor, Hernandarias, is recorded as having unsuccessfully sought to discover and rescue them.

GAONA, JUAN BAUTISTA. President, December, 1904 -
December, 1905, following the August, 1904 Liberal
Revolution terminating the Colorado Party's first long
era of political control.

GAONA, FATHER SILVIO, 1912-   . Catholic priest at
Asunción and historian noted for his El clero en la
guerra de 70, published at Asunción, 1957, a well-
documented history of church activities and representatives during the Triple Alliance War.

GARAY, BLAS MANUEL, 1873-1899. Until his early and
tragic death, a noted historian, research authority on
the Chaco, and founder of the newspaper La Prensa.

GARAY, CRISTOBAL DE. Governor of Paraguay 1653-1656,
noted for his actions in repelling Indian raids through
use of mission Indian forces.

GARAY, COLONEL EUGENIO ALEJANDRINO see also
PAMPA GRAN, BATTLE OF and YRENDAGUE, BAT-
TLE OF, 1874-1937. One of the Paraguayan field
commanders under José Félix Estigarribia at the Chaco
War victory of Pampa Gran late in 1933. Colonel
Garay also commanded the flanking movement which
featured the major Paraguayan victory at Yrendagüe in
December, 1934. He was posthumously named hero of
Paraguay's Infantry and promoted to General.

GARAY, JUAN DE, 1528-1583. Founder of the city of Santa
    Fe, Argentina, in 1573, and of the new city of Buenos
    Aires in 1580, the earlier settlement by Pedro de
    Mendoza having previously been abandoned. Sailed
    down the Paraguay-Paraná River from Asunción to ac-
    complish these missions; most of his force was com-
    posed of "mancebos de la tierra," or men born of
    Paraguayan Indian and Spanish unions commencing after
    1537. Also credited with having introduced the cultiva-
    tion of sugar cane in Paraguay from roots brought by
    him from Peru.

GARAY, MAJOR JUAN MANUEL. Paraguayan army chief-
    of-staff during the Chaco War, and the officer who
    carried the basic attack plan, approved by President
    Eusebio Ayala, to Colonel José Félix Estigarribia in
    September, 1932.

GARCIA, ALEIXO. Near legendary Portuguese explorer to
    whom credit is usually given for the first penetration
    from the east in 1525 of the region now comprising
    Paraguay. He is alleged to have died in northern Para-
    guay on the return from his expedition toward the Chaco
    and Bolivia.

GARCIA, ALEIXO, JR. Rumored and non-existent son of
    the original Portuguese discoverer and explorer of
    Paraguay. His reported existence as an Indian pris-
    oner encouraged Alvar Núñez Cabeza de Vaca to dis-
    patch a fruitless rescue expedition in the early colonial
    period.

GARCIA, DIEGO. Early Spanish navigator and explorer who
    commanded an expedition to the Brazilian Atlantic
    coast at São Vicente and to La Plata in 1526-1527.
    Joined the Sebastián Cabot expedition in La Plata.

GARCIA COSSIO, JUAN. Envoy sent by Governor Bernardino
    Rivadavia of Buenos Aires in 1823 in an unsuccessful
    effort to establish relations with the Paraguay of Dr.
    José Gaspar Rodríguez de Francia. García Cossio was
    unable to proceed north of Corrientes, and Dr. Francia
    refused even to communicate with him since Paraguay
    was viewed as still an Argentine province rather than
    an independent nation.

GARCIA DE MOGUER, DIEGO. Member of the ill-fated

first La Plata expedition of Juan de Solís, who subsequently was commissioned to perform another exploration concurrently with that of Sebastián Cabot. The
two met in La Plata and jointly explored the Paraná
River area in 1528-1530. Both then returned to Spain
where García de Moguer brought charges of duty dereliction against Cabot. Though convicted, the latter
served only a relatively short sentence and then returned to England.

GARCIA DE PANES, PEDRO B. DE. Bishop of Asunción
deposed by Dr. José Gaspar Rodríguez de Francia as
part of his policy to establish state supremacy over
the church.

GARCIA MELLID, ATILIO, ? -1972. Argentine poet, diplomat and historian, widely known for his careful and
documented research of the histories of the River
Plate republics. His Proceso a los falsificadores de
la historia del Paraguay, one of the most competent
and detailed accounts of Paraguay's evolution, published
at Buenos Aires in 1963, brought him a decoration by
the Paraguayan government.

GARCIA ROS, BALTAZAR. Spanish governor at Buenos
Aires in the early eighteenth century. Led a mission
Indian campaign in 1705 which succeeded in capturing
the La Plata port city of Colônia do Sacramento. An
enemy of José de Antequera y Castro and the Comunero movement, he also commanded a mission Indian
invasion army to Paraguay which was soundly defeated
by Antequera at the Tebicuary River in August, 1724.

GARMENDIA, GENERAL JOSE IGNACIO. Argentine veteran
of the Triple Alliance War whose memoirs of the Humaitá campaign are an interesting though colorful and
partial source.

GARMENDIA, PANCHA. A young Asunción lady who allegedly spurned the passion entertained for her by Marshal
López in his earlier years. Pancha was later included
among Paraguay's "destinadas" in the 1869 retreat, and
was subsequently among those executed during the long
trek.

GASCA, PEDRO DE LA. Special representative sent by
Spain in the early sixteenth century to settle Peruvian

problems. Became involved in the 1548 Ñufrio de Chaves-Martínez de Irala controversy over the governorship of Paraguay. Eventually appointed Diego Centeno to the post, but Centeno's subsequent death voided the appointment.

GAVILAN, DR. ERNESTO. Unsuccessful candidate sponsored by the Directorio Revolucionario del Partido Liberal in the 1963 presidential elections.

GELLY, JUAN ANDRES, 1790-1856. Special envoy sent by Carlos Antonio López to Brazil in the late 1840's on a fruitless mission to establish satisfactory boundaries with the empire. Also accompanied Francisco Solano López as a secretary on his 1853-1854 European mission. Editor of El Paraguayo Independiente during the administration of Carlos Antonio López.

GELLY Y OBES, JUAN ANDRES. Son of Juan Andrés Gelly, the Paraguayan diplomat, editor of El Semanario and assistant to Francisco Solano López. Gelly y Obés was born at Buenos Aires and was a General in the Argentine army during the Triple Alliance War.

GENERAL GENES, FORTIN. One of the string of small fortified Paraguayan outposts in the central Chaco at the outbreak of the Chaco War.

GENES, CAPTAIN IGNACIO. Commander of an unsuccessful but ingenious canoe boarding attack against the Brazilian naval squadron in March, 1868, in an effort to prolong the defense of the besieged Humaitá position during the Triple Alliance War.

GICANES, ALEJANDRO. One of Paraguay's more notable poets in the modern era.

GILBERT, HENRY. Recorded as an American citizen resident at Buenos Aires who, in 1842, was contracted by the Paraguayan government for the minting of 30,000 copper coins, among the first in the national monetary system. The November 27, 1842 law authorizing the contract stipulated that Gilbert would be paid 30,000 arrobas of yerba maté put free on board at the riverport of Pilar.

GILL, ANDRES, 1796-1865. Commissioned by the Congress

of 1842 to proceed to Buenos Aires to explain the actions taken by the Congress and to solicit recognition
of Paraguay's independence by Governor Juan Manuel
de Rosas. Rosas side-stepped the independence question but agreed to commercial interchange. Gill's assignment represented independent Paraguay's first diplomatic mission. Also served as Secretary of Government and Chargé of Foreign Affairs in the administration of Carlos Antonio López. In the latter office, he
is recorded as Paraguay's first minister of foreign affairs.

GILL, EMILIO. Brother of President Juan B. Gill, and assassinated with him on a downtown Asunción street on
April 12, 1877.

GILL, JOHN THOMAS. Irish national who reached Paraguay
in 1737. Father of Juan Miguel Gill, a member of the
1811 congress which declared Paraguay's independence,
and grandfather of Andrés Gill, diplomat and foreign
minister in the Carlos Antonio López administration.

GILL, JUAN BAUTISTA, 1840-1877. Politician and statesman. Regarded as the strongest personality in the
early postwar governments following the Triple Alliance
War. Noted in particular for his rejection and disa-
vowal of the Sosa-Tejedor Treaty which contemplated
the acknowledgment of Argentine claims to the Chaco.
President from November, 1874 to April, 1877, when
he was assassinated in downtown Asunción.

GILL AGUINAGA, JUAN BAUTISTA, 1910-   . Widely respected Asunción businessman, author of historical essays, and collector of antiquities. Noted for his "Co-
lección Juan Bautista Gill Aguínaga," one of the most
important numismatic collections in Latin America.

GILL DE CORBAL, CARMELITA. Anti-López Asunción so-
ciety matron, reportedly one of American Minister
Charles Ames Washburn's contacts during the Triple
Alliance War era.

GIMENEZ, LEOPOLDO RAMOS see RAMOS GIMENEZ,
LEOPOLDO.

GIMENEZ, REMBERTO. Noted musicologist and composer,
and an early director of the Escuela Normal de Música

at Asunción.   Conductor of the Symphonic Orchestra,
and composer of the official arrangement of the national
anthem.

GOCERAS, MIGUEL.   Spanish carpenter who is recorded as
having accompanied the 1541 Cabeza de Vaca overland
expedition from Brazil's Atlantic coast to Asunción.

GODOI, JUANSILVANO, 1850-1926.   Statesman, jurist and
historian.   Prominent member of the post Triple Alliance War convention which promulgated the Constitution of 1870, Supreme Court justice, leader of the 1877
and 1879 revolutions, and from 1902 to 1926 director
general of the Biblioteca, Museo and Archivo de la
Nación at Asunción.   Lived much of his life in exile
at Buenos Aires where he amassed an outstanding art
collection.   The collection, known as the "Museo Histórico y de Bellas Artes" de Juansilvano Godoi, was established in 1885 and later moved to Asunción where it
is today one of Paraguay's most notable collections of
art works, numismatics and historical relics.

GODON, REAR ADMIRAL S.W.   Commander of the U.S.
South Atlantic squadron in the early Triple Alliance
War period who became embroiled with Minister Charles
Ames Washburn regarding the latter's desire to return
to Paraguay in 1866 via U.S. naval vessel.   Later succeeded by Rear Admiral C.H. Davis.   Both were later
absolved of dereliction of duty charges in an 1869 congressional inquiry into Paraguayan affairs.

GODOY, COLONEL JULIAN, 1834-1889.   Personal aide to
Marshal President Francisco Solano López who served
throughout the Triple Alliance War, falling prisoner to
Brazilian troops at Cerro Corá, March 1, 1870.   Wrote
an as yet unpublished account of his wartime experiences
which is held in an Asunción private collection.

GODWIN, HENRY see also YBYCUI.   British engineer
whose services were contracted for in Brazil by Juan
Andrés Gelly, and who helped established the Ybycuí
iron foundry in 1850.

GÕES, VICENTE and SCIPION DE.   Brazilians who accompanied the second expedition of Juan de Salazar in 1555,
bringing with them the first seven cows and one bull to
Paraguay.

GOMEZ, LEANDRO. Commander of the Uruguayan Blanco
    government garrison at the Uruguay River port city of
    Paysandú in late 1864. Executed following the city's
    capture by Brazilian forces. The siege of Paysandú
    and the death of Gómez were incidents leading to the
    outbreak of the Triple Alliance War.

GOMEZ, RODRIGO. Spanish conquistador and follower of
    Martínez de Irala. Recorded as having participated in
    a 1542 Chaco exploration expedition together with Juan
    de Fustes and Alvaro de Chaves.

GOMEZ RIOS, EMILIANO, 1898-1957. Historian and edu-
    cator. Served in numerous high administrative positions
    in the national education system, including the post of
    Inspector General of Schools. Author of several his-
    torical works including the widely used and officially
    approved text entitled El Paraguay y su historia.

GONDRA, BATTLE OF. Like that of Nanawa, this Chaco
    War action was a bloody defensive struggle in early
    1933 by Paraguayan troops against mass assaults in the
    Bolivian general offensive of that year. Paraguay's
    commander, Colonel Rafael Franco, later became the
    leader of the Febrerista Revolt of February, 1936.

GONDRA, FORTIN MANUEL see GONDRA, BATTLE OF.

GONDRA, MANUEL see also GONDRA TREATY, 1871-
    1927. Prominent scholar and statesman known partic-
    ularly for his work in international affairs on the peace-
    ful solution of questions between the American republics.
    Twice president of Paraguay, in 1910 and 1920. His
    extensive library was acquired after his death by the
    University of Texas at Austin.

GONDRA TREATY. Named in honor of Manuel Gondra,
    noted Paraguayan scholar and statesman of the early
    twentieth century who was largely responsible for its
    negotiation. Signed at the Fifth International Confer-
    ence of American States at Santiago, Chile, in 1923,
    the pact is entitled Treaty to Avoid or Prevent Con-
    flicts between the American States. Regarded as a
    major step toward the development of the present OAS
    peace maintenance system.

GONZALEZ, ANASTASIO. Diplomatic representative who

with Bernardo Jovellanos attended a conference at Montevideo in 1846 to review matters arising from British and French intervention in La Plata. Their principal achievement was the bringing back to Paraguay of the verse of the future national anthem, composed by the Uruguayan poet Francisco Acuña de Figueroa.

GONZALEZ, ANTONIO E., 1906-   . Chaco War veteran, government official and diplomat. Author of several historical works including La guerra del Chaco (1941), La rebellión de Concepción (1947), and Preparación del Paraguay para la guerra del Chaco (1958).

GONZALEZ, BARTOLOME. Spanish conquistador at Asunción in 1544 who is recorded as having participated in the successful movement to depose Governor Alvar Núñez Cabeza de Vaca in favor of Martínez de Irala.

GONZALEZ, EMETERIO, 1863-1939. Jurist, educator and statesman. Remembered for his career as an instructor at the Escuela Normal de Maestros, the Universidad Nacional, and as a Supreme Court judge.

GONZALEZ, GUILLERMO, 1851-1945. Triple Alliance War veteran who fought at the battle of Acosta Ñú, August, 1869. His memoirs, Reminiscencias históricas de la guerra del Paraguay, were published in 1914 at Asunción.

GONZALEZ, DR. GUSTAVO, 1898-   . Prominent Asunción physician and past president of the Liberal Radical Party, one of the political parties officially inscribed in opposition to the Colorado Party.

GONZALEZ, JUAN GUALBERTO. President, 1890-1893; overthrown in the latter year by a coup of dissident Colorado Party members. Noted principally for his success in defeating a Liberal Party revolt against him in 1891.

GONZALEZ, JUAN NATALICIO, 1897-1966. President briefly from August, 1948, to January, 1949, when he was overthrown by a coup d'etat. One of modern Paraguay's most prominent figures, known for his literary efforts as well as his political record as a director of the Guión Rojo faction of the Colorado Party. Essay-

ist, historian, literary critic, diplomat and author of
short stories. His Geografía del Paraguay, published
in Mexico in 1964, is an outstanding study of Paraguay's evolution.

GONZALEZ, LUIS J., 1912-   . Soldier, journalist, nov-
elist and historian. Noted for his interpretive study,
Paraguay, prisionero geopolítico, published at Buenos
Aires in 1947.

GONZALEZ DE SANTA CRUZ, ROQUE, 1576-1628. Major
figure in Paraguay's missionary history, and today the
nation's foremost candidate for sainthood by virtue of
his exploration and conversion exploits among native
tribes in the unknown regions of Paraguay and neighboring Argentina and Uruguay. Brutally sacrificed by Indians in 1628, his heart was torn out, reportedly still
beating, and thrown into a fire. Later "recovered,"
it is still a venerated religious object attesting to
Roque Gonzalez' faith and courage. Founder in 1615
of Encarnación de Itapúa on the Upper Paraná River.

GONZALEZ ESCOBAR, FATHER AMANCIO, ? -1811. Native of Emboscada, north of Asunción, and one of the
more notable clerics in the pre-independence era.
Assisted in founding the Melodía settlement in 1786,
later to become Nueva Burdeos and today's Villa Hayes.
Known as the "Apostle of the Chaco" for his evangelizing efforts among Chaco Indian tribes.

GONZALEZ NAVERO, EMILIANO, 1861-1934. Jurist, president of the Supreme Court, government cabinet minister, twice vice president, and temporary president.
One of the most respected high government officials of
the early twentieth century. Member of the Liberal
Party committee which planned the August, 1904, revolution bringing the Liberal Party into power for the
first time.

GOULD, G. Z. Secretary of the British Legation at Buenos
Aires during the Triple Alliance War. Noted for his
1867 aborted efforts to secure an acceptable mediation
plan for peaceful termination of the war. His proposals were rejected by Francisco Solano López.

GOVERNORS OF PARAGUAY see APPENDIX I.

GRAN CLUB DEL PUEBLO   see also   GREAT CLUB OF
THE PEOPLE.   Early political organization formed in
1870 by Juan José Decoud in the post-Triple Alliance
War period.   Largely composed of ex-members of the
Paraguayan Legion, the anti-López faction based at
Buenos Aires before the war and a unit within the war-
time allied army.   Considered a forerunner of the
Centro Democrático which eventually became Paraguay's
Liberal Party after the 1904 revolution.   Its opponents
formed the "Club Unión," the "Club del Pueblo," the
"Club Libertad," and finally the Asociación Nacional
Republicana, the modern-day Colorado Party.

GRAN HOTEL DEL PARAGUAY.   Asunción's oldest hotel,
and until the 1960's and the construction of the Hotel
Guaraní, its largest.   Noted for its ornate nineteenth
century dining room which was the theater/ballroom
designed and constructed by Mme. Elisa Alicia Lynch,
famed Irish-born mistress of Marshal President Francisco Solano López.

GRANJA   see also   ESTANCIA.   Commonly used name for
a small "estancia" or farm or ranch.   Granjas are
more frequent in eastern Paraguay while estancias are
typical of the Chaco.

GRAPPLER, H. M. S.   see   BUZZARD, H. M. S.

GREAT CLUB OF THE PEOPLE   see   GRAN CLUB DEL
PUEBLO.

GRILLOS.   A version of leg fetters comprising iron anklets
at the extremes of an iron bar.   Used during the nineteenth century, especially in the era of El Supremo and
the 1868 conspiracy period of the Triple Alliance War.

GUAIENI INDIANS.   Extreme north Chaco tribe encountered
by Martínez de Irala on his 1543 exploration expedition.

GUAIRA   see also   GUAYRA DISTRICT.   Name incorporating
the general area in east central Paraguay stretching to
the Paraná River, especially in the vicinity of Villarrica.   The name appears frequently in histories of early
Spanish and Jesuit colonization efforts, and the attacks
upon them by Portuguese Mamelucos and Bandeirantes.

GUAIRA FALLS.   Located about 120 miles north of the bet-

ter-known Yguazú Falls on the Upper Paraná River,
the eastern border of Paraguay with Brazil--the center
of the so-called Guairá region, site of some of the
earliest settlement projects in Paraguay following the
founding of Asunción. Nearby the falls are the original
sites, long since abandoned, of the Ontiveros and Ciudad Real colonial posts. The Guairá Falls, until recent years almost totally isolated, are said to have the
largest volume of any in the world and geologically to
be one of the world's oldest. In about 40 miles length,
the Upper Paraná descends over a series of 18 cas-
cades in a narrow channel in a fall of about 125 yards.
Estimates by hydroelectric engineers place the energy
output potential at 10 million kilowatts. This considera-
tion in the 1960's revived acrimonious diplomatic disputes between Paraguay and Brazil regarding frontier
limits at the fall's vicinity. Lengthy negotiations resulted in a mutually satisfactory agreement providing
for joint utilization of hydroelectric production. Looking to the future, the electric energy plan developed for
Guairá suggests that it will be the key to the full economic valorization of the entire La Plata basin.

GUALEGUAY, S. S. Small Argentine river steamer captured
    at Corrientes by the Paraguayan invasion army in April,
    1865. Used effectively by the Paraguayans to hamper
    allied plans to cross the Paraná River in early 1866;
    sunk purposely when the Paraguayan army retreated to
    the Humaitá lines, and later refloated and returned to
    her original owners.

GUANES, ALEJANDRO, 1872-1925. Regarded as the first
    great national poet. His works frequently reflect a
    midway stage between romanticism and modernism.
    All were published posthumously in a volume entitled
    De paso por la vida.

GUANES, JUAN N., 1846-1940. Triple Alliance War veteran
    who left a personal wartime memoir entitled Recuerdo
    histórico de la Guerra del Paraguay contra la Triple
    Alianza, 1865-1870.

GUARAMBARAE INDIANS. Branch of the Guaraní family
    found by Juan de Ayolas and Juan de Salazar living in
    the vicinity now occupied by Asunción. Their friendly
    welcome of the Spaniards contrasted with the hostility
    exhibited by the Uruguayan and Argentine tribes pre-
    viously encountered.

GUARANI, CURRENCY. Approved as the national monetary
    unit in 1943 during the administration of President Hi-
    ginio Morínigo. Replaced the former peso. One of
    Latin America's most stable currencies in the last half
    of the twentieth century and valued in 1970 at approxi-
    mately 125 to $1.00 U.S. Name derived from the Gua-
    raní Indian cultural group inhabiting Paraguay at the
    time of its discovery and conquest.

GUARANI INDIANS. Name commonly used with reference to
    Indian tribes residing in Paraguay and the periphery
    areas in Brazil, Uruguay and Argentina who speak
    Tupí-Guaraní language dialects. Thus, scholars and
    observers of Paraguay, its history and peoples, usually
    refer to "Guaraní Indians" as the indigenous peoples
    found in the area by the Spanish. Distinct tribal groups
    within the overall "Guaraní" classification were given
    separate identifying names.

GUARANI WAR. In 1750, under the terms of the "Tratado
    de Permuta," or Treaty of Exchange, Portugal relin-
    quished its claims to the Río de La Plata port of Co-
    lônia do Sacramento in exchange for possession of the
    area occupied by seven Jesuit reductions along the up-
    per left bank of the Uruguay River. The Guaraní In-
    dians resident there refused to accept Portuguese sov-
    ereignty, thereby producing the "Guaraní War." Their
    armies were defeated at the battle of Caa-ybaté in 1756.

GUARANIA see also FLORES, JOSE ASUNCION. A lilting
    and rhythmatically slow form of music highly popular
    in Paraguay since its introduction by composer José
    Asunción Flores.

GUAYAHIBITI, BATTLE OF. An episode of the Comunero
    movement, fought September 15, 1733, near the village
    of Itá about 20 miles southeast of Asunción. Royal
    Governor Manuel Agustín de Ruiloba y Calderón was
    killed and his army totally defeated by a rebel Comune-
    ro force. Subsequently in January, 1735, the Comune-
    ros suffered final defeat at the battle of Tavapy.

GUAYCURU INDIANS. Name customarily applied to the In-
    dian tribes living in the Chaco at the time of the Span-
    ish exploration and conquest of Paraguay. Recorded
    as much fiercer and hostile to the Spanish than the
    Guaraní tribes living in eastern Paraguay. Probable

descendents of the Guaycurús still inhabit remote Chaco regions and continue to resist civilization.

GUAYRA DISTRICT   see also   GUAIRA, CIUDAD REAL, ONTIVEROS, and VILLARRICA DEL ESPIRITU SANTO. Also known as the Guairá District.   An area roughly radiating out about 100 miles from a center at today's Guairá or Sête Quedas Falls, the major cascade on the Upper Paraná River north of Yguazú Falls.   The Guairá region, not a formal administrative district of Paraguay, and now only of legendary fame, was once the locale of early Spanish settlement in the late sixteenth century.   Abandoned due to constant Bandeirante/Mameluco slave raids from Brazil, it may reflect a revival with development of the hydroelectric potential at the Guairá Falls.

GUERILLEROS DE LA MUERTE, IN CHACO WAR   see also JARA, PLACIDO.   The famed "Guerillas of Death" who performed demoralizing raiding operations under their leader Plácido Jara behind Bolivian lines in the Chaco War.

GUERRA, FATHER ALONSO.   Dominican Bishop of Asunción credited with having initiated the first request in the late sixteenth century for the assignment of Jesuit missionaries to Paraguay.   The first three arrived in 1588.

GUERRA DE '70   see also   PARAGUAYAN WAR, and TRIPLE ALLIANCE, WAR OF THE.   In terms of military operations, the war reflected four separate phases. Phase 1 included: a) the seizure in November, 1864, of the Brazilian river steamer Marquês de Olinda, an act inaugurating formal warfare; b) Paraguay's subsequent successful invasion of Brazil's Mato Grosso Province to the north; c) the declaration of war against Argentina in March, 1865; d) the subsequent two-pronged Paraguayan attack south along the Uruguay and Paraná Rivers; e) the total defeat of the eastern arm at the seige of Uruguayana, and the defeat of the navy at the battle of Riachuelo which stopped the advance of the western arm down the Paraná; f) the decision by Marshal President López to retire his forces and to assume a defensive position at Humaitá, the main Paraguayan bastion above the confluence of the Paraguay and Paraná Rivers.   Phase II, from the spring of 1865 to

August, 1868: a) the eventual success of the allied
army in forcing a crossing of the Paraná and the establishment of positions before Humaitá on Paraguayan
territory; b) the almost three years of siege operations
around Humaitá, including the major battles at Tuyuty
and Curupaity; c) the gradual encirclement of the Paraguayan bastion and the steady attrition of Paraguay's
manpower; d) the forcing of the Paraguay River defenses at Humaitá and its bombardment of Asunción;
e) the successful withdrawal northward by Marshal
López of his remaining forces and the fall of Humaitá.
Phase III, the war of maneuvers until December, 1868:
a) the conspiracy episode during which Marshal López
effected a purge of civilian elements of the government
based on reports of their scheming for his overthrow;
b) the withdrawal of the Paraguayan army to fortified
positions along the Pikysyry River, south of Asunción;
c) the renewel allied attack in December including the
battles of Ytororó, Avay and Itá-Ybaté, following which
the Paraguayan forces were all but annihilated; the
evacuation and occupation of Asunción, and the pro-
nouncement by Brazil's Marquês de Caxias that the
war was ended.   Phase IV: the war of the Cordillera
until March, 1870: a) beginning January, 1869, Paraguay's Marshal President López achieved the near incredible task of organizing a new army at Azcurra and
Piribebuy, composed, however, almost solely of old
men, young boys and escaped former prisoners; b) the
new Paraguayan army was defeated and forced to retreat in August after victories at Piribebuy and Acosta
Ñú by the allied army now composed entirely of Brazilian forces; c) during the following six months until
March, 1870, Paraguay's remaining survivors retreated
slowly northeastward in a tragic march known as the
nation's Vía Crucis; d) the long war ends with the final
action at Cerro Corá in which Marshal López and many
of his staff are killed while fighting to the end.

GUERRA GUARANITICA see GUARANI WAR.

GUERRERO, MANUEL ORTIZ see ORTIZ GUERRERO,
    MANUEL.

GUEVARA, LEONARDO. Asunción citizen recorded as hav-
    ing participated in the 1820 conspiracy plot against Dr.
    José Gaspar Rodríguez de Francia, and to have sub-
    sequently disappeared as a victim of El Supremo's re-
    pression.

GUGGIARI, COLONEL AUGUSTO see also BORCHE, CAR-
LOS. Commandante of the Chaco Military Zone during
the World War II administration of Higinio Morínigo.

GUGGIARI, JOSE PATRICIO, 1884-1957. President 1928-
1932. Noted for his efforts to unite the Liberal Party
in the face of growing national discord, and for his
participation in proposals to resolve the growing Chaco
dispute with Bolivia. Founder of the Liga de la Juventud Independiente in 1906, and president of the Liberal Party. The 1928 elections in which Guggiari won
over his opponent, Eduardo Fleitas, were regarded as
the most honest and democratic to that date in Paraguay's history. Guggiari died at Buenos Aires after
long exile.

GUIDO, GENERAL TOMAS. Argentine emissary who signed
a treaty at Asunción in 1856 with Paraguayan Foreign
Minister Nicolás Vásquez covering commerce and navigation matters. Boundary questions were left in obey-
ance because of extreme Argentine claims, but Paraguay's independence was recognized.

GUIDO Y SPANO, CARLOS see also NENIA. Argentine
poet and author who composed "Nenia," a celebrated
poem in La Plata eulogizing Paraguay's peoples and
emphasizing the tragedy of their defeat in the Triple
Alliance War. A climactic line refers to the plaintive
call of the "Urutaú," a nearly extinct Paraguayan bird
species.

GUION ROJO see also COLORADO PARTY and GONZALEZ,
JUAN NATALICIO. Translated as "red dash." Name
given to a faction of the Colorado Party which supported
the candidacy for the presidency in 1947 of Juan Natalicio González. The more vocal members were exiled
with the election of Federico Chaves.

GUTIERREZ, FATHER ANASTASIO. Asunción priest recorded as having heard the confession of a conspirator
against Dr. José Gaspar Rodríguez de Francia and of
informing El Supremo of the plot's details prior to the
1820 conspiracy episode.

GUYRA VERA, CHIEF. Chieftain of a tribe in the Guairá
region in 1630 to whom Jesuit missionaries reportedly
appealed for aid on the eve of a Mameluke slaving

raid. Though alleged himself to be plotting against the Jesuits, Guyrá Verá was taken prisoner in battle with the Mamelukes and sent to São Paulo.

GUZMAN, FATHER FRANCISCO DE see also ANUNCIA-CION, FATHER GABRIEL DE LA. Brother of early explorer and author Ruy Díaz de Guzmán, who, with his brother Gabriel de la Anunciación, accompanied the first Franciscan missionaries in Paraguay and taught them Guaraní.

GUZMAN, RUY DIAZ DE see DIAZ DE GUZMAN, RUY, and ARGENTINA (LA).

- H -

HACIENDA see ESTANCIA. Name occasionally used for a large farm or ranch, with "estancia" being the preferred term.

HALSEY, THOMAS LLOYD. American citizen who, according to some experts, obtained permission to engage in commercial navigation of the Paraguay River during the early independence era.

HARRIS, WILLIAM A. American diplomatic representative at Buenos Aires in 1846. Proposed mediation between Argentina's Juan Manuel de Rosas and Paraguay's Carlos Antonio López to reduce friction stemming from Paraguay's support of the Corrientes movement under General José María Paz.

HAYES, RUTHERFORD B. see also HAYES ARBITRATION and VILLA HAYES. United States president, 1877-1881, greatly admired in Paraguay for his arbital award in 1878 denying Argentine claims to the Chaco. The present Paraguay River port city of Villa Hayes, north of Asunción, is named after him.

HAYES ARBITRATION see also VILLA HAYES. The arbitral reward rendered by United States President Rutherford B. Hayes in 1878, giving Paraguay sovereignty over the Chaco northward from the Pilcomayo River across the Paraguay River from Asunción. The decision rejected Argentina's claims stemming from the Triple Alliance Treaty protocol of May 1, 1865, and pressed after the Triple Alliance War.

HENDERSON, C.A. British consul at Asunción in the 1850's
who sought unsuccessfully to secure the release of
Santiago (James) Canstatt, a Uruguayan claiming British
citizenship imprisoned by Carlos Antonio López.

HERNANDARIAS see ARIAS DE SAAVEDRA, HERNANDO.
Frequently used popular name referring to one of Paraguay's most significant colonial governors.

HERNANDARIAS, VILLAGE OF. Oldest inhabited point in
extreme east central Paraguay, located about 220 miles
due east of Asunción near the terminus of Highway
Route 2 and the Friendship Bridge at the Paraná River,
and about five miles north of the new dam and electric
power plant on the Acaray River. Named after Paraguay's first creole governor in the early 1700's. Now
a center for yerba maté production.

HERNANDEZ, PERO. Secretary to Spanish explorer and
early governor of Paraguay Alvar Núñez Cabeza de
Vaca. Possibly the author of the latter's Comentarios,
one of the first records of the discovery and conquest
era in Paraguay.

HERRERA, JUAN JOSE DE. Uruguayan foreign minister in
the Blanco Party government of President Atanasio
Cruz Aguirre. Sought unsuccessfully to secure Paraguay's support for the Blancos on the eve of the Triple
Alliance War.

HERRERA, NICOLAS DE. Envoy sent by Buenos Aires to
Asunción in 1812, who failed to obtain Paraguayan acceptance of treaty amendment proposals.

HERRERIA, JULIAN DE LA see also CAMPOS CERVERA,
ANDRES, 1888-1937. Paraguay's major contributor to
internationally known art.

HIGUERA, ANTON. Member of the 1544 Alvar Núñez Cabeza de Vaca expedition to Puerto de los Reyes on
the upper reaches of the Paraguay River. Mentioned
in accounts as having warned the governor of a coming
rebellion at the Pueblo Grande Indian site.

HIMNO NACIONAL. Verse composed by the Uruguayan poet
Francisco Acuña de Figueroa and presented to Paraguay's government in 1846. Origin of the music score

is unclear, but may have been the work of either a
French or Hungarian composer. The current official
score was prepared by Remberto Jiménez and approved
in 1934.

HINESTROSA, GREGORIO DE see also CARDENAS, FA-
THER BERNARDINO DE. Governor of Paraguay in the
1640's noted for his support for the Jesuit missions,
and for his exceptional difficulties with Asunción's
Franciscan Bishop Bernardino de Cárdenas.

HISTORIA PARAGUAYA. Annual yearbook of the Instituto
Paraguayo de Investigaciones Históricas, foremost contemporary Paraguayan historical society. Contains
significant research monographs on the nation's history.

HISTORIOGRAPHY - PARAGUAYAN HISTORIANS see AP-
PENDIX II.

HOHENAU see COLONIA HOHENAU. Located about 35
miles north of the Paraná River port city of Encarnación, settled in 1900, and designed as a model colony
for German immigrants in extreme southern Paraguay.
Regarded as the most successful foreign colonization
project until the arrival of the Mennonites in the late
1920's.

HOPKINS, CLEMENT see also HOPKINS, EDWARD AU-
GUSTUS. Brother of Edward Augustus Hopkins. His
inopportune and cavalier treatment of a Paraguayan
soldier in 1854 precipitated the celebrated Hopkins
case, resulting in a rupture of U.S./Paraguayan relations.

HOPKINS, EDWARD AUGUSTUS. Enterprising American
who in the early 1850's traveled to Paraguay and obtained approval of President Carlos Antonio López to
establish joint Paraguayan-American commercial ventures. Falling into bad graces because of inopportune
actions by his brother, Hopkins was expelled from
Asunción. His projects were completely ruined by the
shipwreck along the Brazilian coast of two vessels carrying his equipment and supplies. His expulsion and
the coincidence of the Water Witch affair were matters
which ruptured Paraguayan-U.S. relations. The subsequent Bowlin naval mission produced a return to har-
mony with regard to the latter. The former issue,

however, was only settled later in 1860 in an arbital
award favoring Paraguay's position.

HORQUETA.   Terminus of the short 33-mile long state-
owned railway east of the Paraguay River port city of
Concepción, north of Asunción.   Center of an important
cattle-breeding and lumber industry area.

HOTHAM, SIR CHARLES.   British envoy accredited to the
Argentine Confederation who traveled in the HMS Locust
to Paraguay in December, 1852.   His arrival and subsequent reception by Carlos Antonio López signified
Britain's recognition of Paraguayan independence.   Sir
Charles failed in his efforts to persuade López to accept a friendship, commerce and navigation treaty.

HUBER, DR. O.   Director of a pro-Nazi organization in
Paraguay during the World War II period.

HUMAITA.   Located about 15 miles north of the confluence
of the Paraguay and Paraná rivers, and about 200
miles south of Asunción, the small river port of Humaitá was the focal point of almost three years of
siege operations in the Triple Alliance War.   Paraguay's main defensive bastion, it is historically South
America's Sebastopol or Vicksburg.   Like Vicksburg
its strategic importance stemmed from its commanding
position at a narrow bend in the river.   Its siege included the most sanguinary and costly battles in Latin
America.   Stubbornly defended by Paraguay's army
under Marshal President López, it fell to an allied
naval and land combined envelopment only after a heroic defense involving near total attrition of Paraguay's
manpower.   The shell-blasted ruins of the Humaitá
church still stand as a national memorial, as does a
replica in Asunción's suburbs.

HURTADO, PEDRO.   Son of Isabel the mestizo daughter of
Martínez de Irala, who became a prominent official of
Paraguay and La Plata during the colonial era.

HUTTERITES see also   COLONIA PRIMAVERA.   German
and English in composition, and also known as the Society of Brothers.   Paraguay's most recent colonization project involving a religious group.   Like the
Mennonites, they abhorred war and searched for an
isolated spot where they could live in peace.   Arriving

from England in 1941, they founded the Primavera colony near the Mennonite Friesland colony north of Asunción, and sought to organize a communal society similar to the earlier Nueva Germania and Nueva Australia projects. By the 1960's, the rigors of isolation had sapped the colony, and the remaining survivors elected to sell their holdings and move to other areas.

- I -

IBAÑEZ, MIGUEL. Commandante at Villa Concepción who was accused of being implicated in the 1820 conspiracy plot against Dr. Francia. Died in prison.

IBARRA, ALONSO, 1889-   . Journalist and historian. Collaborated on several Asunción newspapers, and author of numerous historical monographs on the colonial era and the Triple Alliance War.

IBARRA, IGNACIO, 1854-1897. Journalist and politician. Co-founder and editor of the Asunción newspaper La Democracia, founded in 1881. Triple Alliance War telegraphist, and member of the "Club Liberal" and "Centro Democrático," forerunners of the modern-day Liberal Party.

IBICUI see YBYCUI. Paraguay's sole domestic iron-works, totally abandoned today, but important in the pre-Triple Alliance War era and during the war. Raided and razed by Allied troops in 1869.

IBR see INSTITUTO DE BIENESTAR RURAL.

IBYRAY (TRINIDAD) see YBIRAI. The preserved colonial era residence of Dr. José Gaspar Rodríguez de Francia, located in the Trinidad suburb of Asunción.

IGNACIO DE BARROS, VICE-ADMIRAL JOAQUIM JOSE see BARROS, VICE-ADMIRAL JOAQUIM JOSE IGNACIO DE.

IGUASSU, FALLS see YGUAZU FALLS. The Brazilian spelling for one of the world's largest and most scenic cataracts.

INCIDENT OF OCTOBER 23, 1931. Regarded as the nadir of Liberal Party government in Paraguay. Occurring

during the last year of the José P. Guggiari administration, the incident involved the indiscriminate killing
by troops of eleven persons among student demonstra-
tors gathered in front of the presidential palace.

INDEPENDENCE, RECOGNITION OF. Following the 1852
battle of Monte Caseros at which Buenos Aires Governor Juan Manuel de Rosas was finally defeated, and at
Brazil's insistence, Argentina formally recognized
Paraguay's independence. Argentine Confederation
leader, Justo José de Urquiza, sent special commissioner Santiago Derqui to Asunción, and the formal an-
nouncement was made July 17, 1852.

INDEPENDENCIA see also COLONIA INDEPENDENCIA.
Located about 100 miles due east of Asunción near
Villarrica. Settled in January, 1920, largely by im-
migrants from the old German African colonies. South
Germans, who arrived after 1924, have built a modest
grape-growing industry.

INDEPENDENCIA O MUERTE. A Paraguayan motto, similar
to that of Brazil, which was first used as the motto of
El Paraguayo Independiente, the republic's first news-
paper directed by President Carlos Antonio López.
Also a popular patriotic war-cry in the Triple Alliance
War.

INDIAN ASSOCIATION OF PARAGUAY. Cultural organization
at Asunción for the promotion and protection of native
Indian welfare and interests. Established in 1944.

INDIAN TRIBES see AGACE, ALBAIA, CARIO, CHIRIGUA-
NO, GUAIENI, GUARANI, GUAYCURU, ITATIN,
MAKKA, MBAYA, OREJON, PAYAGUA, QUERANDI,
TAPE, TOBA, TUPI, TUPI-GUARANI, XARAYES.

INDIGENAS. Spanish term meaning peoples of pure Indian
race. Native peoples.

INDIO, JOSE EL. Guaraní Jesuit-trained Indian sculptor who
went to Buenos Aires following the expulsion of the
Jesuits in 1767. Remembered there for his striking
works at La Merced Church.

INGAVI, BATTLE OF. Last major battle of the Chaco War,
a Paraguayan victory, fought June 7, 1935.

INLAND JAPAN.   Term applied by many historians to Paraguay with reference to the age of Dr. José Gaspar Rodriguez de Francia, the noted El Supremo of the Republic's formative years.   His isolationist policy of restricting entry or departure from his nation and of only minimal contact with the outside world suggest historical comparison to Japan before Commodore Perry.

INSAURRALDE, AMANCIO, 1862-1950.   Jurist, journalist, and politician.   Noted member of the Liberal Party and participant in the 1904 Revolution.   Remembered for his news editorials against the proposed Benítez-Ichazo Treaty of 1898 regarding the Chaco problem with Bolivia.

INSAURRALDE, CASILDA.   Mother of Marshal José Félix Estigarribia, Paraguay's second most important national hero of Chaco War fame.

INSAURRALDE, DR. CRISPIN.   Prominent member of the Guión Rojo faction of the Colorado Party in the late 1940's.

INSFRAN, PABLO MAX   see   YNSFRAN, PABLO MAX.

INSTITUTE OF NUMISMATICS AND ANTIQUITIES OF PARAGUAY.   Located at Asunción and one of the most active organizations for the preservation of national historical sites and the conservation of archives, relics, and historical objects in general.   Founded June 12, 1943.

INSTITUTO DE BIENESTAR RURAL (IBR).   Paraguay's government-directed Rural Welfare Institute was established by Law No. 852 of March 22, 1863, to replace the old Agrarian Reform Institute.   The IBR is responsible for the distribution of land to new homesteaders and the issuance of titles, the development and preservation of national forest reserves, and the supervision of the current project to stimulate the development of agricultural colonies in the more sparsely settled and remote areas of the national territory. The latter program, one of the most significant in modern Paraguay's history, seeks to promote the transfer of poorer people from the more heavily populated central zone to interior areas under the policy

of "consolidating the national territory." Such projects,
or "marchas" as they are known, have been reasonably
successful in founding farming colonies in the extreme
eastern zone along the upper Paraná River, in the
north, and in the south.

INSTITUTO DE NUMISMATICA Y ANTIGUEDADES DEL PA-
    RAGUAY see INSTITUTE OF NUMISMATICS AND
    ANTIQUITIES OF PARAGUAY.

INSTITUTO PARAGUAYO. Prominent and influential intel-
    lectual organization founded at Asunción in 1895. Pub-
    lished a review which achieved recognition throughout
    Latin America. Merged with the Gimnasio Paraguayo
    in 1933. Its director was the prominent historian Juan
    Francisco Pérez Acosta.

INSTITUTO PARAGUAYO DE INVESTIGACIONES HISTO-
    RICAS. Contemporary Paraguay's foremost historical
    society, founded at Asunción August 15, 1937.

INSTITUTO PARAGUAYO DE LA VIVIENDA. Government
    department responsible for the development of housing
    projects, established by Law No. 759 of February 9,
    1962.

INSTITUTO PARAGUAYO DE LETRAS. Founded at Asunción
    July 31, 1943. Society for the advancement of all ac-
    tivities related to the national literature sector.

INTENDENCIAS. An administrative device based on the
    French system introduced into Spain's New World col-
    onies in the eighteenth century as a part of the "Bour-
    bon reforms." The Provincia del Paraguay thus be-
    came the Intendencia del Paraguay in 1782. The de-
    centralization and bureaucratic reform expected from
    this change developed too late to halt rising popular
    dissatisfaction with Spanish rule.

INTENDENTE. Term applied to the government's represent-
    ative responsible for civil affairs in Paraguay's urban
    centers. Similar to "mayor" but without the extensive
    prerogatives and responsibilities of the United States
    system.

INTER-AMERICAN CONFERENCE FOR THE MAINTENANCE
    OF PEACE, 1936. Held at Buenos Aires December 1

to December 23, 1936. Occurred during the final
stages of the Chaco War Peace negotiations but had no
appreciable effect upon them.

INTER-AMERICAN TECHNICAL SERVICE FOR AGRICUL-
TURAL COOPERATION see SERVICIO TECNICO IN-
TERAMERICANO DE COOPERACION AGRICOLA.

INTERNATIONAL CONFERENCE OF AMERICAN STATES ON
CONCILIATION AND ARBITRATION see CONCILIA-
TION AND ARBITRATION CONFERENCE OF 1929, and
CONFERENCE ON CONCILIATION AND ARBITRATION,
1929.

IPACARAI see YPACARAY, LAKE. Variant in the spelling
of Lake Ypacaray, Paraguay's foremost resort and
tourist attraction located near Asunción.

IPANE RIVER (YPANE). Drainage stream in northern Paraguay which flows into the Paraguay River near Concepción. Navigable by river vessels for a short distance.

IRALA, ADRIANO, 1894-1933 see also LIGA NACIONAL
INDEPENDIENTE. Poet, journalist and law professor. Colleague of Dr. Juan Stefanich in developing the
Liga Nacional Independiente in 1928, an ideologically
based association which looked to improvement of all
facets of Paraguayan life. Irala died from illness contracted in the Chaco War. Frequently used the pseudonym I. R. Alita.

IRALA, ANA DE. Daughter of Governor Martínez de Irala
and his Indian servant María.

IRALA, ANTOLIN, 1878-1921. Attorney, jurist, statesman
and authority on international law. Served both as
Minister of Justice and Minister of Foreign Affairs.

IRALA, ANTONIO DE. Son of Governor Martínez de Irala
and his Indian servant María, daughter of the Guaraní
Indian chief Pedro de Mendoza. Antonio's brother and
sister were Diego Martínez de Irala and Ginebra Martinez de Irala.

IRALA, DIEGO MARTINEZ DE. Mestizo son of Governor
Irala by María, daughter of an Indian chief named

Pedro de Mendoza. Diego was the founder of Corrientes, Argentina, and a prominent colonial official of that riverport.

IRALA, DOMINGO MARTINEZ DE, 1510-1556 see PACTO DE SANGRE. First and one of the most capable of Spanish governors in Paraguay. Held position from 1539 to 1542, and from 1544 to 1556. Strengthened Spanish control of Asunción. Abandoned the earlier Buenos Aires base because of Asunción's greater proximity to Peru and the friendliness of the Guaraní Indians. A native of the Basque provinces, he died at Asunción in 1556. Frequently referred to in history as the Father of Paraguay for his efforts in promoting miscegenation.

IRALA, GINEBRA MARTINEZ DE. Daughter of Governor Irala and sister of Diego Martínez de Irala. Her marriage to Pedro de Segura Zavala produced a son, Juan de Irala, a noted colonial official and writer.

IRALA, ISABEL DE. Daughter of Governor Martínez de Irala and his servant Agueda. Isabel's son by her first marriage, Hernando de Mendoza, was one of the founders of Buenos Aires. Pedro Hurtado, the son of her second marriage, was a high official both in Paraguay and La Plata.

IRALA, JUAN DE. Grandson of Martínez de Irala who attained prominence both as a colonial official and as a writer.

IRALA, MARIA DE. One of Governor Martínez de Irala's mestizo children, daughter of the servant Beatríz.

IRALA, MARTIN PEREZ DE. One of Governor Martínez de Irala's mestizo children, son of the servant Scolástica.

IRALA, URSULA DE. Daughter of Governor Martínez de Irala and his Indian servant Leonor. Her son by her marriage to Alonso Riquelme de Guzmán y Ponce de León was Ruy Díaz de Guzmán, author of La Argentina, famed early account of Paraguay and La Plata.

IRALA BURGOS, JERONIMO, 1930-   . Author, jurist and history professor at the Universidad Nacional.

Author of several studies of the colonial and independence eras and of the Chaco War.

IRENDAGUE, BATTLE OF see YRENDAGUE, BATTLE OF.

IRRAZABAL, COLONEL LUIS, 1891-1958 see also NANA-
WA, BATTLE OF. Paraguayan Chaco War hero famed
for his tenacious defense of the Nanawa position during
the Bolivian general offensive of early 1933, and for
his participation in the Campo Vía operation which resulted in the surrender of two Bolivian divisions.

ISASI, CARLOS LUIS, 1871-1944. Journalist and statesman.
Editor of El Cívico, news organ of the "Cívicos" faction of the Liberal Party in the early twentieth century,
and cabinet minister in the administration of Benigno
Ferreira and Eligio Ayala.

ISLA. Small clusters of trees which commonly dot Paraguay's plain or prairie areas.

ISLA MADAMA. A small inhabited point between the northeastern border city of Pedro Juan Caballero and Cerro
Corá alleged to have been a temporary halting place
for Mme. Elisa Alicia Lynch during the Paraguayan
army's long 1869-1870 retreat. In some accounts, the
site is called Isla Piano stemming from unfounded hear-
say that Mrs. Lynch may have abandoned her cherished
piano there on the retreat.

ISLA PIANO see ISLA MADAMA and PIANO.

ISLA POI, FORTIN. Paraguayan central Chaco fortified
post and temporary headquarters in 1932 during the
early stages of the Chaco War.

ITACURUBI DEL ROSARIO. Small inhabited point about 120
miles north of Asunción, and location of the estancia
of Carlos Antonio López, to which he had retired during
the later stages of the Dr. Francia regime. He was
residing there when called to participate in the new
government formed in 1841 after the death of El Supremo.

ITALO-AMERICAN COLONIZATION SOCIETY see PATER-
NO, DR. STEFANO, COLONIA NUEVA ITALIA, and
COLONIA TRINACRIA.

ITAPIRU see also WATER WITCH. Former Paraguayan
    small river fort located along the Paraná River slightly
    above its confluence with the Paraguay River. The
    scene in February, 1855, of the Water Witch incident
    in which a U.S. sailor was killed during an exchange
    of gunfire with the battery. Also the locale during the
    Triple Alliance War of fighting during the allied ad-
    vance across the Paraná River toward the Paraguayan
    lines around Humaitá. Itapirú is still a Paraguayan
    military post, and the remains of its original fortifica-
    tions are still visible.

ITAPIRU, ACTION AT. Sharp and bloody Triple Alliance
    War action fought April 10, 1866, on a sand-bar in the
    Paraná River between Paso de Patria and the old Ita-
    pirú Fort of Water Witch fame. Allied victory over a
    Paraguayan landing force permitted the subsequent
    crossing of the Paraná by the entire allied army.

ITAPUA see also ENCARNACION. The original name for
    the Paraná River port city of Encarnación. During the
    Jesuit era and especially during the age of Dr. Francia
    in the early nineteenth century, this was the only port
    at which Paraguay's limited foreign trade was permitted.

ITATIN INDIANS. Guaraní tribe originally found in extreme
    northern Paraguay. Held to have been forced by other
    marauding tribes to retreat south to Argentina's Mi-
    siones and Corrientes provinces just prior to Spanish
    discovery and conquest of Paraguay.

ITAUGUA see also ÑANDUTI LACE. Situated about 20
    miles (30 kms) east of Asunción on Route 2, this city
    was founded in 1728 by Martín Barua. Noted in the
    modern era for the handicraft production of Ñandutí,
    a "spider-web" type of extremely delicate lace much
    desired by tourists.

ITA-YBATE, BATTLE OF see also LOMAS VALENTINAS,
    CAMPAIGN OF. Comprising the final phase of the
    Lomas Valentinas campaign of the Triple Alliance War,
    this series of actions between December 21-27, 1868,
    on a line of small hills east of the riverport of Villeta,
    ended in the virtual disappearance of Paraguay's army.
    Coming under direct fire of enemy troops for the first
    time in the war, Marshal President López was forced
    to retire from the action with only about 60 surviving

soldiers.   The victory encouraged allied forces to believe the war had ended.

ITURBE, SUB-LIEUTENANT VICENTE IGNACIO, 1786-1836.
Military officer who participated in the 1811 battles of
Paraguarí and Tacuarí against Belgrano's Argentine
force.   Principal collaborator with Pedro Juan Caballero in the May, 1811, revolution, and the person selected to carry the ultimatum to Spanish Governor Velasco.   Executed in 1837 on charges of complicity in
the conspiracy plot of 1820.

- J -

JAEGGLI, ALFREDO L.   Asunción intellectual, and author
of Albino Jara - un varón meteórico, 1963, a study of
one of Paraguay's early twentieth-century political figures.

JARA, COLONEL ALBINO.   Minister of war in the Liberal
Party government in 1908 noted for his reorganization
of the army.   Leader of a successful military revolt
in that year, and briefly president in 1911.

JARA, COLONEL JULIO.   One of the leaders of an aborted
revolt in September, 1937, which sought to oust President Félix Paiva and promote the return to power of
the Febrerista leader Colonel Rafael Franco.

JARA, PLACIDO see also GUERILLEROS DE LA MUERTE.
Leader of a famed Paraguayan detachment which raided
behind Bolivian lines during the Chaco War.   Known
popularly as "Gaucho del Chaco."

JARDIN BOTANICO, ASUNCION.   Located about five miles
north in the suburbs of Asunción, this large riverside
park comprises the former estate and the well-preserved residence of President Carlos Antonio López.

JEFFERS, LIEUTENANT WILLIAM NICHOLSON see also
WATER WITCH.   Temporary commander of the USS
Water Witch in the absence of Lieut. Thomas Page,
during the 1855 shooting episode at Fort Itapirú which
severely strained United States-Paraguayan relationships.

JEJUI, S. S.   Paraguayan naval gunboat sunk at the battle of
    Riachuelo, June 10, 1865, only naval battle of the Tri-
    ple Alliance War and largest in Latin America's his-
    tory.

JEJUI RIVER.   North central Paraguay drainage stream,
    navigable for a short distance by shallow-draught ves-
    sels, which flows into the Paraguay River about mid-
    way between Asunción and Concepción.

JESUIT COLEGIO, ASUNCION.   One of Paraguay's oldest
    institutions of learning, dating to the early seventeenth
    century.   Forced to halt operations and mobbed several
    times during the vicissitudes of the Jesuit mission era,
    notably during the Comunero Revolt.

JESUITS see also REDUCTIONS, TRINIDAD and JESUS.
    Arriving in Paraguay in the early 1600's at the inspira-
    tion and request of Governor Hernandarias, the mis-
    sionaries of Loyola's Society of Jesus gave ample proof
    in Paraguay of their abilities as "soldiers of Christ."
    During more than 150 years, they developed a system
    of missions which closely resembled an empire within
    an empire.   Independent of and resisting civil and po-
    litical power, they established perhaps the world's only
    successful experiment in true communal living until the
    twentieth century.   Their organized strength enabled
    them to resist periodic depredations by Brazilian Ma-
    meluke and Paulista marauders.   By 1767 the Spanish
    monarchy came to regard their independent enclave as
    a political threat, and Paraguay's encomenderos looked
    upon their commercial success as an economic threat.
    Upon their expulsion in that year the approximate
    150,000 Guaraní Indians living in the missions reverted
    back to a forest-dwelling life.   The ruins of 30 im-
    mense missions or reductions remained in southeast
    Paraguay and along both banks of the upper Paraná
    and Uruguay Rivers.   Only a few have survived to be-
    come national monuments of historical interest.

JESUITS, EXPULSION OF.   Decree expelling the Jesuits
    from the Spanish colonies signed March 27, 1767 by
    Carlos III on the recommendation of his minister Count
    Aranda.   Order carried out in July, 1767, by Intendente
    Francisco Bucareli at Buenos Aires.   The expulsion
    ended a 169-year record of humane effort which is re-
    corded as the world's first and probably only wholly

successful effort at communal living. Jesuit successes, their profitable operation and their aloofness from co- lonial administrative control, were factors which aroused royal suspicions against them.

JESUS, REDUCTION OF   see also   JESUS-MARIA, MISSION and TRINIDAD. Located about six miles distant from the ruins of the Trinidad Mission and about 25 miles northeast of the Paraná River port of Encarnación in southeastern Paraguay. The second largest of the re- maining Jesuit reductions in Paraguay's Misiones De- partment. Noted for the extremely large size of its central church structure. Now a national monument.

JESUS-MARIA, MISSION   see also   GUYRA VERA, CHIEF. Jesuit mission in the extreme eastern Guairá region in 1629-1630 which suffered attacks by Brazilian mame- luke raiders and was eventually abandoned.

JOHNSON, CAVE   see also   HOPKINS, EDWARD AUGUSTUS, and UNITED STATES AND PARAGUAY NAVIGATION CO.   American representative at the 1860 Washington arbitration proceedings who heard the United States and Paraguay Navigation Company case with Paraguay's José Berges.

JOVELLANOS, BERNARDO. One of the two Paraguayan representatives who returned from a mission to Monte- video in 1846 with the verse of the future national anthem, composed by the Uruguayan poet Francisco Acuña de Figueroa.

JOVELLANOS, SALVADOR. Paraguay's second president in the postwar period following the Triple Alliance War. As vice president, he assumed the presidency follow- ing the overthrow of Cirilo Antonio Rivarola in Decem- ber, 1871. His administration until November, 1874, was marred by four revolts and by two notorious loan operations negotiated in England in an effort to recoup the national treasury.

JUICIO DE RESIDENCIA. The obligation on the part of all authorities under the Spanish colonial administrative system to remain at their posts for six months after expiration of their terms of office in order to reply to all accusations of malfeasance which might be brought against them.

JUNTA DE BUENOS AIRES DE 1810. Governing Board of
Buenos Aires established after the Argentine independence movement against Spanish rule on May 25, 1810.
A principal objective of the new government was retention as dependencies of Buenos Aires and the provinces
of the former Spanish viceroyalty, including Paraguay.

JUNTA DE DOCTOS. Special board of inquiry convened at
Asunción in 1656 to resolve a controversy arising from
the claims of Bishop Bernardino de Cárdenas that a
Jesuit version of the catechism was blasphemous. The
highly controversial issue was resolved in favor of the
Jesuits.

JUNTA DE GOBIERNO DEL PARTIDO COLORADO see also
COLORADO PARTY. The Governing Board of the Colorado Party with headquarters in one of Asunción's
most modern office buildings.

JUNTA ELECTORAL CENTRAL. Paraguay's central election board, a dependency of the executive branch responsible for the administration of all national elections. Comprised of a president and board members
representing all officially authorized political parties.
Organizes, scrutinizes, and tabulates the results of
political elections. Voting is compulsory for all of 18
years of age or older, of both sexes, and is performed
under the Australian secret ballot version. Women obtained the franchise in 1963.

JUNTA GUBERNATIVA, JUNE, 1811. Established by the
Congress convoked June 17, 1811, following the May
independence movement and the ousting of Spanish Governor Bernardo Velasco on June 9. Paraguay's first
governing Junta was composed of Fulgencio Yegros,
Dr. José Gaspar Rodríguez de Francia, Pedro Juan
Caballero, Francisco Xavier Bogarín, and Fernando de
la Mora. Superseded by the First Consulate, established by the Special Congress of October, 1813.

JUNTA MUNICIPAL. Municipal boards or councils acting
in advisory capacity to the Intendente, the official responsible for direction of civil affairs in Paraguay's
urban centers. Elected by popular vote, and thus a
gauge of political currents.

JUNTA OF ASUNCION see JUNTA GUBERNATIVA, JUNE,
1811.

JUNTA PROVISORIA OF 1840.   Provisional governing Board
    organized in 1840 upon the death of Dr. Francia and
    composed of Alcalde Manuel Antonio Ortiz and the com-
    manders of Asunción's military barracks.   Subsequently
    dissolved by a coup led by Romualdo Duré on its failure
    to summon a National Congress.

JUSTINIANO, BARTOLOME.   Royal messenger, detained
    briefly in Brazil, who brought the official order to
    Asunción in 1555 naming Domingo Martínez de Irala as
    governor.

- K -

KERR, DR. JOHN AUSTIN.   American Rockefeller Founda-
    tion doctor in Paraguay during 1928-1929 who directed
    the Foundation's Campaña Sanitaria health campaign
    aimed at eradicating disease in the Paraguayan country-
    side.

KIDD, FREDERICK see NUEVA AUSTRALIA.   Member of
    the Australian Cooperative Society colonization experi-
    ment of 1893.   Became director of the Nueva Australia
    colony following the splitting of the original group and
    the departure of William Lane.

KILOMETER SEVEN, CONTEST FOR.   Locale of particularly
    vicious fighting on the southern front along Paraguay's
    string of fortified positions during the 1932-1933 initial
    phases of the Chaco War.   Known in Bolivian histories
    as Campo Jordán.

KING JOSEPH OF PARAGUAY see also ANTEQUERA Y
    CASTRO, JOSE DE.   Name by which Dr. José de
    Antequera y Castro, Paraguay's Comunero leader, was
    popularly known abroad, especially at Lima where he
    was imprisoned and subsequently executed in 1731.

KIRKLAND, CAPTAIN W. A.   Captain of the USS Wasp,
    American warship of the South Atlantic squadron.   Sent
    by Admiral C. H. Davis to Asunción in August, 1868,
    to procure the safe release of Minister Charles Ames
    Washburn, embroiled with President Francisco Solano
    López as a suspected conspirator against him.

KRUGER.   Reportedly an American national of as yet un-

known origins who apparently traveled to Paraguay immediately prior to the Triple Alliance War to offer his
services to Paraguay's army. A munitions expert and
possibly a Civil War veteran, he produced naval mines
and torpedoes for use against Brazil's river warships.
A disaster involving one of the devices cost Kruger his
life during the Humaitá campaign.

KUNDT, GENERAL HANS. German instructor of Bolivia's
army, and commanding general in the early stages of
the Chaco War of the 1930's. Addicted to direct mass
frontal assault tactics, Kundt was defeated with heavy
losses in consecutive battles, and was forced to re-
linquish his command.

- L -

LA. Phrases and place names beginning with an article,
with few necessary exceptions, are found under the
word following the article.

LACERDA, CORPORAL JOSE FRANCISCO see also DIABO,
CHICO. The full name of the Brazilian soldier who
is alleged to have mortally wounded Paraguay's Francisco Solano López at Cerro Corá, March 1, 1870,
terminating the Triple Alliance War.

LACONICH, MARCO ANTONIO, 1902-   . Journalist and
historian. Author of several works on the Paraguayan
and Chaco Wars which were prohibited from sale in
Paraguay, including La paz del Chaco - un pueblo
traiciondo (1938) and El Paraguay mutilado (1939). In
1948 he published Caudillos de la conquista, a study
of leaders of the conquest and colonial eras.

LAFTA. Latin American Free Trade Association. Paraguay signed the Montevideo Pact which created LAFTA
on February 18, 1960. Since 1961, the other partic-
ipating republics have granted Paraguay special foreign
trade concessions because of its status as a lesser
developed nation. Paraguay now carries on the highest
trading percentage of the LAFTA nations within the
area encompassed by the agreement.

LAGUNA, RETREAT FROM see also TAUNAY, VISCONDE
DE. An ill-fated Brazilian Triple Alliance War army

expedition in 1867 which was aimed at invasion of
north Paraguay from Mato Grosso Province. Defeated
and turned into a near rout by hunger, illness and
harrassment by pursuing Paraguayans. The episode
was recorded by participant Visconde de Taunay in one
of the best wartime stories entitled Retreat from Laguna.

LAGUNA VERA, ACTION AT. Fought August 1, 1868, this
action involved a last attempt by the surviving members of the Humaitá garrison to break the allied encirclement. Featured by a canoe attack in which both
women and children participated, much to the admira-
tion of defending allied troops.

LAMAS, ANDRES. Uruguay's Blanco government minister
to Argentina in the immediate pre-Triple Alliance War
period who sought unsuccessfully to prevent an Argen-
tine-Brazilian accord with Uruguay's Colorado Party
under Venancio Flores. A major figure in the complex
pre-war diplomatic negotiations.

LAMAS CARISIMO DE RODRIGUEZ ALCALA, TERESA.
One of Paraguay's most honored feminine authors.
Her book, Tradiciones del hogar, published in 1925,
is recorded as the first literary work published by a
woman in Paraguay. Also wrote La casa y su sombra
in 1925.

LAMBARE see also CERRO LAMBARE. Former Indian
village site located near the Cerro Lambaré slightly
south of Asunción on the east bank of the Paraguay
River. The Indians at Lambaré were defeated by the
Spanish under Juan de Ayolas just prior to the founding of Asunción.

LANE, WILLIAM see also NUEVA AUSTRALIA. English-
born Australian Socialist-journalist who conceived the
Australian Cooperative Society for the purpose of establishing a socialist communal colony in Paraguay.
The experiment failed shortly after arrival of the immigrants in 1893. Surviving members remained to
build a colony along non-socialist lines after Lane departed from Paraguay.

LANUS, ANARCASIS. Wealthy Buenos Aires merchant authorized secretly by President Bartolomé Mitre in

early 1865 to supply reports on Paraguay during his
visit to Asunción. In the early post-Triple Alliance
War era, Lanús was alleged to have profited immense-
ly from the trade of furnishing supplies to the allied
occupation army and from other business ventures in
defeated Paraguay.

LAP   see   LINEAS AEREAS PARAGUAYAS.

LAPIDO, OCTAVIO. Uruguayan Blanco government diplomat
sent on pre-Triple Alliance War missions to Buenos
Aires and Asunción in efforts to stop Argentine support
of Venancio Flores, and to encourage support of the
Blancos by Paraguay's Francisco Solano López. Both
missions were unsuccessful.

LA PLATA, VICEROYALTY OF   see also   VICEROY. Established by a royal order of 1776 to include the areas
of Paraguay, Uruguay and Argentina. Until that date,
the Province of Paraguay was under the administrative
jurisdiction of the Viceroyalty of Peru. A cornerstone
of Argentine foreign policy since the independence era
has been to maintain at least nominal hegemony over
the break-away republics of Uruguay and Paraguay,
originally included in the old viceroyalty. By the Real
Ordenanza of January 28, 1782, the Viceroyalty of La
Plata was divided into eight intendencias of which Paraguay was one.

LARA, JOSE MARIA DE, 1781-1836. Paraguayan who
studied at the University of Charcas, took a prominent
part in Bolivia's independence movement, and in 1829
was named minister in the cabinet of General Santa
Cruz.

LARA, DOÑA JUANA DE. Famed heroine of the independence movement of May 14, 1811, who allegedly aided
the conspiracy in Asunción's Casa de la Independencia.
The next day, May 15, she reportedly presented Pedro
Juan Caballero a bouquet of flowers whose colors may
have stimulated the choice of red, white and blue for
the national flag.

LARA, NUÑO DE. Member of the 1526 Sebastián Cabot expedition to La Plata. Left by Cabot in 1530 as commander of the small Sancti Spíritu fort on the lower
Paraná River. Subsequently killed in an Indian attack

which destroyed the fort and massacred most of the garrison.

LARA CASTRO, MARIANO LUIS, 1913-   . Lawyer and history professor. Author of numerous studies in the field of civil and constitutional law, and of the Chaco War.

LAS.   Phrases and place names beginning with an article, with few necessary exceptions, are found under the word following the article.

LASCANO, FATHER JUAN GABRIEL DE. Envoy sent by Governor Martínez de Irala in an unsuccessful effort in 1545 to negotiate peace terms with Chief Abacote and the Agacé Indians.

LATIFUNDIA.   Large land estates as compared to "minifundia" or small landholdings. Such large farms and ranches in Paraguay are known as "haciendas," "estancias," or "granjas."

LATN see LINEAS AEREAS DE TRANSPORTE NACIONAL.

LAUREL-TY.   A small country zone about five miles east of Asunción between Luque and San Lorenzo where the descendents of a group of Negro soldiers brought to Paraguay from Uruguay by General José Artigas still reside.   During the Paraguayan War, men from this singular ethnic group largely comprised a battalion known as the "Nambi-í," or "small ears" in Guaraní. They were an elite unit assigned to Paraguayan ships for boarding enemy vessels at the naval battle of Riachuelo.

LEAGUE OF NATIONS, CHACO WAR.   Though it sought to resolve the Paraguayan/Bolivian dispute by every means in its early stages, the League was singularly unsuccessful in preventing the outbreak of a full-scale war. In May, 1935, due to its lack of success, the League withdrew from the affair in favor of deliberations of the Buenos Aires mediation group.   It was never again to intervene in Latin American affairs.   Paraguay resigned from the League in February, 1935.

LEALES.   "Loyalists," the opponents of the "Comuneros" in Paraguay during the entire colonial period. Leales

believed in the supremacy of the Spanish kings as the
foundation of society, while Comuneros supported public
defense of certain rights and privileges even though
they ran counter to those of the crown. Rivalry between the two factions dates from the overthrow of
Adelantado Alvar Núñez Cabeza de Vaca at Asunción
in 1544.

LEBRON, FATHER ALONZO. Franciscan missionary who,
with Father Bernardo de Armenta, reached the Brazilian Atlantic coast in 1538 with the Alonso Cabrera expedition. Accompanied Alvar Núñez Cabeza de Vaca
as an interpreter-guide on his 1541 overland expedition
to Paraguay. Later arrested for his efforts to return
to Brazil.

LEDESMA VALDERRAMA, MARTIN DE. Appointed governor
of Paraguay in 1536. Noted for his hostility against
the Jesuit missions. Succeeded by Gregorio de Hinestrosa, who in turn was pro-Jesuit in his policies.

LEGION PARAGUAYA see also ASOCIACION PARAGUAYA.
Group of Paraguayan exiles opposed to President
Francisco Solano López and resident at Buenos Aires.
Became associated with the allied army at the outbreak of the Triple Alliance War, and were greatly
despised by López. Legion members formed the
Triumvirate of 1869, a provisional government organized after the fall of Asunción. Most legionnaires returned to Paraguay after the war to assume prominent
official and private positions during Paraguay's "reconstruction" era.

LEGUA. A measure of distance equal to five kilometers or
approximately three miles. Still commonly used by
the peoples of interior Paraguay.

LEGUIZAMON, MAJOR J. ESTANISLAO, 1846- ? . Aide-
de-camp of Paraguay's General Bernardino Caballero
during the Triple Alliance War, and also his collaborator in the 1873 postwar revolution. Wounded at the
1868 battle of Ytororó and subsequently captured by
Brazilian forces. His Apuntes biógrafo-históricos was
published at Asunción in 1898.

LEITE PEREIRA, JOSE MARIA. Portuguese national and
acting consul at Asunción during the Triple Alliance

War period. Accused of complicity in the suspected 1868 conspiracy plot against Marshal President Francisco Solano López, he was arrested, tried and condemned in spite of efforts by American Minister Charles A. Washburn to extend him diplomatic immunity.

LEMMON, ROBERT B. see also COLEGIO INTERNACIONAL. Successor in 1926 to Clement Manly Morton as director of Asunción's Colegio Internacional, Paraguay's best private institution of learning.

LEON GARABITO, ANDRES DE. Governor, 1650-1653. Appointed by the Audiencia of Charcas at the height of the anti-Jesuit episode stimulated by Bishop Bernardino de Cárdenas. His forces defeated in battle, Cárdenas left Asunción for his native Bolivia in 1651. In 1652, forces led by León Garabito also defeated a large Mameluke slave raiding party.

LEON Y ZARATE, SEBASTIAN DE. Commander of a mixed Spanish and mission Indian army which defeated the forces of Bishop Bernardino de Cárdenas at the climax of the anti-Jesuit episode of 1650. Cárdenas later returned to his native Bolivia.

LEONOR. Mestizo servant-mistress of Governor Martínez de Irala, who bore him a daughter, Ursula de Irala.

LEVI RUFFINELLI, DR. CARLOS, 1919-   . see also LIBERAL PARTY. Prominent Asunción medical doctor and university professor. President of the governing directorate of the Liberal Party since 1961.

LEVI RUFFINELLI, FERNANDO, 1922-   . see also LIBERAL PARTY. Asunción attorney, journalist, and member of the governing directorate of the Liberal Party. Brother of Carlos Levi Ruffinelli, president of the governing directorate of the Liberal Party.

LEY DE EDUCACION COMUN. Promulgated in the late 1880's, possibly with the stimulation of ex-Argentine President Domingo Faustino Sarmiento, and a basic document providing for Paraguay's new educational system following the Triple Alliance War.

LEYES DE PARTIDA. Old Spanish ordinances still in force in Paraguay during the Triple Alliance War period,

under which two-member military tribunals were appointed to investigate persons suspected of treason
against Marshal President Francisco Solano López.

LIBERAL (EL).   Liberal Party newspaper at Asunción especially active in the early twentieth century as a
mouthpiece for publicizing party principles and philosophy.

LIBERAL PARTY.   Officially inscribed in 1961 as a political
party in opposition to the governing Colorado Party.
Generally espouses the conservative philosophies of the
traditional Liberal Party.   A split within its organization produced the Liberal Radical Party, a less aggressive organization officially inscribed as a political party in 1967.

LIBERAL PARTY - ORIGINAL   see also   PARTIDO LIBERAL
and PARTIDO LIBERAL RADICAL.   Founded in 1887
by Antonio Taboada, and traditionally one of Paraguay's
most important political parties, the other major organization being the Colorado Party.   The Liberals
were in control of Paraguay from 1904 to 1936.   Since
1947, and especially since 1954, they continue as the
major opponents of the Colorados.   Their effectiveness
as a party was seriously impaired in the 1960's by the
party's splitting into two groups, the Liberals and the
Liberal Radicals.   Ideologically, there is small differ-
ence between the party's basic doctrinary philosophy of
government and that of the ruling Colorado Party.
Some observors feel that if anything the Liberals belie
their name and are actually more conservative than the
Colorados.   Traditional party differences have thus
primarily been more formal than of a doctrinal nature.

LIBERAL RADICAL PARTY   see also   LIBERAL PARTY.
Officially inscribed in 1967 as a political party in opposition to the ruling Colorado Party.   Espouses a platform somewhat less aggressive than the traditional philosophy of the Liberal Party.   Its president in 1970
was Dr. Efraím Cardozo, prominent Asunción historian
and author.

LIGA DE LA JUVENTUD INDEPENDIENTE.   Independent
student political organization founded at Asunción in
1906.   Its aim was to require strict adherence to the
1870 Constitution and to seek a general election reform.

It superseded the Centro Alón, formed in 1900; its official paper was also named Alón, founded in 1903.
Known popularly as the "Partido Constitucional." Dissolved after the 1908 revolt which unseated President
Benigno Ferreira, with most of its members electing
to join the Liberal Party.

LIGA NACIONAL INDEPENDIENTE   see also   STEFANICH,
JUAN.   Association of intellectuals organized in the
late 1920's for the purpose of providing an ideological
orientation for the "new" Paraguay which they hoped
would develop.   Not a political party, although their
leadership and philosophy merged into the Febrerista
Party born of the 1936 revolt headed by Colonel Rafael
Franco.   The Liga dissolved in 1936 following the appearance of the Unión Nacional Revolucionaria.

LILIEDAT, AUGUST.   French engineer and iron foundry expert whose services were contracted for during the
period of internal development sponsored by Carlos
Antonio López.   Became director of the Ybicuí foundry
following its establishment by Henry Godwin in 1850.

LIMA, AUDIENCIA OF.   Highest court of jurisdiction during
the colonial era, especially during the Comunero period,
with responsibility over Paraguayan affairs.

LIMA, CESAR SAUVAN VIANNA DE   see   VIANNA DE LI-
MA, CESAR SAUVAN.

LIMA E SILVA, LUIS ALVES DE   see also   CAXIAS, DU-
QUE DE.   Brazil's foremost soldier and the only official to receive the title of Duque during the imperial
reign of Dom Pedro II.   Allied commander in chief
during the Triple Alliance War from the departure of
Argentina's Bartolomé Mitre in 1866 until the fall of
Asunción in early 1869.   His major achievements were
the successful termination of the Humaitá siege operations and the subsequent Lomas Valentinas campaign
which culminated in the near-extinction of Paraguay's
army.

LINCOLN, RICHARD.   English blacksmith from Plymouth
who is recorded as having accompanied the early Pedro
de Mendoza expedition and who probably initiated Paraguay's iron industry.

LINCOLNSHIRE FARMERS. Term referring to an 1872 colonization project involving British immigrants to be
settled on land grants at Itá and Ypané near Asunción.
The "farmers," who in the majority turned out to be
the dregs of London and other large cities, were soon
decimated by harsh living conditions. With few exceptions, the survivors gave up and returned to Buenos
Aires.

LINEAS AEREAS DE TRANSPORTE NACIONAL (LATN).
Domestic air carrier offering both passenger and cargo
service. Established as a private company in 1941,
it was nationalized in 1954 and subsequently reorganized
as an autonomous operating department of the Ministry
of Defense in June, 1955.

LINEAS AEREAS PARAGUAYAS--LAP. Paraguay's international air carrier established in March, 1963, and
operating as a state-owned autonomous branch of the
Ministry of Defense.

LISBOA, ADMIRAL JOAQUIM MARQUES see TAMANDA-
RE, BARÃO DE.

LISBOA, DR. MELITÃO BARBOSA. Brazilian army doctor
who, with his colleague Dr. Manoel Cardozo da Costa
Lôbo, performed an autopsy on the corpse of Paraguay's Francisco Solano López after the battle of Cerro
Corá, March 1, 1870.

LLANAS, RAMON DE LAS. Aide to Dr. José de Antequera
y Castro who succeeded in a 1723 mission to sequester
Diego de los Reyes Balmaceda, Paraguay's official
governor who had fled to Corrientes, Argentina. Prelude to the fall of the Comunero movement.

LOCRO. A heavy soup-type food made of white corn and
meat widely consumed in Paraguay.

LOIZAGA, CARLOS. Member of the Legión Paraguaya, a
group of Paraguayan exiles opposed to Marshal López
and associated with the allied army. Member of the
Triumvirate of 1869. Paraguay's representative in the
negotiation of the Loizaga-Cotegipe Treaty of 1872
which established post-war boundary limits between
Paraguay and Brazil.

LOIZAGA-COTEGIPE TREATY, JANUARY 9, 1872 see also
    COTEGIPE-LOIZAGA TREATY. Formal boundary lim-
    its treaty signed at Asunción between Paraguay and
    Brazil following the Triple Alliance War. With no dif-
    ficulty, imperial Brazil managed to obtain the maximum
    of her pre-war territorial claims including an unexpected
    further southward strip to the southernmost boundary of
    one of the afluents of the Apa River. Total territorial
    gains for Brazil were established at 62,325 sq. kms.

LOMAS, LAS see PIKYSYRY CAMPAIGN. Numerous his-
    tories of Paraguay by American and other foreign schol-
    ars use this term, or Lomas Valentinas (Valentine
    Hills), in referring to the December, 1868, campaign
    which ended in the near annihilation of Paraguay's Tri-
    ple Alliance War army and the evacuation of Asunción.
    Paraguayan scholars prefer the term "Pikysyry Cam-
    paign," and battle of Itá Ybaté for battle of Lomas Va-
    lentinas.

LOMAS VALENTINAS, CAMPAIGN OF. Occurring in Decem-
    ber, 1868, and known also as the Pikysyry Campaign,
    this series of actions, taking place about 20 miles
    south of Asunción, terminated the formal stages of the
    Triple Alliance War including the evacuation and oc-
    cupation of Asunción. Included in it were the bloody
    contests at Ytororó, Avay and Itá Ybaté which all but
    resulted in total extermination of Paraguay's army.

LONGCHAMPS, MARCELINE. One of the few foreign trav-
    elers to Paraguay who left a primary source record of
    the Dr. Francia era. With his Swiss companion, Jo-
    hann Rudolph Rengger, Longchamps entered Paraguay in
    1819 and stayed there five years before El Supremo au-
    thorized departure. Their Essai historique sur la révo-
    lution du Paraguay was subsequently published in 1827.

LOPEZ, ANGEL BENIGNO, ? -1868. Younger brother of
    Marshal President Francisco Solano López. Alleged
    in several contemporary accounts to have harbored the
    desire to supplant his older brother as president. Sus-
    pected of being a leader of the 1868 conspiracy, Be-
    nigno was arrested, tried and executed in late 1868 on
    the eve of the Lomas Valentinas battles.

LOPEZ, FATHER BASILIO ANTONIO, ? -1859. Brother of

Carlos Antonio López, uncle of Francisco Solano López, and Bishop of Asunción until his death there in
1859.

LOPEZ, CARLOS ANTONIO, 1792-1862. The second in
Paraguay's great authoritarian triumvirate in the formative independence era. Carlos Antonio López introduced a republican form of government during his administration between 1844-1862, while retaining many
of the characteristics of the previous personal rule of
Dr. José Gaspar Rodríguez de Francia. Sometimes
known as El Ciudadano--the Citizen, he opened Paraguay to the world and promoted an astonishingly varied
number of innovations which stimulate reference to his
administration as the nation's Golden Age.

LOPEZ, CIRILO. Allegedly a creole shoemaker living near
Asunción, and father of President Carlos Antonio López.

LOPEZ, ENRIQUE SOLANO, 1859-1917. Son of Francisco
Solano López and Elisa Alicia Lynch. Accompanied
the Paraguayan army on the retreat to Cerro Corá,
and with his mother buried his father after he was
killed there March 1, 1870. Returning to Paraguay
after a brief postwar exile, Enrique Solano sought pa-
tiently to redeem his father's name under extremely
hostile conditions. Journalist for La Patria, organ of
the Colorado Party, and superintendent of primary instruction. Left a notable private library and archives.

LOPEZ, ESTANISLAO. Governor of Argentina's Santa Fe
province during the early years of Dr. Francia's regime who posed a worry to El Supremo over the possibility that he would unite with other provincial caudillos to invade Paraguay.

LOPEZ, MESTRE FERMIN. A school teacher from Villarrica who on August 12, 1869, allegedly marshaled his
pupils in Paraguay's defensive trenches at Piribebuy
in a bloody but futile effort to stop attacking Brazilian
forces. The episode is included among the republic's
deeds of valor of the Triple Alliance War.

LOPEZ, FRANCISCO SOLANO, 1826-1870. Paraguay's
foremost national hero. Ascending to the presidency
upon the death in 1862 of his father, Carlos Antonio

López, Solano López sought to continue the economic development of Paraguay and to secure for it a significant role within the balance of power in La Plata. Such ambitions clashed with those of Paraguay's neighbors, notably Brazil, and were ultimately destroyed in the holocaust of the Triple Alliance War. As Paraguay's Marshal President, he led the armed forces during more than five years of campaigning against incredible odds. Killed while resisting pursuing Brazilian troops at Cerro Corá, March 1, 1870, he became the only chief executive in the history of the Americas to die fighting his enemies in formal war while still in office. Resurrected to highest national prestige in the twentieth century, Solano López is regarded today as the epitome of the Paraguayan.

LOPEZ, GASPAR, ? -1868. Like Andrés Maciel, a Paraguayan student granted a scholarship for studies abroad during the Carlos Antonio López administration. Official translator of the Ministry of Foreign Relations, he was arrested on suspicion of conspiracy and executed along with Maciel at Pikysyry during the Triple Alliance War.

LOPEZ, COLONEL JUAN FRANCISCO. 15-year-old son of Marshal President López. Killed by a Brazilian cavalryman at Cerro Corá, March 1, 1870, after his father had likewise been killed in the last engagement of the Triple Alliance War.

LOPEZ, JUANA CARILLO DE see CARILLO DE LOPEZ, JUANA PABLA. Variant in the spelling of the name of the mother of Francisco Solano López and wife of Carlos Antonio López.

LOPEZ, LEON BASILIO see LOPEZ, BASILIO ANTONIO. Variant in the spelling of the name of the brother of Carlos Antonio López who was named Bishop of Asunción.

LOPEZ, MARIANO. Director at mid-nineteenth century of a Latin school at Villarrica, one of the few institutions of learning outside of Asunción existing in that period.

LOPEZ, FATHER MARTIN. Brother of Carlos Antonio López and Bishop Basilio Antonio López. A priest,

he served in several parishes near Asunción but led an
otherwise undistinguished life.

LOPEZ, MIGUEL SOLANO, 1911-   . Son of Enrique Solano López and grandson of Marshal President Francisco Solano López. Author and diplomat noted for
his studies of the Chaco War in which he participated.

LOPEZ, RAFAELA see LOPEZ DE BEDOYA, RAFAELA.
Daughter of President Carlos Antonio López, sister of
Francisco Solano López.

LOPEZ, COLONEL VENANCIO, ? -1869. Younger brother
of Marshal President Francisco Solano López. Served
as Minister of War and Marine in the latter's Triple
Alliance wartime cabinet until arrested as a suspected
conspirator during the 1868 conspiracy episode. Executed during the last stages of the Paraguayan army's
final retreat to Cerro Corá.

LOPEZ, VENANCIO VICTOR, 1862-1929. Son of Colonel
Venancio López and grandson of Carlos Antonio López.
Jurist, journalist, poet and educator. Educated at
Buenos Aires and returned to Asunción in 1887 to become a Supreme Court justice. Occupied several cabinet posts and was professor at the National University
until the 1904 revolution, when he returned to Buenos
Aires. Professor at the University of La Plata in his
later years.

LOPEZ CARILLO DE BARRIOS, INOCENCIA see also
BARRIOS BEDOYA, GENERAL VICENTE. Daughter
of President Carlos Antonio López and Juana Pabla
Carillo Viana; married to General Vicente Barrios,
prominent Paraguayan army commander in the early
Triple Alliance War period.

LOPEZ DE AVIEGA, PEDRO. One of the Asunción colony's
first carpenters. Arrived with the Alvar Núñez Cabeza de Vaca 1541 overland expedition from the Brazilian Atlantic coast.

LOPEZ DE BEDOYA, RAFAELA see BEDOYA, RAFAELA
DE.

LOPEZ DE BLOMBERG, ERCILIA. Daughter of Colonel
Venancio López and granddaughter of Carlos Antonio

López.   Raised and educated at Buenos Aires where
she wrote for La Prensa and produced poems, literary
critiques and short stories.   Mother of the Argentine
author Héctor Pedro Blomberg.

LOPEZ DECOUD, ARSENIO, 1885-1945.   Son of Benigno
López, the brother of Francisco Solano López.   Government official and diplomat in the early twentieth
century.   Occasional literary critic and author of
Album gráfico de 1911, his only notable literary work.

LOPEZ-FERREIRA DE OLIVEIRA TREATY   see also   OLI-
VEIRA, ADMIRAL PEDRO FERREIRA DE.   Paraguayan-Brazilian agreement signed in 1855 covering
only commerce and navigation matters and not boundary limits.

LOPEZ PEQUEÑO, CRISTOBAL.   A basket-weaver and recorded as one of the new Asunción colony's early
craftsmen.

LORENCANA, FATHER MARCELLO.   One of the first Jesuit missionaries who arrived in Paraguay in the late
sixteenth century.   Active at Asunción in 1604, and
later aided in the establishment of the first reductions
in southern Paraguay.

LORETO, MISSION.   First Jesuit mission in the Guairá
region established in 1610 by Fathers José Cataldino
and Simón Maceta.   Abandoned about 1636 due to
heavy mameluke slaving raids from Brazil, and relo-
cated south of the Upper Paraná River near Posadas,
Argentina.

LORETO, TRANQUERA DE.   The corridor of shortest distance between Encarnación/Posadas on the Upper Paraná river and the Uruguay River to the south.   Now
a part of the Misiones department of modern Argentina.
In 1865 it embraced the old Jesuit reduction area
south of Posadas, and claims to it were disputed by
Argentina and Paraguay.   The former's refusal to let
Paraguayan troops cross the area was the factor which
caused President Francisco Solano López to declare
war against Bartolomé Mitre's Argentina in March,
1865.

LOS.   Phrases and place names beginning with an article,

with few necessary exceptions, are found under the word following the article.

LOYOLA, BISHOP MARTIN IGNACIO DE. Noted as the sponsor in 1603 of a home and training institution for orphans, the first in Paraguay.

LOYOLA, ST. IGNATIUS DE see JESUITS and REDUCCIONES. The famous Catholic saint and founder of the militant Society of Jesus. His Jesuit missionaries were "Soldiers of Christ" in their determined evangelizing efforts in Spain's New World colonies.

LOZANO, PEDRO, 1697- ? . Jesuit historian whose Descripción corográfico, published in 1733, offers an absorbing survey of conditions in pre-colonial and colonial Paraguay. Official chronicler of the Jesuit Society in La Plata. Also wrote Historia de la Compañía de Jesús en el Paraguay and Historia de la conquista del Paraguay, Río de la Plata y Tucumán, both noted primary source works. Either died in Paraguay or returned to Europe about the time the Jesuits were expelled in 1767.

LUGO, PEDRO BENITEZ DE. Spanish official of the early Asunción colony recorded as among those witnessing the assumption of the governorship in 1542 by Alvar Núñez Cabeza de Vaca.

LUGO, PEDRO DE. Governor of Paraguay in 1629, and one of the first to employ mission Indians to repel mameluke slave raiders from Brazil.

LUIS, SIMON. One of the Asunción colony's first skilled craftsmen, mentioned in historical accounts.

LUQUE. Located about ten miles (15 kms) northeast of Asunción near President Stroessner International Airport, this city became the second wartime capital of Paraguay after the bombardment of Asunción by the Brazilian fleet in 1868. It was founded in 1675 by Governor Martín de Ledesma Balderrama.

LYNCH, ELISA ALICIA, 1835-1886. Perhaps the most tragic feminine figure in Latin America's history, Mrs. Lynch was an Irish-born lady whose name in now firmly linked with that of Marshal President Francisco So-

lano López.   Unable to marry her Paraguayan consort
because of her undissolved marital status, she nevertheless accompanied him to Paraguay from his pre-war
mission to Europe.   She contributed strongly to the
maturing of Paraguayan society, and remained faithful
to the marshal president through the entire war.   She
buried Solano López and her oldest son with her own
hands after their deaths at Cerro Corá.   Sent to Europe
by the allies with her surviving sons, she eventually
died penniless in Paris.   Her ashes were returned to
Asunción in 1964.   Though much maligned in earlier accounts of the war, she is now recognized as a prominent figure in the national epic.

- M -

McCOY, MAJOR GENERAL FRANK R.   see also   COMMIS-
SION OF INQUIRY, BOLIVIA AND PARAGUAY.   United
States member of special 1929 commission selected to
seek a means for amicable settlement of the Paraguay-
Bolivia Chaco dispute.

MACETA, FATHER SIMON   see also   LORETO, MISSION.
Early Jesuit missionary arrival in Paraguay credited
with having assisted in the establishment of the first
missions or reductions in the Guairá region.

MACHAIN, ESTANISLAO.   Prominent Asunción citizen and
reportedly one of Dr. Francia's enemies, who was arrested and who died in prison in the 1820 conspiracy
episode against El Supremo.

MACHAIN, DR. FACUNDO, 1847-1877.   Foreign minister in
the post-Triple Alliance War 1874 administration of
President Juan Bautista Gill, and a founder of the new
political organization Gran Club del Pueblo.   Member
of the commission selected to draft the 1870 Constitution.   Especially noted for his negotiation of the final
1876 treaty with Argentina establishing Chaco boundary
limits.   Assassinated October 29, 1877, for his defense
of the suspected murderers of President Juan Bautista
Gill.

MACHAIN, JOSE.   Diplomatic representative accredited to
the United States early in 1876 during the post-Triple
Alliance War period of allied occupation of Paraguay.

His mission was alleged to have been motivated partly
from fears that the former allied nations entertained
designs of annexing Paraguay.

MACIEL, ANDRES, ? -1868.   Educated in Europe.   Officer
in the Triple Alliance War noted for his chronicles of
life in the army's camps.   Executed at Pikysyry during
the 1868 conspiracy episode.

McMAHON, MAJOR GENERAL MARTIN T.   Civil War veteran and last United States minister accredited to Paraguay during the era of the Triple Alliance War.   Replaced previous minister Charles A. Washburn, and
remained next to the government of Francisco Solano
López from December, 1868, to July, 1869.   Highly
sympathetic to the cause of Paraguay and a friend of
López and Mme. Lynch, McMahon rendered impressive
testimony at subsequent U. S. Senate hearings in refuta-
tion of depositions presented by Mr. Washburn.

McROBERTS, GENERAL SAMUEL.   American financier who
figured in the early stages of the Mennonite Chaco colony project.   Purchased a substantial land tract in
1921 from the Casado interests, and then exchanged it
for Mennonite-owned land in Canada.

MAIZ, FATHER FIDEL, 1833-1920.   Priest, journalist and
aide to Marshal Francisco Solano López during the
Triple Alliance War period.   Once accused of conspiracy and treason against Paraguay's leader, Maiz survived the accusations to become a principal inquisitor
of prisoners during the 1868 conspiracy episode.   A
witness at the last battle at Cerro Corá, he later
wrote one of the more interesting first hand accounts
of the war from Paraguay's side entitled Etapas de mi
vida.

MAIZ, FATHER MARCO ANTONIO see also ACADEMIA
LITERARIA, ? -1848.   Credited as the founding director of the Academia Literaria at Asunción on November 30, 1841, one of the first progressive acts of the
Carlos Antonio López regime.   The Academia was
Paraguay's first lay institution of higher learning.   Father Maiz was consecrated at the same time as Bishop
Basilio Antonio López, brother of Carlos Antonio López.   He also spent 14 years in Dr. Francia's prison
for having opposed the planned perpetual dictatorship
at the Congress of 1816.

MAKKA INDIANS see also COLONIA FRAY BARTOLOME
DE LAS CASAS. Remnants of a Chaco tribe of primi-
tive indigenous Indians who now live in a Toldería, on
an island in the Paraguay River slightly to the north
of Asunción. Easily visited, they provide a fascinating
example of the appearance and customs of the Chaco's
original inhabitants.

MALLET, GENERAL EMILIO LUIS. French-born Brazilian
army artillery expert, veteran of the Ituzaingó 1827
battle against Argentina, who fought through the entire
Triple Alliance War. His stand at the May, 1866,
first battle of Tuyuty was largely responsible for blunting the Paraguayan attack. Still remembered in Brazil's military as the "Patron of the Artillery."

MALLORQUIN, JUAN L., 1882-1947. Educator and statesman. Professor at the Colegio Nacional, author of
several works regarding Paraguay's Chaco boundary
problems with Bolivia and Argentina, president of the
Supreme Court, and president of the Asociación Nacional Republicana, the Colorado Party.

MAMELUCOS. Tough Brazilian marauders usually of mixed
racial origin who periodically raided the Paraguayan
missions region in the seventeenth and eighteenth centuries for the purpose of enslaving Guaraní Indians.

MANCEBOS DE LA TIERRA. Translated as "children of the
land," this term refers to the vast number of offspring
of Spanish/Indian unions appearing in Paraguay almost
immediately after the settlement of Asunción. The
modern Paraguayan stems directly from such efforts as
the "Pacto de sangre," the "Blood Compact" urged
upon his men by early Governor Martínez de Irala.
"Mancebos de la tierra" largely composed the subsequent expeditions from Asunción down the Paraná River to found the Argentine cities of Rosario and Buenos
Aires.

MANDIOCA. Manioca, also known as yucca and casava in
other areas--a root-like tuber which is a basic ingre-
dient of the Paraguayan diet.

MANDUVIRA RIVER. Central Paraguayan drainage stream,
navigable for a short distance, which flows into the
Paraguay River to the north of Asunción. The remaining vessels of Paraguay's navy were burned and scut-

tled on one of its tributaries in 1869 near the end of
the Triple Alliance War.

MANGORE, CHIEF. Chief of the Timbú Indians living in
the vicinity of Fort Sancti Spíritu, built about 1526 by
the Sebastián Cabot expedition up the Paraná River.
Mangoré was killed in attacking the fort reportedly for
vengeance because his love for the wife of one of the
conquistadors was spurned.

MANGRULLOS. High wooden observation towers used by
both armies during the Triple Alliance War, especially
in the siege of Humaitá.

MANLOVE, MAJOR JAMES. Along with the torpedo expert
Kruger and the balloonist Allen brothers, one of the
curious American actors in the Triple Alliance War.
An ex-Confederate from Maryland, Manlove succeeded
in reaching Paraguayan lines in 1866, and presented
Marshal President López with a blockade-running and
privateering scheme aimed at damaging the allied navy.
López declined the offer, and Manlove subsequently
died a prisoner during the 1868 conspiracy episode.

MANSO, CAPTAIN ANDRES. Commander of an ill-fated
Spanish expedition into the Chaco along the Pilcomayo
River in 1556. All were killed by Chiriguano Indians.

MARCHAS. Term given to the colonization movements organized and supervised by the Instituto de Bienestar
Rural (IBR), since its establishment in 1963. The
"marchas," moderately successful to date, are principally designed to attract poorer people living in the
heavily populated central area to new agricultural sites
in less populated and more remote areas where they
can own their land. The program has the political objective of "consolidating the national territory."

MARCY, WILLIAM L. American secretary of state in 1853-
1854 who attempted to correct the text of the United
States-Paraguay 1853 treaty because of alleged numerous errors found in the text. President Carlos Antonio López had already ratified it, however, and United
States approaches for modifications were unsuccessful.

MARGINADOS. Term used in Paraguay for those poor sectors of the national population who live a marginal ex-

istence, i.e., those whose standard of living is station-
ary or even declining in relation to national income and
production levels.

MARIA. Servant-mistress of Governor Martínez de Irala,
and mother of his children Diego Martínez de Irala,
Antonio de Irala and Ginebra Martínez de Irala.

MARIA, JOSE DE see also ROBERTSON BROTHERS.
Spanish merchant at Buenos Aires contracted by J. P.
and W. P. Robertson for an import-export business
venture with Dr. Francia's Paraguay. María arrived
at Asunción in 1818, and though successful in his enterprise, was only allowed to depart by El Supremo in
1825 after intercession by the British consul.

MARIN IGLESIAS, ALEJANDRO, 1907- . Journalist,
history professor, president of the Chamber of Deputies and cabinet minister. Noted for his interpretive
study, Cartas a la juventud paraguaya, published at
Buenos Aires in 1937, a searching analysis of the national character directed toward Paraguay's youth.

MARINA. Servant-mistress of Governor Martínez de Irala,
to whom she bore a daughter, Ana de Irala.

MARISCAL (EL) see LOPEZ, FRANCISCO SOLANO. "The
Marshal." Title used commonly in reference to Marshal President Francisco Solano López, Paraguay's
foremost national hero, chief executive and commander-
in-chief during the Triple Alliance War. Frequently
referred to as "El Mariscal de Hierro"--the Iron Marshal.

MARISCAL ESTIGARRIBIA, FORTIN. Paraguayan Chaco
military post and now an important way-point on the
new Trans Chaco highway near the Mennonite center
of Filadelfia. Formerly Fortín Camacho.

MARISCAL LOPEZ, FORTIN. Paraguayan southern Chaco
military post attacked and taken by Bolivian forces in
a December, 1928, pre-Chaco war incident.

MARQUES DE OLINDA. On instruction from President
Francisco Solano López at his Cerro León headquarters,
this Brazilian river steamer was seized by a Paraguayan gunboat while proceeding upstream from Asunción, November 11, 1864. The warning shot fired by

the pursuing Paraguayan vessel began the War of the Triple Alliance.

MARQUEZ, LUIS. Special Buenos Aires Junta envoy sent to Asunción in 1810 with José Espínola y Peña on an unsuccessful mission to secure Paraguay's adhesion to the new Junta. A prelude to the 1810-1811 Manuel Belgrano military expedition to Paraguay.

MARQUEZ LISBOA, ADMIRAL JOAQUIM see also TAMANDARE, BARÃO DE. Commander-in-chief of Brazil's naval fleet in the early years of the Triple Alliance War and one of Brazil's greatest naval heroes.

MARTINEZ, COLONEL FRANCISCO. Successor in command of the Paraguayan garrison at Humaitá during the Triple Alliance War following the suicide of Colonel Paulino Alén. Colonel Martínez surrendered Humaitá to the allies upon its encirclement in August, 1868. His wife, Juliana Ynsfrán de Martínez was subsequently executed during the 1868 conspiracy episode.

MARTINEZ, RAMONA. Paraguay's Molly Pitcher. This 15-year-old girl, a personal servant to Marshal López, stiffened Paraguayan resistance to Brazilian attacks at the battle of Itá-Ybaté, December, 1868, by her heroic participation in the trenches alongside the men.

MARTINEZ DE IRALA, DOMINGO see IRALA, DOMINGO MARTINEZ DE. Practically all sources use the form "Governor Irala" rather than the correct form "Governor Martínez de Irala, in referring to Paraguay's "Founding Father."

MARTINEZ PITA, GENERAL RODOLFO see CHACO NEUTRAL MILITARY COMMISSION. Argentine general who headed the post-Chaco War commission to oversee troop withdrawals and prisoner exchanges by Bolivia and Paraguay.

MASAMAKLAY, BATTLE OF see SAMAKLAY, BATTLE OF.

MASAMAKLAY, FORTIN see also SAMAKLAY, FORTIN. Both names are used in Paraguay for the small post on the southern Chaco front, scene of a pre-war incident and of heavy fighting in the December, 1933, offensive.

MASTERMAN, GEORGE FREDERICK. British subject and
pharmacist employed in Paraguay who became involved
in the 1868 conspiracy episode against Marshal President Francisco Solano López. Imprisoned at San Fernando, Masterman was eventually released with Cornelius Porter Bliss as members of the American Minister
Charles Ames Washburn's household. His memoirs,
Seven Eventful Years in Paraguay (London, 1869), are
a useful though colorful primary source of the era.

MATE, YERBA see also YERBA MATE. The art or act
of drinking yerba maté, either heated or cold (tereré),
with a "porongo" or small gourd-like receptacle and a
"bombilla" or metal straw/spoon. The most popular
beverage of the River Plate republics.

MATE AMARGO see also YERBA MATE. A form of preparing yerba maté, Paraguay's national beverage.

MATO GROSSO PROVINCE, BRAZIL. Borders Paraguay to
the north. Frontier questions with Mato Grosso, involving the Apa and Blanco rivers, were a disturbing
factor in pre-Triple Alliance War Paraguayan-Brazilian
relations. Paraguay's initial and successful offensive
in December, 1864, was directed at Mato Grosso to
secure the large munitions stores reported in the area.
Post-war treaty provisions established Brazil's claim
to the Apa River as the border with Paraguay, in ac-
cordance with the secret protocol of the Triple Alliance
Treaty of May 1, 1865.

MAYRA, GALIANO DE. Spanish sword-maker in the early
colonial era at Asunción, member of the Martínez de
Irala expedition.

MAZAMORRA. Commonly-used Paraguayan dish taken as a
dessert and prepared from corn cooked with coal ash
and served with milk.

MBAYA INDIANS. Branch of the Chaco Guaycurú tribes who
invaded and settled areas north of Asunción and east of
the Paraguay River prior to the Spanish conquest.
Eventually conquered by the Spanish in the mid-eight-
eenth century.

MBORORE, BATTLE OF. Fought in 1640, a decisive conflict in which armed mission Indians under Jesuit lead-

ership soundly defeated a large Brazilian mameluke
slaving expedition.   The mamelukes never again mounted
large-scale raids into the mission area.

MEDINA, JUAN.   Noted in records as a ship cordage maker
among the early Spanish arrivals at Asunción.

MELO DE PORTUGAL, PEDRO.   Governor during 1778-1785.
Aside from the numerous urban sites founded during his
administration, the first institution of superior learing
was established--the Real Colegio Seminario de San
Carlos.   Founder of the Chaco Indian reducation named
Melodia at the present site of Villa Hayes, across the
Paraguay River north of Asunción.

MELODIA, MISSION   see also   MELO DE PORTUGAL,
PEDRO.   Chaco Indian mission, formerly existed in
the late colonial era at the present site of Villa Hayes.

MENA, JUAN DE.   Paraguayan "Comunero" associated with
Dr. José de Antequera y Castro in the Comunero Revolt of the 1730's.   Tried and executed with Antequera
in Lima in 1731.

MENA BARRETO, GENERAL JOÃO MANOEL.   One of Imperial Brazil's best Triple Alliance War generals; a
cavalry commander, he was killed at Piribebuy, August,
1869, one of the war's last battles.

MENDEZ CALDEIRA, MANUEL.   Uruguayan merchant in
business at Asunción during the Dr. Francia regime.
Exiled to the interior by El Supremo, Méndez Caldeira
spent 11 years before he was finally released.

MENDEZ FLEITAS, EPIFANIO   see also   MOVIMIENTO
POPULAR COLORADO, 1917-   .   Former Asunción
chief of police, president of the Banco Central and
member of the Chamber of Deputies.   In exile since
1956 and one of the directors of the Movimiento Popular Colorado.

MENDOZA, ANDRES HURTADO DE.   Viceroy of Peru who
in 1556 dispatched the ill-fated Andrés Manso expedition to the Chaco to conquer the Chiriguano Indians
residing near the Pilcomayo River.   All expedition
members were massacred.

MENDOZA, DIEGO DE. Brother of Admiral Pedro de Mendo-
za and member of the early 1535-1536 expedition to La
Plata. Killed in an Indian attack near the first site of
Buenos Aires.

MENDOZA, FRANCISCO DE. Spanish conquistador, member
of the early Pedro de Mendoza expedition. Conspirator
in the successful 1544 plot at Asunción to depose Alvar
Núñez Cabeza de Vaca, and subsequently temporary
governor. Executed by Captain Diego de Abreu during
a rebellion in the absence of Martínez de Irala.

MENDOZA, GONZALO DE. Member of the 1535 Pedro de
Mendoza expedition to La Plata, and with Juan de Salazar y Espinosa, a founder of Asunción in 1537. First
husband of Martínez de Irala's daughter Agueda, and
father of Hernando de Mendoza, a founder of Buenos
Aires.

MENDOZA, HERNANDO DE. Son of Agueda, mestizo daughter of Martínez de Irala, and a founder of Buenos Aires.

MENDOZA, PEDRO DE. First Spanish administrator appointed in 1534 by Emperor Charles V to the newly
discovered La Plata region. His directives were to
discover new routes to Peru and to defend Spanish-
discovered lands from Portuguese inroads. Originally
founded "Nuestra Señora de la Santa María del Buen
Aire"--Buenos Aires, in 1536; sent his assistant, Captain Juan de Ayolas on voyages of discovery along the
Paraná and Paraguay Rivers. Deciding to return to
Spain because of illness, Mendoza died at sea June 23,
1537.

MENDOZA, CHIEF PEDRO DE. Chieftain of a Guaraní
tribe in the vicinity of Asunción who took the Christian
name Pedro de Mendoza. His daughter, María, became
a servant-mistress of Governor Martínez de Irala, and
bore him two sons and a daughter.

MENNO COLONY see COLONIA MENNO and MENNONITES.

MENNONITES see also COLONIA MENNO, COLONIA
FERNHEIM, and COLONIA NEULAND. Most successful and certainly the most curious of the numerous and
heterogeneous foreign immigrant colonization experiments in Paraguay. Conceived in the mid-1920's by

Mennonites originally from Russia who were living in
Canada, searching for an area in the world where they
could live in isolated peace, they centered upon the
Chaco on land bought originally by a New York financier. The first group arrived in December, 1926,
and organized themselves as the Colonia Menno. Two
subsequent colonies, Fernheim and Neuland, were established around the experiment's one urban center of
Filadelfia. Of the estimated 20,000 colonists who came
to Paraguay, about 12,000 still remain in the colonies.
They form the largest single foreign ethnic group in
Paraguay. Their moderate success in such isolated
surroundings is credited to their ability to develop a
dairy industry, the products of which find a ready market in Asunción. Isolation handicaps are being reme-
died by improved transport available on the Trans
Chaco Highway, although what the road's impact will
be on the colony's original ideological objectives is
still uncertain.

MENSU. Derived from the word "Mensualero," or planta-
    tion worker living on minimal wages and subject to
    oppressive labor conditions. The "mensú" of Paraguay
    in the late nineteenth century suffered as degrading an
    existence on yerba maté plantations as the Brazilian
    seringueiro on rubber plantations. Author Rafael
    Barret used this theme for his noted essays and sto-
    ries of a social protest nature.

MERCADO, DR. BAILON. Bolivia's diplomatic representa-
    tive to Paraguay on the eve of the Chaco War. De-
    parted from Asunción following the Vanguardia, Fortín
    Mariscal López and Boquerón incidents of December,
    1928.

MESA, CAPTAIN PEDRO IGNACIO see MEZA, CAPTAIN
    PEDRO IGNACIO.

MESTIZO see also MANCEBOS DE LA TIERRA. Term
    applied to the offspring of Spanish-Indian unions, orig-
    inally stimulated by the "Pacto de Sangre" sponsored
    by Governor Domingo Martínez de Irala.

MEZA, CAPTAIN PEDRO IGNACIO see MESA, CAPTAIN
    PEDRO IGNACIO. Highest official in Paraguay's navy
    and fleet commander at the June, 1865, battle of
    Riachuelo, most sanguinary naval conflict in Latin

America's history. Defeated and mortally wounded,
Meza subsequently died at Humaitá and was buried without military honors. Today his name has been resurrected as one of the nation's wartime heroes.

MIGUEL. Indian guide who reportedly aided the 1541 Alvar
Núñez Cabeza de Vaca expedition to reach Asunción.

MILITARY COLLEGE see COLEGIO MILITAR.

MILTOS SOTERO, CAYO, 1843-1871. Politician, orator and
a founder of the "Club del Pueblo." Vice president in
the administration of Cirilo Antonio Rivarola, Paraguay's first president under the 1870 constitution in the
post-Triple Alliance War period. Upon his early death,
Miltos was succeeded by Salvador Jovellanos.

MINEROS. Term applied during the colonial era to Indian
workers, living in virtual enslavement, employed in
eastern Paraguay's yerba maté plantations.

MINGA. A form of voluntary collective labor dating from
the colonial era and still employed in Paraguay's rural
areas in crop harvesting, road construction and house-
building. Strikingly similar to the cooperative devices
of the Far West of the United States' wagon train era.
A sanatarium in the Puerto Presidente Stroessner area
is called "Minga-guazú"--large collective effort.

MINIFUNDIA. Meaning small landholdings as compared to
"latifundia" or large estates or haciendas. Minifundia
are the predominant characteristic of Paraguay's interior land development system, usually stemming from
the fractioning of previous large estates.

MIRANDA, FATHER FRANCISCO. Franciscan missionary
credited with the settlement in 1539 of the village of
Yaguarón, important for its early colonial church, and
of the nearby villages of Itá and Atyrá.

MIRANDA, ROQUE CENTURION, 1900-1960. Principal figure
in the development of a national theater in the post-
Chaco War era. Author, actor, director, and founder
of the Escuela Municipal de Arte Escénico at Asunción.

MIRANDA CUETO DE ESTIGARRIBIA, JULIA. Wife of President and Marshal José Félix Estigarribia, killed with

him in an airplane accident on September 7, 1940,
near Asunción.

MISIONES PROVINCE, ARGENTINA. Northernmost Argentine
province between the Paraná and Uruguay Rivers, bordering Paraguay to the north. Paraguay's southern
riverport city of Encarnación faces Argentina's Posadas
across the Paraná. Once claimed by Paraguay, Misiones department was the stronghold of the Jesuit reduction system, and many majestic ruins of old missions are still visible. Candelaria, near present-day
Posadas, was the mission area's center. Though an
1852 treaty established the Paraná River as the Argen-
tine-Paraguay boundary, Paraguay persisted in its
claims to the area until the definitive frontier agreements reached following the Triple Alliance War.

MISSIONS, JESUIT see JESUITS and REDUCTIONS.

MITA. Compulsory work by Indian levees for Spanish colonial landowners or encomenderos. The rather mild
Paraguayan mita may not be compared with the much
harsher Peruvian and Bolivian versions which involved
forced labor in the silver mines.

MITRE, BARTOLOME. Argentine's foremost national hero
and original commander-in-chief of the allied armies
in the Triple Alliance War. A strong champion of the
"Unitarian" faction in Argentina as opposed to the "Fed-
eralists," he sought to create a united Argentina. His
willingness to ally Argentina with imperial Brazil
against Paraguay engendered unrest in the interior
provinces. Deficient in leadership as a soldier, especially at the battle of Curupaity, he retired in the
Triple Alliance War's later phases in favor of Brazil's
Marquês de Caxias.

MITRE, GENERAL EMILIO. Brother of Bartolomé Mitre,
Argentina's foremost national hero, and last commander of the small Argentine force still in the field in
1869 during the Triple Alliance War.

MOLAS, FATHER JOSE AGUSTIN. Chaplain of Paraguay's
forces at the 1811 battle of Tacuarí against Argentina's
Manuel Belgrano. Defended Paraguay's right to independence in the subsequent discussions with Belgrano,
and left a unique written memoir-dialogue of the conference.

MOLAS, MARIANO ANTONIO, 1780-1844. Asunción attorney
in the early independence period and member of the
first National Congress. Opposed the nomination of
Dr. José Gaspar Rodríguez de Francia as permanent
dictator, and was imprisoned by El Supremo in 1828.
During his 12 years of prison, he wrote Descripción
histórica de la antigua provincia del Paraguay, a unique
contemporary source record.

MOLAS LOPEZ, FELIPE. Paraguay's president for a seven-
month period in 1949 following the brief regime of General Raimundo Rolón. Removed from office by a military revolt in September, 1949, and followed by the administration of Federico Chaves.

MOLINAS, JUAN ESTEBAN. Paraguayan Triple Alliance War
veteran whose 1909 and 1917 depositions contribute useful detail to information regarding the alleged 1868 conspiracy plot against President Francisco Solano López.

MOLINES, FELIPE DE. Spanish artisan recorded as basket
weaver at Asunción in the early colonial era.

MOMFORT, FRANCISCO DE. Governor in 1685; noted for
his success in 1688 in driving marauding Brazilian
Bandeirantes and mameluke slavers from the former
Santiago de Jérez region in extreme northern Paraguay.

MOMPOX Y ZAYAS, FERNANDO DE. Leader of the later
phase of the Comunero Revolt of the 1730's who originally met Dr. José de Antequera y Castro, the revolt's
principal leader while imprisoned at Lima. Mompox
traveled to Asunción and assumed leadership of the
Comunero movement. He fled to Brazil upon Antequera's execution and the success of royalist troops
from Buenos Aires aided by levies of Guaraní Indian
troops from the Misiones district. Reportedly died at
Rio de Janeiro where he had established a small merchant business.

MONDAY RIVER. River draining east central Paraguay
which joins the Paraná River about six miles south of
Puerto Presidente Stroessner near the Friendship Bridge
and Yguazú Falls. Its "Salto de Monday" is a much
smaller but still impressive version of the Yguazú Falls
in Paraguay, and a possible site for another Paraguayan
hydroelectric project similar to that on the Acaray River.

MONEDA, RAFAEL DE LA. Governor of Paraguay 1740-
1747, noted for his efforts in the post-Comunero period
to protect the colony from Indian depredations. Finally
subdued the fierce Mbayá Indians living to the north of
Asunción. Founded numerous additional fortified settlements including Emboscada to the north of Asunción,
which was peopled by blacks and mulattoes. Recorded
as the best Spanish governor in the colonial era following Martínez de Irala and Hernandarias.

MONTE. Named applied to forest-covered areas.

MONTERO, JOSE P. Vice president in the administration
of Dr. Manuel Franco, who served the remainder of
Franco's term in office following his death in 1919.

MONTIEL, PEDRO. Suspected conspirator against Dr. José
Gaspar Rodríguez de Francia who disappeared a prisoner of El Supremo's mass arrests in 1820.

MONTOYA, FATHER ANTONIO RUIZ DE, 1585-1652. One
of the first Jesuit missionaries in Paraguay, active in
establishing missions in the eastern Guairá region in
the early seventeenth century. Credited with having
induced the Spanish government in 1643 to permit the
arming of mission Indians to repel Brazilian mameluke
slaving raids. Also revised the Catechism written in
Guaraní and published a dictionary and vocabulary of the
Guaraní language.

MOPOCOL see MOVIMIENTO POPULAR COLORADO.

MOQUIARACE, CHIEF LORENZO. Carío Indian chief living
near Asunción who was a Spanish ally against the Chaco
Guaycurú Indians. His daughter married García Venegas, regidor and treasurer at Asunción, and who accompanied the arrested Alvar Núñez Cabeza de Vaca
back to Spain in 1545.

MORA, FERNANDO DE LA, 1785-1830. Asunción intellectual
and member of the Superior Governing Board (Junta
Superior Gubernativa) appointed by Paraguay's first National Congress of June 17, 1811. Associate of Dr.
José Gaspar Rodríguez de Francia, but later implicated
in the 1820 conspiracy episode and apparently died in
prison.

MORA DELGADO DE STROESSNER, ELIGIA. Wife of General Alfredo Stroessner, Paraguay's president since 1954.

MORALES, DR. AUGUSTIN. Asunción intellectual discharged from the National University and forced into exile during the restrictive phase of the World War II Morínigo administration.

MORATO, MANOEL. Infamous leader of Brazilian mameluke slaving raids against eastern Paraguay's Guairá Indian missions in the early seventeenth century.

MOREL, PEDRO. Spanish artisan recorded at Asunción after 1555 engaged in casting bells and cannonballs.

MORENO, BONIFACIO, ? -1868. Teacher and director of an Asunción primary school. Captured at the battle of Avay, December 11, 1868, in the last stages of the Triple Alliance War, he was mistakenly executed by Brazilian troops in the belief that he was Paraguay's General Bernardino Caballero.

MORENO, FULGENCIO R., 1872-1933. Noted author, educator, historian and politician. Known especially for his penetrating research and advancement of Paraguay's claims to the Chaco, and for his published works on the city of Asunción and Paraguay's independence era.

MORENO, FATHER JOSE DEL CARMEN, ? -1868. Young priest specializing in the teaching of Latin. Instructor at the College of San Carlos at Asunción. Killed at the battle of Ytororó, December 6, 1868, in the late stages of the Triple Alliance War.

MORENO GONZALEZ, JOSE ANTONIO, 1907-   . Journalist, politician, diplomat and historian. Editor of El Orden, El País, La Epoca, El Diario, El Debate and Jornada, of Asunción; director of several periodicals, and agent for the Associated Press and several Brazilian and Argentine newspapers. Author of numerous studies on the colonial period and of the Chaco War era.

MORENO GONZALEZ, JUAN CARLOS. Son of the historian Fulgencio Moreno,. and a noted musicologist and composer in the modern era.

MORGENSTERN, COLONEL ENRIQUE WISNER VON. Also
referred to frequently as François Enrique or Francisco
Wisner de Morgenstern. A Hungarian national, and one
of the more notable foreign technicians contracted for
service in Paraguay during the Carlos Antonio López
administration. Friendly with and trusted by both
Francisco Solano López and Alicia Lynch, von Morgenstern rendered valuable service for Paraguay. In addition to his plans for the construction of the Humaitá
fortress, he completed one of the best early complete
maps of Paraguay--printed in Vienna in 1873, and left
a collection of documents on the life and times of Dr.
Francia which were later published in Argentina in
1923. Captured at Lomas Valentinas in 1868 during
the Triple Alliance War, he later returned to Paraguay
to become director of railways. Date of death unknown.

MORINIGO, HIGINIO, 1897-   . President of Paraguay
from 1940 to 1948, and one of the most important figures in modern Paraguay's political evolution. Native
of Paraguarí, an east central city about 40 miles from
Asunción. Choosing the army for a career, he was
graduated from the military college in 1922 and subsequently received regular promotions. Following
service in the Chaco War, he became war minister in
the cabinet of Marshal José Félix Estigarribia. He
became president following the latter's death by airplane accident in September, 1940. Reelected in 1943.
As Paraguay's wartime president, General Morínigo
suspended all political activity, developed a strict censorship system, and pursued a neutral policy which to
some observers in the early war years appeared to
be pro-Axis in its sympathies. In 1943, however, he
was the first Paraguayan president to visit the United
States, where he delivered a pro-democracy speech
before Congress at Washington. Unsuccessful in his
efforts to promote a new Nationalist Revolutionary
State which would supplant the traditional political parties, Morínigo in 1947 faced Paraguay's most serious
political revolution. Strong backing by Colorado Party
adherents enabled him to suppress the revolt, largely
composed of Febrerista Party supporters. In 1948,
however, he was removed from office by a coup.
Since then he has withdrawn from politics and normally
resides with his family at Buenos Aires.

MORINIGO, MARCOS A. Vice president to Juan G. Gonzá-

lez who served as president until 1894 following the
overthrow of the latter.

MORINIGO, VICTOR, 1899-   . Prominent member of the
Colorado Party and companion of J. Natalicio González,
principal architect of the party's regeneration after the
1940's. A capable essayist, Morínigo is known for his
penetrating commentaries on local events. Utilized the
pseudonym El pacífico asunceño.

MORPHY, CARLOS. Irishman named governor in 1766;
remembered for having carried out the expulsion edict
against the Jesuits in 1767.

MORTON, CLEMENT MANLY. First director in 1920 of
the Colegio Internacional, regarded as Paraguay's best
private institution of learning.

MOSCOSO, MAJOR OSCAR. Commander of a Bolivian detachment which captured Paraguay's central Chaco
Fortín Pitiantuta on June 15, 1932, regarded by many
historians as the date of formal outbreak of the Chaco
War.

MOSQUEIRA, SILVANO, 1867-1955. Poet and diplomat.
Educated at Asunción and Buenos Aires. Contributor
of poems to numerous periodicals and newspapers.
Also composed poetry in the Guaraní language.

MOSQUERA, CAPTAIN RODRIGUEZ. Presumed member of
the 1526-1527 Sebastián Cabot expedition to La Plata.
Remained in 1530 with Nuño de Lara at Fort Sancti
Spíritu on the lower Paraná River. Possibly a survivor of the Indian attacks on the fort who led the remaining soldiers back to the Brazilian coast.

MOSQUERA, RUI GARCIA. Conquistador captain who with
Alonso Riquelme de Guzmán, extinguished the Agacé
Indian uprising under Chief Abacote near Asunción in
1558.

MOVEMENT OF FEBRUARY 17, 1936 see REVOLUTION
OF FEBRUARY 17, 1936, and FEBRERISTA PARTY.
Name occassionally used with reference to the 1936
Revolution which gave birth to Paraguay's Febrerista
Party.

MOVIMIENTO POPULAR COLORADO see also COLORADO
  PARTY. Splinter faction of the Colorado Party known
  as the MOPOCOL, which opposes the regular Colorado
  Party regime. Its members have been in exile since 1959.
  The principal leader is Epifanio Méndez Fleitas, former Asunción chief of police and ex-president of Paraguay's Central Bank.

MOVIMIENTO RENOVACION see also LIBERAL PARTY.
  Splinter group of the Liberal Party which espouses an
  "active, progressive liberalism," and is influential
  among intellectuals and students.

MOVIMIENTO SOCIAL-DEMOCRATA CRISTIANO see
  CHRISTIAN DEMOCRATIC PARTY and PARTIDO
  DEMOCRATA CRISTIANO.

MOVIMIENTO 14 DE MAYO. Pro-Castro type faction of
  Paraguay's Communist Party. Organized ineffective
  armed invasion parties into Paraguay from Argentina
  in 1959-1960, and was subsequently disbanded.

MOYNIHAN, JOHN OWEN. British sculptor-stonemason who
  presumably was contracted for service in Paraguay
  during the Carlos Antonio López administration. A
  co-worker with Alonso Taylor in the construction of
  Asunción's Government Palace. Some of his sculpture
  work was reportedly of such bad taste that it had to
  be removed and stored in the basement.

MUERO CON MI PATRIA! "I DIE WITH MY COUNTRY!"
  Now nearly a legend, these were reportedly the last
  words of Marshal President Francisco Solano López
  on his death at the hands of a Brazilian cavalryman
  at Cerro Corá, March 1, 1870, terminating the Triple
  Alliance War.

MUJIA, DR. RICARDO. Bolivian diplomatic representative
  in Asunción in 1915 who presented a lengthy Bolivian
  statement of Chaco claims which nullified hopes for
  early settlement under the Ayala-Mujía 1913 protocol.

MUÑOZ, FORTIN. Bolivian fortified post on the south central front, and locale of heavy fighting in the early
  stages of the Chaco War.

MUSEO HISTORICO Y DE BELLAS ARTES DE JUANSILVA-
  NO GODOI see also GODOI, JUANSILVANO. Founded

in 1885 by Juansilvano Godoi, one of Paraguay's most
prominent art collectors, historians and archivists.
Now located in Asunción, it contains an impressive
collection of art works, numismatics and historical
relics.

MUSEO HISTORICO Y MILITAR. Located in Asunción's
Ministry of National Defense, this museum contains
Paraguay's largest and most fascinating collection of
relics, pictures and documents of both the Triple Alliance and Chaco Wars.

MYSKOWSKY, COLONEL LEOPOLDO LUIS. Polish army
officer who reached Paraguay at an unknown date,
fought on Paraguay's side in the Triple Alliance War,
and was killed at the 1866 battle of Curupaity. Mater-
nal grandfather of Julio Correa, popular poet, author
and theatre actor of the early twentieth century credited
with having originated theatrical performances in the
Guaraní language.

- N -

NACION (LA), ASUNCION. Asunción newspaper representing
the views of the "Liga Nacional Independiente" which
began publication in 1926.

NAGY, ARTURO, 1914-1971. Distinguished Hungarian philosophy professor who emigrated to Paraguay in 1949
and was naturalized in 1955. Professor on the faculty
of the Universidad Nacional. Specialist in iconographic
studies and author of numerous specialized studies.

NAMBI-I see also LAUREL-TY. An unusual Paraguayan
army unit assigned for boarding purposes to the navy
during the battle of Riachuelo during the Triple Alliance War. Composed largely of descendents of a
group of Negro troops brought to Paraguay by Uruguay's
General José Artigas in 1820-1821.

NANAWA, BATTLE OF. During January and July, 1933,
Bolivian troops sought desperately to dislodge Paraguayan troops from this fortified position in mass frontal attacks featuring heavy artillery bombardments,
air attacks and the use of tanks. They were persist-
ently repelled by Paraguayan defenders commanded by

Colonel Luis Irrazábal. Scene of some of the Chaco
War's bloodiest fighting, the area still retains a singular resemblance to World War I battlefields with
trench lines clearly visible. Several war studies refer
to it as the "Verdun of America."

NANAWA, FORTIN see NANAWA, BATTLE OF.

ÑANDUTI LACE see also ITAUGUA. A principal native
    Paraguayan handicraft specialty comprised of extremely
    delicate "spider-web" like lace designs. Made at
    Itauguá, 20 miles east of Asunción.

NATIONAL DEVELOPMENT BANK see BANCO NACIONAL
    DE FOMENTO.

NATIONAL FEDERATION OF STUDENTS see also FEDE-
    RACION DE ESTUDIANTES DEL PARAGUAY. Uni-
    versity students organization and traditionally liberal
    radical in its ideology. Responsible for numerous
    riots, protest marches and strikes in Paraguay's mod-
    ern political evolution including the current Stroessner
    regime.

NATIONAL FOREIGN TRADE COUNCIL see CONSEJO
    NACIONAL DE COMERCIO EXTERIOR.

NATIONAL HYMN see HIMNO NACIONAL.

NATIONAL REVOLUTIONARY STATE see NUEVO ESTA-
    DO NACIONALISTA REVOLUCIONARIO and MORINI-
    GO, HIGINIO.

NATIONAL UNIVERSITY, ASUNCION see also UNIVERSI-
    DAD NACIONAL DE LA ASUNCION. Paraguay's fore-
    most institution of higher learning, provided for by
    decree of October 18, 1892.

NATIONAL VETERANS ASSOCIATION see ASOCIACION
    NACIONAL DE EX-COMBATIENTES.

ÑEEMBUCU see ESTERO DE ÑEEMBUCU. Administra-
    tive department in southern Paraguay of which Pilar
    is the capital. Zone in which the Humaitá siege op-
    erations of the Triple Alliance War took place.

NENIA see also GUIDO Y SPANO, CARLOS. Famed

poem written by the Argentine poet Guido y Spano,
which eulogizes the tragic Paraguayan defense in the
Triple Alliance War. Its major lines read "Llora,
llora, urutaú," the urutaú being a near extinct bird
species in Paraguay known for its plaintive call.

NEULAND COLONY   see   MENNONITES and COLONIA
NEULAND.

NOLASCO, PEDRO.   Priest who refuted the accusations of
Bishop Bernardino de Cárdenas in 1648 that the Jesuits
were remiss in their evangelizing duties among mission
Indians.

NUEVA ASUNCION.   Early colonial era Spanish outpost near
the Parapití River in eastern Bolivia.   Founded on
August 1, 1559, by Ñuflo de Chaves, while on an expedition westward from Asunción.   Also referred to in
some records as "La Barranca."

NUEVA AUSTRALIA   see also   LANE, WILLIAM.   Most
important large-scale colonization experiment by Eng-
lish-speaking peoples in Paraguay.   Formed by Australian immigrants in 1893 by William Lane under his
Australian Cooperative Society plan.   The experiment
in socialism failed when colonists refused to follow the
rigorous life demanded of them.   Survivors remained
to establish a moderately successful colony near the
city of Villarrica about 100 miles east of Asunción.

NUEVA BURDEOS.   Name given to the first and ill-fated
colonization experiment attempted in 1855 at the site
of the present riverport city of Villa Hayes, about 12
miles north of Asunción.   Conceived by Francisco
Solano López but poorly organized with French colonists unsuited to agricultural efforts in Paraguay, the
colony failed miserably in circumstances which pro-
voked near rupture of Franco-Paraguayan relations.

NUEVA COIMBRA, FUERTE DE.   Portuguese fort constructed along the Paraguay River north of the present
frontier limits.   Attacked unsuccessfully in 1801 by a
Paraguayan force under Governor Lázaro de Ribera in
an effort to displace growing Portuguese settlement on
the upper Paraguay.

NUEVO ESTADO NACIONALISTA REVOLUCIONARIO   see

also MORINIGO, HIGINIO. Government administrative
program promulgated by President Higinio Morínigo
shortly after his assumption to power in 1940 following
the death of Marshal José Félix Estigarribia. The new
program was announced as based on the motto "Order,
Discipline and Hierarchy," and observers regarded it as
copied from the Italian Fascist model. A clamp-down
on political activity, censorship, and government intervention into most facets of activity were its principal
aspects. The "New State" disappeared at the close of
World War II and the 1947 revolution.

NUEVA GERMANIA see COLONIA NUEVA GERMANIA.

NUÑEZ, ELOY FARIÑA see FARIÑA NUÑEZ, ELOY.

- O -

OCAMPOS, BERARDO. Prominent member of the Colorado
Party "Democrático" faction in the late 1940's and
1950's.

OKES, HENRY. English businessman, agent for the Robertson brothers, who performed a successful commercial
mission to Paraguay for them in 1820. One of the very
few foreigners permitted to enter and leave Paraguay
during the reign of Dr. José Gaspar Rodríguez de
Francia.

OLABARRIETA, DIEGO DE. Spanish notary at Asunción who
officiated at the 1542 inauguration ceremonies for Governor Alvar Núñez Cabeza de Vaca.

O'LEARY, JUAN EMILIANO, 1879-1968. Former dean of
Paraguayan letters and originator in the early 1900's
of the revisionist school of historical writing which
promotes Francisco Solano López as the foremost national hero. Author of numerous literary works on the
subject of the War of the Triple Alliance.

OLIVEIRA, ADMIRAL PEDRO FERREIRA DE. Commander
of a Brazilian fleet sent to Paraguay in 1855 to stimulate a solution to delicate boundary problems. The
subsequent López-Ferreira Treaty in 1855 produced
agreement only to commerce and navigation matters.

OLMEDO, NATALICIO, 1902-   . Journalist, one of the
most prominent newspapermen of northern Paraguay,
contributor, founder and director of several Concepción papers and periodicals. Author of several works
regarding northern Paraguay and the Chaco War.

OÑATE, PEDRO DE. Messenger sent with Ñufrio de Chaves
by Governor Martínez de Irala to Peru in 1548 to seek
a means of obtaining needed supplies for the new Asunción colony. On arrival at Lima, Chaves complained
to Pedro de la Gasca of the need to replace Irala as
governor of Paraguay.

ONTIVEROS. Early Spanish settlement in the Guairá region along the Upper Paraná River probably located
above the site of the modern-day Brazilian frontier
city of Foz de Iguassú. Founded about 1554 by Captain García Rodríguez de Vergara.

OPFERRING. Nazi-oriented political organization in Paraguay during World War II.

OPINION PUBLICA (LA). Post-Triple Alliance War Asunción newspaper.

ORDEN (EL). Asunción daily newspaper founded in 1923
by Félix Paiva and Gualberto Cardús Huerta. Reappeared briefly in 1957 but was forced to suspend publication by government order.

ORDENANZA DE INTENDENTES. One of the most important of the so-called eighteenth century Bourbon reforms in the Spanish colonial administrative system.
Promulgated in 1782, its chief effect in La Plata, including Paraguay, was a strengthening in the powers
of the Viceroy at Buenos Aires.

ORDENANZAS see also ARIAS DE SAAVEDRA, HERNAN-
DO. One of the most important documents related to
Paraguay's sociological evolution. Promulgated by
Governor Hernando Arias de Saavedra, these regula-
tions specified the obligations of the "encomenderos"
or large landowners regarding the treatment, care,
and education of native Indians employed by them.

OREJON INDIANS. Tribe discovered by early Spanish expeditions along the upper reaches of the Paraguay Riv-

er, and noted for their custom of enlarging their ears
through the insertion of discs.

ORLEANS, GASTON LUIS FELIPE DE   see also   EU,
COMTE D'.   French-born son-in-law of Emperor Dom
Pedro II of Brazil who in early 1869 succeeded the
Marqués de Caxias in command of allied forces for the
final Cordillera campaign of the Triple Alliance War.

OROÑO, NICASIO.   Member of a group of Paraguayans who
promoted an unsuccessful scheme in 1874 to end the
allied occupation of Paraguay after the Triple Alliance
War.

ORTEGA, JUAN DE.   Member of the Martínez de Irala expedition and one of the Governor's most trusted followers.

ORTEGA, FATHER MANOEL DE.   Portuguese Jesuit and
one of the first to arrive in Paraguay, reportedly in
1588.   Active in the founding of the first mission in
eastern Paraguay and the Guairá region.

ORTEGA VALLEJOS, LAZARO.   Commander of a military
expedition in the Chaco in the mid-seventeenth century.
Credited with the construction of a series of outposts,
thus forming the basis for later Paraguayan sovereignty
claims.

ORTIGOSA, SERGEANT JOSE MARIA   see also   CUATI,
SERGEANT.   Formal name of one of Paraguay's Triple
Alliance War heroes.

ORTIZ DE VERGARA, FRANCISCO DE.   Governor of Paraguay in the mid-sixteenth century.

ORTIZ DE VERGARA, JUAN.   Briefly the leader of the
Comunero movement in 1733-1734, on the eve of its
final defeat and collapse.

ORTIZ DE ZARATE, JUAN.   Third "Adelantado" of La Plata
at Asunción.   Wealthy Alto Perú (Bolivia) land owner,
he reached Asunción in 1575 and died there in 1576.

ORTIZ DE ZARATE, DOÑA JUANA.   On his death in 1576,
Adelantado Juan Ortiz de Zárate willed his position to
Juana, his daughter by an Inca princess, and to whom-

ever she should marry. In the interim, Paraguay
was to be governed by Juan Ortiz de Zárate's nephew,
Diego Ortiz de Zárate Mendieta. Juana, known as the
Marquesa del Paraguay, eventually married a judge of
the Audiencia of Charcas, Juan Torres de Vera y Aragón, who was governor for a brief period before retiring
to Spain.

ORTIZ DE ZARATE Y MENDIETA, DIEGO. Nephew of Adelantado Juan Ortiz de Zárate, and temporary governor
of La Plata following his death.

ORTIZ GUERRERO, MANUEL, 1899-1933. Early twentieth
century poet proficient in verse in both Spanish and
Guaraní. One of modern Paraguay's best-known literary
figures. His complete works, Obras completas, were
published at Buenos Aires in 1952.

ORTIZ MELGAREJO, FATHER RODRIGO. Franciscan missionary of Paraguayan descent noted for his work among
Indians and as an accomplished orator in both Spanish
and Guaraní.

ORUE, MARTIN DE. Spanish official at Asunción suspected
by Governor Alvar Núñez Cabeza de Vaca of treason
against him.

OSORIO, DIEGO ESCOBAR. Briefly governor of Paraguay
in 1647-1649 during the era in which Bishop Bernardino
de Cárdenas pursued his anti-Jesuit campaign.

OSORIO, GENERAL MANOEL LUIS. Brazilian Triple Alliance War hero, and second only to the Duque de Caxias
among the Empire's greatest soldiers. Remembered
in Brazil's military as the Patron of the Cavalry.
Fought through the entire war until exhaustion forced
his retirement from command after the 1869 battle of
Piribebuy.

OSORIO, JUAN DE. Officer in the 1535 Pedro de Mendoza
expedition, executed for suspected treason against the
admiral at Rio de Janeiro prior to arrival in La Plata.

OTAÑO, JUAN BERNARDO, 1901-1951. Journalist and historian. Editor of the El Orden and La Nación Asunción
newspapers, the Resplandor and Correo del Norte of
Concepción, and contributor to the Revista Militar and

Revista de las Fuerzas Armadas de la Nación.   Author
of several novels and numerous monographs on the
Triple Alliance War, especially on the composition and
participation of Paraguay's navy.

OTAZU, DIONISIO.   Asunción official who opposed the nomination of Dr. José de Antequera y Castro as governor
during the Comunero revolt.

OVIEDO, FLORENTINO.   A famed hero in the Triple Alliance War who was eventually captured by Brazilian
troops at the battle of Acosta Ñú.   The newly developed
city of Coronel Oviedo in eastern Paraguay is named
after him.

OWEN, JOHN.   English designer-sculptor at Asunción during
the Carlos Antonio López administration, credited with
performing the sculpture work at the National Palace.

- P -

PACTO DE SANGRE.   The "Pact of Blood" urged upon the
Spanish by Domingo Martínez de Irala in the early sixteenth century which comprised their marriages with
native Indian women.   These unions initiated the development of a Paraguayan race.   Irala, for his part, is
remembered as the "father" or originator of Paraguay.

PAGE, LIEUTENANT THOMAS JEFFERSON see also WA-
TER WITCH, U.S.S.   Commanding officer of the gunboat U.S.S. Water Witch on a hydrographic mission in
Paraguayan waters in 1853-1855.   The celebrated Water Witch episode, arising from an exchange of shots
between the vessel and a Paraguayan river fort in which
the ship's helmsman was killed, ruptured U.S.-Para-
guayan relations and proved the most serious international incident of the Carlos Antonio López administration.

PAIS (EL).   Liberal Party Asunción newspaper owned by
Dr. Policarpo Artaza which was confiscated during the
World War II Higinio Morínigo regime and became pro-
Nazi in opinion.

PAIVA, FELIX, 1877-1965.   Participant in the Liberal Party
revolution of August, 1904, and provisional president

of Paraguay during 1937-1939 following the overthrow
of the Febrerista regime.   Dean of the Law School of
the National University prior to his selection for the
presidency, and holder of several government cabinet
posts.   Succeeded by Marshal José Félix Estigarribia.

PALACIO DE GOBIERNO.   Paraguay's Government or National Palace in downtown Asunción.   Also known popularly as the "Palacio de López."   Begun in 1860 as
the residence of Brigadier General Francisco Solano
López, its completion was deferred by the Triple Alliance War.   Finally completed in 1892.   Since 1894 it
has served as the official presidential office location.

PALACIOS, BISHOP MANUEL ANTONIO.   Bishop of Asunción
implicated in the alleged conspiracy plot against Marshal President Francisco Solano López during the Triple
Alliance War.   Executed in 1868 during the San Fernando trials.

PALACIOS, MIGUEL, 1840-1875.   Prominent participant in
the post Triple Alliance War political scene.   The
draft of the 1870 constitution was drawn up in his home.
Member of the "Gran Club del Pueblo" and selected by
President Cirilo Antonio Rivarola as his foreign minister.   Holder of numerous high government posts until
his early death in Asunción.

PALOS, FATHER JOSE DE.   Bishop of Asunción in 1724-1725
and an opponent of Dr. José de Antequera y Castro.
His stand against Antequera was a factor in the latter's
decision to flee Asunción in 1725.   Though forced to
leave Paraguay temporarily, Bishop Palos returned to
Asunción in 1735 with the forces of Bruno Mauricio de
Zavala at the close of the Comunero Revolt.

PAMPA GRAN, BATTLE OF.   Paraguayan Chaco War victory
at the close of 1933 which involved an encirclement and
subsequent capture of a large number of Bolivian troops.
War hero José Félix Estigarribia was promoted to Brigadier for his brilliant tactics.

PAN DE AZUCAR.   Geographic point of contention between
Paraguay and Brazil in the late 1840's, located between
the Apa and Blanco rivers on the extreme northern
frontier.   Warfare erupted briefly over Brazil's claims
to the Apa as the border in contrast to Paraguay's
claims to the Blanco.

PANE, IGNACIO ALBERTO, 1880-1920. One of the most
   prominent of modern Paraguayan poets, a brilliant intellectual and a sociologist specializing in Paraguayan
   family and social characteristics. Vocal partisan in
   the movement to revindicate Marshal Francisco Solano
   López, and with Juan E. O'Leary, a leader in the effort to revive a strong Paraguayan nationalism.

PANES, BISHOP GARCIA. Bishop of Asunción during the independence movement of May, 1811. Took no prominent
   part in the overthrow of Spanish Governor Velasco.

PANES, PEDRO BENITO G. DE. Bishop of Asunción during
   Dr. Francia's era. Removed from his position but
   later reinstated during El Supremo's policy of encouraging state supremacy over the church.

PANIAGUA, GONZALEZ. Member of the 1546 Martínez de
   Irala Chaco exploration expedition who is recorded as
   having averted a possible mutiny and civil war within
   the group.

PANTEON NACIONAL. Known also as the Panteón de los
   Héroes and Oratorio, Paraguay's National Pantheon of
   the Heroes stands in downtown Asunción's Plaza de los
   Héroes. Built in 1936 and a smaller version of the
   French Les Envalides Memorial, Paraguay's structure
   contains the remains of Carlos Antonio López, Francis-
   co Solano López, José Félix Estigarribia, General
   José Díaz, and others.

PARADISE ISLAND. Like El Dorado and Sierra de la Plata,
   Paradise Island was another of the legendary, fabulously rich areas which attracted early Spanish conquistadores exploring the upper Chaco area west of Paraguay.
   Scouts sent by Martínez de Irala on his 1543 expedition
   to the headwaters of the Paraguay River reported the
   existence of Paradise Island in the region inhabited by
   the Xarayes Indians. Further searches to locate the
   site were, of course, fruitless.

PARAGUARI. Capital city of the administrative department
   of the same name, Paraguarí is located about 40 miles
   (63 kms) southeast of Asunción. It was founded in
   1771 by Fernando de Pinedo. During the War of the
   Triple Alliance it was the terminus of Paraguay's railway, one of the first constructed in South America.

The original railway station, which still exists, was
reportedly the site of a secret meeting of conspirators
later involved in the 1868 treason episode during the
Triple Alliance War. Located nearby is Cerro Porteño,
a small, circular tree-covered hill in a prairie-like
area which was the site of the defeat of General Manuel
Belgrano and his Argentine forces by a Paraguayan army in 1811. The army's artillery training grounds is
also located in the vicinity, as are the Grutas de Santo
Tomás, a curious cave formation containing as yet undeciphered hieroglyphics.

PARAGUARI, BATTLE OF see also PARAGUARI and
CERRO PORTEÑO. Also known popularly in Paraguay
as the battle of Cerro Porteño. Fought January 19,
1811, near the interior city of Paraguarí, between the
Argentine invasion force commanded by Manuel Belgrano and a Paraguayan army under Generals Cavañas and
Gamarra. Belgrano's defeat here and at the subsequent
battle of Tacuarí spelled the end of the Argentine invasion attempt and were significant events leading to Paraguay's independence movement on May 14, 1811.

PARAGUAY. South America's smallest republic after Uruguay, and with Bolivia, one of the continent's two landlocked nations. Located at approximately the continent's
geographic center (coordinates: between 19° 17' and
27° 30'S and 54° 30' and 62° 28'W), and bounded by Brazil, Argentina and Bolivia. Paraguay is profoundly
divided by the Paraguay River which, with the Paraná,
forms its life-line to the Atlantic at Buenos Aires. Its
western region, equal to about two-thirds of the republic's area, comprises the desolate Chaco. The eastern
region, east of the Paraguay River, is a fertile area
often described as a paradise or arcadia. Largely a
riparian state, Paraguay is bounded on the south and
east by the Paraná River and on much of its west and
north by the Paraguay and its tributaries. Midway
adjacent to its eastern border with Brazil are the majestic Yguazú Falls, a major scenic attraction. Of
Paraguay's approximate 2.2 million inhabitants, about
one-quarter reside at Asunción, the capital. Agriculture is by far the most economically important activity,
and average annual per capita income is only slightly
above $200. Historically, Paraguay is far more im-
portant than its physical profile suggests. Recorded
in its evolution: (1) site of the first permanent Euro-

pean settlement in southern South America--Buenos
Aires was permanently founded by colonists from Asunción; (2) Spain's only New World colony where the Indian rather than the European proved largely the victor
--Paraguay's peoples still prefer usage of the Guaraní
language to Spanish; (3) the locale of the Jesuit's Empire within an Empire--world's only large-scale successful experiment in communal living; (4) site of the
Comunero Revolt, the New World's first serious and
large-scale rebellion against Spanish rule; (5) locale
for the continent's most intriguing experiments in auto-
cratic government--the administrations of Dr. Francia,
and Carlos Antonio and Francisco Solano López; and
(6) the stage for Latin America's two largest and most
sanguinary wars--the 1864-1870 Triple Alliance War,
and the 1932-1935 Chaco War. In the late twentieth
century, Paraguay is the Last Frontier of the Americas,
a land where the clocks once stopped which still possesses a distinct colonial flavor and a Chaco which reflects much of the Far West of the United States a
century ago.

PARAGUAY, S. S. see also HOPKINS, EDWARD AUGUSTUS.
River steamer of the United States and Paraguay Navigation Company, formed by Edward Augustus Hopkins,
which foundered off the Brazilian coast in 1853.   Loss
of the company equipment it carried was a major blow
to Hopkins' plans for commercial success in Paraguay.

PARAGUAY CENTRAL RAILWAY see also FERROCARRIL
PRESIDENTE CARLOS ANTONIO LOPEZ--FPCAL.
Constructed originally in the 1850's, and one of South
America's first rail lines. A major achievement in
Paraguay's record of progress registered during the
administration of Carlos Antonio López. Built by British engineers of the Burrel, Valpy and Thompson Company and serviced by British-made equipment, it had
reached the Cerro León military encampment and the
city of Paraguarí by 1864. In 1869 during the Triple
Alliance War, it recorded another Latin American
"first" when used by Marshal President López for the
operation of an armored train mounting a field gun.
Sold after the war to British interests, extended to the
Argentine border at Encarnación-Posadas, and purchased
by the Paraguayan government in 1961.

PARAGUAY RIVER. One of South America's major rivers

running about 1,000 miles from its origin in Brazil's
Mato Grosso state in the area known as "Lake Xarayes"
to its confluence with the Paraná River about 200
miles south of Asunción. At the confluence the two
rivers join to form the Paraná, running a further 800
miles to the Río de la Plata and Buenos Aires. The
Paraguay is navigable upstream from Asunción by river
vessels to Corumbá, Brazil. It divides Paraguay into
two distinct regions--the eastern and more fertile one-
third, and the western two-thirds and desolate area of
South America known as the Chaco. The Paraguay is
traditionally the republic's life-line to the Atlantic at
Buenos Aires. Maintenance of free navigation rights
along its course is a prime factor in Paraguay's foreign policy since the colonial era.

PARAGUAYAN LEGION see LEGION PARAGUAYA and
    ASOCIACION PARAGUAYA.

PARAGUAYAN WAR see TRIPLE ALLIANCE, WAR OF
    THE. Variant in the name given to Latin America's
    bloodiest and most prolonged conflict occurring 1864-
    1870 between Paraguay and Argentina, Brazil and Uru-
    guay. Though generally known as the Triple Alliance
    War, some historians, especially among the allied na-
    tions, refer to it as the Paraguayan War--Guerra del
    Paraguay.

PARAGUAYO (EL). Official newspaper of the Higinio Mo-
    rínigo administration of the World War II period.

PARAGUAYO INDEPENDIENTE (EL). Paraguay's first
    newspaper, published at Asunción between April 26,
    1845, and September 18, 1852. Both founded and ed-
    ited by Presidente Carlos Antonio López, it had as its
    principal objectives the recognition by Argentina of
    Paraguay's independence, and free navigation of the
    Paraguay and Paraná Rivers. Its motto, "Independencia
    o muerte," was a patriotic battle-cry for Paraguayan
    troops during the Triple Alliance War.

PARANA RIVER. One of South America's major river sys-
    tems and the most important economically in the twen-
    tieth century. It drains the central basin of southern
    South America and is navigable by ocean-going vessels
    for approximately 800 miles. It forms the southern
    and eastern boundaries of Paraguay from its confluence

with the Paraguay River, about 200 miles south of
Asunción, to the Guairá Falls, about 60 miles north
of the Friendship Bridge and Yguazú Falls on the Paraguayan-Brazilian border east of Asunción. Maintenance of free navigation rights on the Paraná was a
cardinal factor of Paraguayan foreign policy since the
colonial era. Likewise, control of the Paraná represented for Argentina an effective means of maintaining
hegemony over Paraguay. Blockade of the river in
1865 strangled Paraguay's hopes in the nineteenth century Triple Alliance War.

PARANHOS, JOSE MARIA DA SILVA see also RIO BRANCO,
VISCONDE DE. Imperial Brazil's foremost diplomat
in the latter half of the nineteenth century, specializing
in La Plata affairs. Commencing in 1858 when he un-
dertook his first mission to Paraguay, Paranhos was
the empire's prime negotiator and participant in Paraguayan affairs throughout the war and the early post-
war period. Paraguayan historians, for example, al-
lege that he was responsible for the negotiations of the
1865 Triple Alliance Treaty which allied Brazil, Argentina and Uruguay against Paraguay.

PARAPITI RIVER. Chaco frontier zone stream within Bolivian territory, and actually crossed by Paraguayan
offensive forces in the late stages of the Chaco War in
1935.

PAREDES, COLONEL RAMON. Army officer who directed
a military revolt in August, 1937, which forced the
resignation of Colonel Rafael Franco's Febrerista cabinet and subsequently, the departure of Franco himself.
Later in 1940 briefly a member of the early cabinet of
the Higinio Morínigo government.

PARISH, SIR WOODBINE. British consul general at Buenos
Aires who in 1825 was successful in encouraging the
release of several foreigners held in Paraguay under
Dr. Francia's Inland Japan policy.

PARKINSON, JAMES S. see also PARAGUAY CENTRAL
RAILROAD. English engineer, probably associated
with Burrel, Valpy and Thompson, who was contracted
for the construction of the railroad between Asunción
and Paraguarí during the administration of Carlos Antonio López.

PARLETT, DR. English physician who traveled to Paraguay in the early years of the Dr. Francia regime, and was permitted to practice there by El Supremo until his death in 1825.

PARNAIBA, S.S. also PARNAHYBA. Brazilian naval vessel at the Paraná River naval battle of Riachuelo, June 11, 1865, which was boarded and nearly captured by Paraguayans in the action's most desperate fighting.

PARODI, DR. DIEGO DOMINGO. Italian national who reached Paraguay in 1856. Physician during the Triple Alliance War era. Left in charge of the wounded at Caacupé after the August, 1869, battle of Piribebuy. Marshal President Francisco Solano López reportedly gave him his remaining money for their care. Also a photographer, he is credited with having made the last and most widely reproduced picture of Paraguay's marshal president.

PARODI, ENRIQUE D., 1857-1917. Son of Domingo Parodi, Paraguayan field doctor captured at Caacupé in the Triple Alliance War, who received his higher education at Buenos Aires and lived there the remainder of his life. Founder and director of the Revista del Paraguay, periodical published at Buenos Aires, 1891-1898. Poet and author utilizing Paraguayan subjects.

PARQUE CABALLERO. Large municipal park in downtown Asunción along the banks of the Paraguay River. Occupies the site of the residence of General Bernardino Caballero, Triple Alliance War hero and founder of the Colorado Party.

PARTIDO COLORADO see ASOCIACION NACIONAL RE-PUBLICANA.

PARTIDO COMUNISTA see also CREYDT, OSCAR A., and BARTHE, OBDULIO. Although active in politics in 1946, Paraguay's Communist Party has been permanently proscribed from the nation since the 1947 revolution. Effective supporters estimated at 5,000. Made its original appearance in Paraguay about 1925. Its perennial leaders, Oscar A. Creydt and Obdulio Barthe, remain active in exile.

PARTIDO CONSTITUCIONAL see LIGA DE LA JUVENTUD INDEPENDIENTE.

PARTIDO CONSTITUCIONALISTA. Dissident faction of the
    old Liberal Party active in the late nineteenth and
    early twentieth century, and reunited with the old Lib-
    erals by Manuel Gondra, president in 1910.

PARTIDO DEMOCRATA CRISTIANO see also CHRISTIAN
    DEMOCRATIC PARTY and MOVIMIENTO SOCIAL-
    DEMOCRATA CRISTIANO. Appearing in the 1960's and
    the youngest of Paraguay's modern political parties.
    Its development, though strong among Catholic faith
    adherents, has suffered through lack of effective leader-
    ship.

PARTIDO FEBRERISTA see also FEBRERISTAS, FEBRE-
    RISMO and FRANCO, GENERAL RAFAEL. One of
    modern Paraguay's four most important political par-
    ties. Founded in 1936 by Colonel Rafael Franco, it
    held power from February, 1936, to August, 1937,
    when it was overthrown by a military-backed coup. The
    extreme liberal left in terms of Paraguay's political
    spectrum, it espoused a socialistic program based on
    the ideologies of Europe in the 1930's. Overthrown by
    an army-backed coup, it suffered an eclipse during
    which its leaders were periodically forced into exile.
    In modern Paraguay, its prestige and popular support
    have declined to nominal proportions.

PARTIDO LIBERAL see LIBERAL PARTY and LIBERAL
    RADICAL PARTY. Second most important of modern
    Paraguay's political organizations.

PARTIDO NACIONAL REPUBLICANO see ASOCIACION
    NACIONAL REPUBLICANA. Seldom used name for the
    Colorado Party which refers to its ideological bases
    stemming from a general "Partido Nacional" or National
    Party historically incorporating the best of Paraguayan
    traditions since the eras of Dr. Francia, Carlos Antonio
    López and Francisco Solano López.

PARTIDO REVOLUCIONARIO FEBRERISTA see FEBRE-
    RISTA PARTY. Official title for Paraguay's third most
    important political party, formed in the February revo-
    lution of 1936.

PASO CARRETA. One of the approaches on higher ground

over the Estero Bellaco marshes from the Humaitá position south towards the Paraná River. Strategically
important during the May, 1866, Triple Alliance War
battle of Tuyuty.

PASO DE LA PATRIA, ARGENTINA see also PASO DE
PATRIA. Argentine riverport facing the Paraguay
points of Paso de Patria and Itapirú across the Paraná
River near its confluence with the Paraguay.

PASO DE PATRIA. Small port on an inlet on the Paraguay
side of the Paraná River located about three miles east
of the confluence of the Paraná and Paraguay Rivers in
extreme southwestern Paraguay. Across from it on the
opposite bank of the Paraná is the Argentine port of
Paso de la Patria, and near it in close proximity to
the confluence is the historic river battery of Itapirú,
still an important Paraguayan river and border control
point. The original foundations, dating to the 1850's
are still visible. Paso de Patria/Paso de la Patria
was the river crossing area for both armies during the
Triple Alliance War. The preserved house utilized by
Marshal President López as a general headquarters is
located in the former. Nearby is the historic Tuyuty
battlefield area.

PASO PIRIS. One of the passes over the swampy Estero
Bellaco area south of Humaitá toward the Paraná River.
Strategically important in the 1866 battles and siege of
Humaitá in the Triple Alliance War.

PASO PUCU. Headquarters of Marshal President López during the siege of Humaitá in the Triple Alliance War.

PASO SIDRA. One of the passes over the swampy Estero
Bellaco area south of Humaitá toward the Paraná River. Strategically important in the 1866 battles and
siege of Humaitá during the Triple Alliance War.

PASSO DE SÃO BORJA, ACTION AT. Small Brazilian riverport on the upper Uruguay River at its nearest point
to Paraguay. Scene in June, 1865, of the crossing of
the Paraguayan eastern invasion force under Colonel
Antonio de la Cruz Estigarribia during the early stages
of the Triple Alliance War.

PASTOR BENITEZ JR., JUSTO, 1925-   . Son of one of

Paraguay's most distinguished intellectuals, and active journalist. Member of the directorate of the Liberal Radical Party, officially inscribed as a political organization in opposition to the Colorado Party.

PASTOR BENITEZ, JUSTO (SR.), 1895-1962. Prominent Paraguayan intellectual and foreign minister during the era of the Chaco War. Author of numerous works on Paraguay's history, most of which were written while he was in political exile. Noted particularly for his detailed studies of Dr. Francia, Carlos Antonio López and General José Félix Estigarribia.

PASTORE, CARLOS A., 1907-   . Noted journalist, historian and Liberal Party leader. Founder and editor at Montevideo while in exile of El Paraguayo Independiente, periodical opposing the Colorado Party regime. The author of El Paraguay y la tiranía de Morínigo (1947), and La lucha por la tierra en el Paraguay (1949), both published at Montevideo.

PATACONES. Principal Paraguayan currency used in the period from independence to the Triple Alliance War. Divided into eight metallic coins known as "reales."

PATAPILAS. Name used by Bolivian soldiers for Paraguayans during the Chaco War.

PATERNO, DR. STEFANO see COLONIA NUEVA-ITALIA and COLONIA TRINACRIA. Principal director of the Italo-American Colonization Society, and founder in the late nineteenth century of the two Italian agricultural colonies of Nueva Italia and Trinacria.

PATIÑO, POLICARPO. Personal secretary to Dr. José Gaspar Rodríguez de Francia, Paraguay's famed El Supremo of the early independence period.

PATIÑO-CUE. A small, delightful summer resort village on the western shores of Lake Ypacaray east of Areguá, about 20 miles (30 kms) from Asunción. Location of the former summer residence, now destroyed, of Mme. Elisa Alicia Lynch, consort of Francisco Solano López.

PATRIA (LA). One of Asunción's three modern daily newspapers, the current series of which was founded in

1953.   The official mouthpiece, "vocero," of the governing board of the Colorado Party. La Patria was originally first published in 1917, and reappeared briefly again in 1931.

PAULISTAS   see also   MAMELUKES and BANDEIRANTES.
Portuguese and Brazilian pioneers who explored westward from the São Paulo area in the sixteenth and seventeenth centuries into the Mato Grosso region and Paraguay.   Credited with the discovery and occupation of Brazil's "west."   Many were aimed at enslavement of the Guaraní Indians living in the Jesuit missions of southeastern Paraguay.

PAYAGUA INDIANS.   Member of the Guaraní Indian family who lived along the banks of the Paraguay River from below Asunción north to the vicinity of Bahía Negra.   Noted for their ferocity and maraudings against other tribes as well as the newly arrived Spanish.   The last of them were reportedly not exterminated until Dr. Francia's era.

PAYSANDU, URUGUAY   see also   GOMEZ, LEANDRO.
Uruguay River port in west central Uruguay.   Its siege and capture by Brazilian troops in late 1864 terminated Uruguayan Blanco government opposition to Brazil's invasion force and represented another incident in the chain of events leading to the Triple Alliance War.

PAZ, GENERAL JOSE MARIA.   Argentine commander of Corrientes Province forces in the short-lived 1845-1846 war against Buenos Aires dictator Juan Manuel de Rosas.   Paraguay's 5,000 army under command of 20-year-old Brigadier Francisco Solano López crossed the Paraná River and joined General Paz, but was subsequently forced to retreat following the defeat of the Corrientes forces.   The episode comprised General López' only first-hand experience with warfare prior to the Triple Alliance War.

PAZ Y JUSTICIA.   Peace and Justice, Paraguay's formal motto appearing on one side of the national flag.   The other side contains a different escudo, Paraguay being the only republic possessing a flag which has distinct escudos on each side.

PEACE CONFERENCE OF 1935.   Inaugurated deliberations

at Buenos Aires on July 1, 1935, following the Chaco
War cease-fire agreed to in the Peace Protocol of
June.   Participants included Argentina, United States,
Brazil, Chile, Peru, and Uruguay.   Its first proposals
of October 15, 1935, were fruitless when Paraguay refused to accept a formula whereby Bolivia would receive a large portion of Chaco area including a port
on the Paraguay River.   Complete final agreement on
Chaco boundaries was not reached until 1938 when the
definitive treaty was signed July 21.

PEACE CORPS (CUERPO DE PAZ).   Active in Paraguay on
a modest scale since 1966, generally on the basis of
one or two members assigned to or near the principal
urban centers.   Highly regarded for its accomplish-
ments in technical assistance in rural education, health
and sanitation, animal husbandry and agriculture.

PEACE PROTOCOL OF JUNE, 1935.   Signed at Buenos
Aires between Bolivian and Paraguayan representatives
on June 12, following negotiations since May by representatives of a group of neutral nations including the
United States.   Two days later on June 14, a cease-
fire was ordered which terminated the Chaco War.   In
addition to the cease-fire, the protocol also provided
for the immediate convocation of a peace conference
to resolve the causes of the Chaco dispute.

PEDRO II, EMPEROR OF BRAZIL, 1831-1889.   Though a
peaceful man dedicated to the empire's policy of seeking to resolve questions with its neighbors without re-
sorting to force, Dom Pedro saw in the rise of Paraguay's Francisco Solano López a menace to the empire's
policies in La Plata.   Particularly vexing were Paraguay's claims to border areas in the Mato Grosso region, and the new policy of securing for Paraguay a
firm position in the international balance of power in
La Plata.   Paraguay's armed response to Brazil's
Uruguayan intervention in the form of the seizure of
the river steamer Marquês de Olinda and the invasion
of Mato Grosso, were regarded by Dom Pedro as matters impugning the national honor.   The Triple Alliance War thus became for him one of revindication.
His determination that there could be no peace until
President López was overthrown was central to the
war's prolongation.   The war proved the most serious
problem of his near 50 years reign as Latin America's

only successful experiment in monarchy.   Forced into
exile by the republican movement of 1889, he died
subsequently in Europe in 1891.

PEDRO JUAN CABALLERO, CITY OF.   Border city in extreme northeastern Paraguay facing the Brazilian border city of Ponta Porá.   Terminus of a major highway
linking these frontier points with the Paraguay River
port of Concepción.   Named in honor of Pedro Juan
Caballero, hero of Paraguay's 1811 independence movement from Spain.

PEIXOTO, COLONEL FLORIANO VIEIRA.   Brazil's Iron
Marshal and "Consolidator of the Republic" who, like
his comrade Manuel Deodoro da Fonceca--first president of Republican Brazil, fought through the entire
Triple Alliance War.   Commander of an infantry regiment at Cerro Corá, the war's last action during which
Marshal President Francisco Solano López was killed.
Peixoto reportedly obtained López' manta or horse-
blanket as a souvenir.

PEÑA, MANUEL PEDRO DE, 1811-1867.   Paraguayan ex-
patriate who wrote a series of derogatory newspaper
commentaries on the regimes of Carlos Antonio and
Francisco Solano López, most of which appeared in the
Buenos Aires La Tribuna in the early 1860's.   Peña,
formerly a government official at Asunción, persisted
in claiming an unauthenticated family relationship with
the López family.   His "Cartas del ciudadano paraguayo Manuel Pedro de Peña dirigidas a su querido
sobrino Francisco Solano López" reflected the hatred
of exiled Paraguayans resident at Buenos Aires.

PEÑA, MANUEL PEDRO DE LA.   Paraguayan representative sent to Buenos Aires in 1842-1843, following the
successful mission of Andrés Gill, to negotiate the
purchase of arms and supplies from the government of
Juan Manuel de Rosas.   An early and successful effort
to modify the isolationist policies of Dr. José Gaspar
Rodríguez de Francia who died in 1840.

PEÑA, PEDRO.   Assuming the presidency during the early
twentieth century's era of anarchy, Peña held office
for the shortest term on record, from March 1 to
March 15, 1912.

PEÑA DE GONZALEZ, ROSA, 1843-1899. Remembered for
her successful efforts to promote facilities for the improved education of women.   Educated at Buenos Aires,
and later a director of one of the schools founded by
Argentina's statesman-educator, Domingo F. Sarmiento.
Returning to Paraguay after 1870, she married Juan
G. González, later president of the republic, and em-
barked on a plan to establish schools for girls.   By
1883, 24 girls primary schools were in operation.
She is also known as the founder of the Asilo Nacional,
the National Asylum.

PEÑA HERMOSA ISLAND.   Modern Paraguay's most dreaded
encarceration camp located on an island in the Paraguay River near its confluence with the Apa River north
of Concepción.   A military prison since 1933, it is reportedly still used to hold criminals and political prisoners.

PEÑARANDA, GENERAL ENRIQUE.   Bolivian field commander who succeeded German General Hans Kundt after the
latter's early Chaco War disasters.   Highly successful
in temporarily blunting Paraguay's 1934 offensive at
Ballivián.

PENDLETON, JOHN S.   American representative who negotiated the first attempt at a friendship, commerce and
navigation treaty between the United States and Paraguay at Asunción in 1853.

PENINSULARES see also GACHUPINES.   Term referring
to those in the Spanish colonies who were born in
Spain, as compared to those born in the New World
who were known as Criollos.   The widening split between the two classes was a major factor in the development of independence movements in the late eighteenth and early nineteenth centuries.

PEQUIRI RIVER.   Small stream north of Yguazú Falls on
the banks of which the settlement of Ontiveros was
founded in the mid-sixteenth century.

PERALTA, DOMINGO DE.   Regidor in the Asunción government during the early sixteenth century governorship
of Alvar Núñez Cabeza de Vaca.

PERCY, CAPTAIN JOCELYN.   Captain of HMS Hotspur

in La Plata in 1815. Instrumental in obtaining the release of J.P. Robertson, who was detained along with
his ship by forces of Uruguay's José Artigas while sailing up the Paraná River to Paraguay.

PEREIRA, TOMAS ROMERO see ROMERO PEREIRA, TO-
MAS. A principal architect of the modern Colorado
Party.

PEREIRA LEAL, FELIPE JOSE. Brazilian charge d'affairs
expelled from Paraguay in 1853 over a dispute regarding Paraguayan-Brazilian frontier problems in the north.

PEREZ, FERNANDO. Noted in historical records as one of
the first skilled craftsmen to arrive at Asunción in the
early colonial period.

PEREZ, JUAN. Blacksmith-veterinarian recorded among
the early mastercraftsmen arrivals at Asunción in the
colonial era.

PEREZ, FATHER MANUEL ANTONIO. Presided at the fu-
neral in September, 1840, of Dr. José Gaspar Rodríguez de Francia.

PEREZ ACOSTA, JUAN FRANCISCO, 1873-   . Regarded
as the dean of contemporary Paraguayan lettres. Journalist, government official, diplomat and historian.
Founder of the Instituto Paraguayo and director of several major Asunción newspapers. Noted for his careful
and penetrating research of historical subjects, particularly the life and times of Dr. José Gaspar Rodríguez
de Francia. His prolific and well-prepared works rank
him, in the opinion of his colleages, with Manuel Domínguez, Fulgencio R. Moreno and Blas Manuel Garay.

PERON, JUAN DOMINGO. Argentine president 1946-1955
whose administration had strong influence on Paraguay.
Asunción was a temporary place of exile for Perón following his downfall in 1955. Perón sought to promote
both friendship and hegemony over Paraguay, with one
notable act being the return of war trophies taken by
Argentina during the Triple Alliance War.

PESOA, JUANA. Early common-law consort of Paraguay's
Marshal President Francisco Solano López. A native
of the Paraguay River port of Pilar, she bore him sev-

eral children prior to his union with Mme. Elisa
Alicia Lynch.

PESOA, MANUEL, 1925-   . Historian and political scientist. Co-founder of the "Club Liberal Alón" and of
the "Ateneo Liberal." Author of several works regarding Paraguay's political evolution and the Liberal
Party.

PETIT-GRAIN OIL see also BALANSA, DR. BENJAMIN.
A high-grade extract of bitter orange leaves used as
a perfume base, and of which Paraguay is the major
source of world supply.

PETTIROSSI, SILVIO, 1887-1915.   Father of Paraguayan
aviation, and with Santos Dumont of Brazil, Jorge
Chaves of Peru, and Jorge Newbery of Argentina, one
of the great names of early Latin American aviation.
Trained in France. Winner of the International Aviation Contest at the 1915 San Francisco World Exposi-
tion. Died in a plane accident at Buenos Aires, October 17, 1915.

PIANO see ISLA MADAMA. Name used in some histories
of the Triple Alliance War for a small inhabited point
in extreme northeastern Paraguay near the border city
of Pedro Juan Caballero and better known as Isla Madama. According to unfounded tales, Mrs. Elisa
Alicia Lynch is said to have discarded her cherished
piano there on the long retreat to Cerro Corá.

PICUIBA-CARANDAYTY, BATTLE OF see also YRENDA-
GUE, BATTLE OF. Spectacular Paraguayan envelopment movement of early December, 1934, culminating
in the defeat and near annihilation of a Bolivian army
at Yrendagüe, December 8. Perhaps the most grue-
some and conclusive action of the Chaco War.

PIKYSYRY CAMPAIGN see also LOMAS VALENTINAS
CAMPAIGN. Known in Paraguay as the Pikysyry Campaign, this series of actions in December, 1868 terminated the formal phase of the Triple Alliance War
up to the evacuation and allied occupation of Asunción.

PIKYSYRY LINES. A strong line of fortifications erected
on orders of Marshal President Francisco Solano López
during the Pikysyry or Lomas Valentinas campaign of

December, 1868, in the Triple Alliance War. Located
along the Arroyo Pikysyry from Itá Ybaté to the river
fortification of Angostura, below Villeta about 10 miles
south of Asunción.

PILAR. Located in extreme southwestern Paraguay above the
confluence of the Paraná and Paraguay Rivers, Pilar is
an important river port and industrial center specializing in cotton textiles. Historically, it is significant for
its location near the Humaitá area, site of the approximate three and a half years siege of Paraguay's major
fortified bastion by allied forces in the Paraguayan War.
The shell-torn ruins of the Humaitá church and the
house in which Marshal President Francisco Solano
López pledged loyalty to the flag of Paraguay still remain as major historical sites.

PILAR (EL). Paraguay's southernmost important riverport
on the Paraguay River is commonly known as "El Pilar"
or "El Pilar de Ñeembucú."

PILCOMAYO PACT see also REVOLUTION OF 1904.
Signed December, 1904, between the Colorado and Liberal Parties following mediation by the Asunción diplomatic corps. Terminated the major 1904 Revolution,
held as the first large-scale popular revolt in Paraguay
since the Triple Alliance War, ended the long period of
Colorado Party rule, and ushered in the Liberal Party
for its first time. Juan Bautista Gaona became the
first Liberal Party president on December 13.

PILCOMAYO RIVER. Born in Bolivia's highlands, the Pilcomayo runs about 1,000 miles southeast to its confluence
with the Paraguay River shortly below Asunción. Originally known as the Araguay. Since the 1878 Hayes
Arbitration, it forms the Paraguayan/Argentine Chaco
border. Non-navigable by ships, it is a sluggish and
winding stream of shallow depth which drains much of
the Chaco. Near its mouth is located Clorinda, an
Argentine Chaco city which serves both as a contraband
commerce traffic center with Asunción, and as a convenient haven for Paraguayan political exiles.

PIMENTA BUENO, JOSE ANTONIO. Imperial Brazil's envoy
to Paraguay who announced on September 14, 1844,
Brazil's recognition of Paraguayan independence.

PINEDO, AGUSTIN FERNANDO DE. Governor during 1772-
1778. Noted for his efforts to abolish the encomienda
system in Paraguay, to promote the establishment of a
formal provincial militia force, and for his project to
develop colonies in the Chaco. Founder of the city of
Concepción, north of Asunción on the east bank of the
Paraguay River, as a settlement to contain possible
further southward Brazilian encroachment.

PINEDO, ANTONIO DE. Recorded as a locksmith, one of
the first artisans to arrive at Asunción in the early
colonial period.

PINILLA-SOLER PROTOCOL OF 1907. The most auspicious
of the several pre-Chaco War proposals for settlement
of the Paraguay-Bolivia Chaco dispute. The 1907 protocol stipulated that the President of Argentina would
arbitrate the boundary question after lines were fixed
by direct negotiations. It failed because of persistent
claims of boundary violations by both sides.

PIQUETES see also POTREROS. Small fenced pastures
for cattle grazing. Frequently around a water-hole and
near the estancia residence.

PIRAYU. Small interior village about 35 miles east of Asunción near the Cerro León site of the Paraguayan army's
former Triple Alliance War training camp. Noted historically as the birthplace of General José E. Díaz,
popular wartime hero and commander at the Paraguayan
victory of Curupaity.

PIRIBEBUY. Situated on the plateau of the Cordillera de Los
Altos about 45 miles (75 kms) east of Asunción, the
city was the third of Paraguay's capitals in the final
phase of the War of the Triple Alliance. The city was
founded in 1640 by Pedro Lugo de Navarra. On August
12, 1869, it was attacked and taken by Brazilian forces
in one of the most sanguinary actions of the Triple Alliance War. It remains today a perfect example of the
many Paraguayan towns in which the clocks literally
stopped in 1869.

PIRIBEBUY, BATTLE OF see also PIRIBEBUY. Opening
action of the 1869 Cordillera Campaign, the final phase
of the Triple Alliance War. At Piribebuy, on August
12, 1869, the Conde d'Eu's Brazilian flanking forces

stormed a Paraguayan defensive position in one of the
war's bloodiest combats, killed or captured most of
the defenders, and seized Paraguay's official state archives which later became the Rio Branco Collection.
From Piribebuy the Paraguayan army retreated northeastward to fight the holding battle of Acosta Ñú, and
then onwards on the long retreat which finally ended at
Cerro Corá and the death of Francisco Solano López,
March 1, 1870.

PITIANTUTA, FORTIN see PITIANTUTA, LAKE.

PITIANTUTA, LAKE. A lagoon in the central Chaco, one
of the area's few water sources. Paraguay's Fortín
Carlos Antonio López, on its east bank, was attacked
by Bolivian troops June 15, 1932, in an action which
began the Chaco War.

PLA GUERRA GALVANY, MARIA JOSEFINA, 1909-
Emigrated from the Canary Islands to Paraguay in
1927. Josefina Pla figures prominently in modern
Paraguay's cultural evolution for her popular poems,
short stories, dramas for the theatre, and studies of
Jesuit religious art. One of the outstanding foreign-
born contributors to modern Paraguayan culture. Married to noted artist Andrés Campos Cervera, better
known as Julián de la Herrería, who died in 1937.

PLANO DE PIRAYU see also PIRAYU. Attack plan pre-
pared under direction of the Conde d'Eu, commander
of allied forces in the 1869 final phase of the Triple
Alliance War, aimed at dislodgement of the regenerated
Paraguayan army positioned along the Cordillera de
Azcurra. Name derived from village of Pirayú, the
allied headquarters near the old Paraguayan army's
Cerro León encampment.

PLATANILLOS, FORTIN. Bolivian fortified outpost in the
central Chaco at the beginning of the Chaco War.

PLAYAS. Low-lying but slightly elevated areas of either
forest or open grass cover found in the flood plains of
stream channels. Literally translated as "beaches."

PLAZA DE LA INDEPENDENCIA. Formerly Plaza Unión,
a major park in downtown Asunción, so-named since
1811 in memory of a contemplated confederation with

Buenos Aires. Re-named Plaza de la Independencia in 1892 as a result of public outcry against reports at Buenos Aires that Paraguay desired annexation to Argentina.

PLUNKETT, DR. RICHARD J. First director of the Inter-American Public Health Service office in Paraguay, opened in 1944.

POLITICAL PARTIES see CHRISTIAN DEMOCRATIC PARTY, CONTRABANDOS, COLORADO PARTY, COMMUNISTS, FEBRERISTAS, LIBERAL PARTY, LIBERAL RADICAL PARTY, LIGA NACIONAL INDEPENDIENTE, and UNION NACIONAL REVOLUCIONARIA.

POLLAROLO, VICENTE, 1905-   . Prominent sculptor in the modern period noted for his busts of Paraguay's major national heroes.

PONTA PORA, BRAZIL. Brazilian frontier city located adjacent to Paraguay's Pedro Juan Caballero in extreme northeastern Paraguay. Brazil enjoys free port privileges at the Paraguay River port of Concepción, served by highway from Ponta Porá.

PORONGO. The small gourd or "calabasa" shell used as a receptacle for taking maté.

PORTEÑOS. Name used historically in Paraguay and elsewhere in La Plata referring to the peoples of Argentina's port city of Buenos Aires. For example, "Cerro Porteño"--the hill near Paraguarí where Manuel Belgrano's army from Buenos Aires was defeated in 1811. "Porteños" were also occasionally referred to in Paraguay as "Los de Abajo," or those from below, meaning from down the Paraná River.

PORTO ALEGRE, BARÃO DE see also SOUZA, MANOEL MARQUES DE. One of Brazil's most able corps commanders during the Triple Alliance War, and a professional soldier since he was 13 years of age. Commander of the Brazilian army which defeated Buenos Aires dictator Juan Manuel de Rosas at the 1852 battle of Monte Caseros. His heroic actions at the second battle of Tuyuty, November, 1867, turned almost certain defeat into victory for the allied army.

PORTOCARRERO, COLONEL HERMENEGILDO DE ALBU-
QUERQUE. Commander of the Brazilian Mato Grosso
riverport Fort Coimbra at the outbreak of the Triple
Alliance War. The fort was evacuated on December
28, 1864, in the face of Paraguayan siege operations.
However, the colonel's wife, Ludovina Portocarrero,
was later named Patroness of the Mothers and Wives
of Brazil's Soldiers for her work in helping to load
cartridges during the brief siege.

PORTUGAL, PEDRO MELO DE see MELO DE PORTUGAL,
PEDRO. Variant in the spelling of the name of a governor of Paraguay in 1778-1785.

POSADAS, ARGENTINA. Argentine Paraná River port facing
Encarnación, Paraguay. The northern terminal of the
Argentine railway system which links with Paraguay's
Presidente Carlos Antonio López Railway by ferry
across the river. Near Posadas lie the ruins of many
of the old Jesuit reductions of the Mission era.

POTREROS. Large fenced pasture areas for cattle grazing.

POWELL, LIEUTENANT WILLIAM L. Officer of the USS
Water Witch in Asunción in 1854. Advised Lieutenant
Thomas J. Page, then at Corrientes with the ship, of
the Edward Augustus Hopkins affair. Page subsequently proceeded to Asunción and arranged for the departure of Hopkins.

PRESIDENTIAL MESSAGE OF 1854. One of the more unique
documents in Paraguay's history, this statement by
Carlos Antonio López outlined his ideology for his nation's future evolution. In striking similarity to modern Paraguayan governmental doctrine, he noted that
Paraguay had not suffered the near anarchy reflected
in the other republics which had transferred abruptly
from colonial absolutism to democracy, and that the
key to orderly development lay in gradual reform as
the population became educated to their responsibilities.

PRESIDENTS OF PARAGUAY see APPENDIX I.

PRIETO, JUSTO, 1897-   . Prominent Liberal Party
member, author, educator, journalist and statesman.
Regarded as having followed the Liberal doctrinary
approach of Dr. Cecilio Báez. Holder of cabinet

posts in the Eusebio Ayala and Estigarribia administrations. Author of several noteworthy studies in the fields of both sociology and history. Noted particularly for his La provincia gigante de las indias (1951), a sociological study of Paraguay.

PRIETO, JUSTO JOSE, 1928-   . Journalist and professor of literature, history and sociology. Author of an outline work entitled Bosquejo de la literatura paraguaya.

PRIMAVERA   see   COLONIA PRIMEVERA and HUTTERITES.

PRIMOLI, FATHER JUAN BAUTISTA   see also   JOSE BRASONELLI, ANTONIO RIBERA and ANTONIO SEPP, 1673-1747.   Italian Jesuit from Milan, sent to Paraguay as engineer and sculptor in the construction of the Jesuit missions or reductions.   Arrived in La Plata in 1717, constructed the Jesuit College and several churches in Buenos Aires, a cathedral and church at Córdoba, and the famed church at the Trinidad mission in Paraguay.

PRONUNCIAMIENTO.   Call-to-arms and political manifesto issued by a military leader announcing his entry into the political arena to "save the nation." Usually the prelude to a "Cuartelazo" or barracks revolt.

PROPRIEDAD DE DIOS.   Translated literally as "God's property." An area of cultivated ground at Jesuit missions or reductions used for the production of commodities for the common welfare.   Such commodities were frequently sold in export trade, the proceeds of which were used for "God's work"--defrayment of general mission expenses.

PROTEST NOTE OF AUGUST 30, 1864.   Directed by Paraguay's government to the Brazilian government protesting the latter's ultimatum of August 4 to the Uruguayan Blanco government.   The protest stated that any Brazilian intervention in Uruguay would be held as an attempt to destroy the political equilibrium of La Plata, and that Paraguay could not be held responsible for the consequences.   Since Brazil subsequently used armed force to intervene in Uruguay, this protest note is widely regarded as the basis for Paraguay's adoption of war against Brazil--the outbreak of the Triple Alliance War.

PROVINCIA GIGANTE DE LAS INDIAS. "Gigantic Province
of the Indies," recorded as the first known name for
Paraguay. Used during the early discovery and conquest age, it considered Paraguay as embracing all
of La Plata, the Chaco, and the area north to the
Amazon Basin. Subsequent repartitions and divisions
progressively reduced Paraguay to its present size.

PUCHERO. Boiled meat and vegetables similar to Irish
stew. "Locro" and "puchero" are among the most
commonly eaten foods in Paraguay.

PUEBLO GRANDE, INDIAN VILLAGE. Indian village located near Puerto de los Reyes on the upper reaches
of the Paraguay River. Attacked and destroyed by
Alvar Núñez Cabeza de Vaca during his 1544 expedition on reports of suspected Indian hostility.

PUENTE DE LA AMISTAD (FRIENDSHIP BRIDGE). One of
Latin America's potentially most important highway
bridges connecting the Brazilian and Paraguayan road
systems at the Paraná River near Yguazú Falls, about
205 miles east of Asunción. Inaugurated in 1964 and
consisting of a 500-meter span over the Paraná River.
It opened an important variant of the Pan American
Highway, and provided Paraguay with a road transport
route eastward through Brazil to the Atlantic port of
Paranaguá.

PUERTO CASADO see also PUERTO SASTRE. Puerto
Casado, located on the Chaco bank of the Paraguay
River about 500 miles north of Asunción, was by the
1970's the only quebracho tannin extract exporting
port still in operation.

PUERTO DE AYOLAS. Originally discovered by Juan de
Ayolas of the Pedro de Mendoza expedition in 1537.
Located above Bahía Negra on the headwaters of the
Paraguay River, and first named Nuestra Señora de
la Candelaria. Used as a base during the early colo-
nial era for Chaco exploration expeditions.

PUERTO DE CHAVES see PUERTO SAN FERNANDO.

PUERTO DE LAS PIEDRAS. Site located about 200 miles
north of Asunción along the Paraguay River probably
in the vicinity of modern Concepción. Used as a base

in the early colonial era for Chaco exploration expeditions.

PUERTO DE LOS REYES. Small bay in the extreme upper reaches of the Paraguay River in the Lake Xarayes region of Brazil's Mato Grosso. Discovered by the Martínez de Irala expedition in 1543 and used by subsequent expeditions as a base in searches for a route west to Peru.

PUERTO GUARANI see PUERTO SASTRE.

PUERTO PINASCO see PUERTO SASTRE.

PUERTO PRECISO. River or seaports selected by the Spanish government in the colonial era for the compulsory debarkation of water-borne commerce. In 1735, for example, the Paraná River port of Santa Fe was declared a "Puerto Preciso" for all river traffic from Paraguay as an economic penalty for the 1717-1735 Comunero Revolt at Asunción.

PUERTO PRESIDENTE FRANCO. Riverport village along the Paraná River about five miles south of the Friendship Bridge and 205 miles east of Asunción. Named after President Manuel Franco, and declining in importance since the building of Puerto Presidente Stroessner in 1957.

PUERTO PRESIDENTE PACHECO see also BAHIA NEGRA. Name given to Paraguay's Bahía Negra riverport on the upper Paraguay River after its capture by Bolivian troops in the 1880's. Subsequently, on September 13, 1888, a Paraguayan expedition recaptured the port which reassumed its original name. Incident preluding the later Chaco dispute.

PUERTO PRESIDENTE STROESSNER. Situated to the extreme east, approximately 200 miles (327 kms) from Asunción at the terminus of Route 2, this is one of Paraguay's newer inhabited points. Constructed and inaugurated in 1957, it is located in close proximity to the famed Yguazú Falls, and the 500-yard long Friendship Bridge over the Paraná River, which connects Paraguay and Brazil. Completion of the bridge in 1964 permitted direct highway connections between Asunción and the Brazilian Atlantic port of Paranaguá.

The nearby Acaray River hydroelectric plant, completed
in 1968, now supplies all electric current for Asunción.

PUERTO REPSA. Paraguay River port for the new Refinaría
Paraguaya, S.A., Paraguay's petroleum refinery, located slightly to the south of Asunción.

PUERTO SAN FERNANDO. Originally known as Puerto de
Chaves, and located near the Lake Xarayes region of
the extreme northern headwaters of the Paraguay River.
Used as a base and departure point for expeditions to
Peru during the early colonial period.

PUERTO SASTRE. Once a major quebracho tannin extract
exporting port on the Chaco bank of the Paraguay River north of Asunción. With the twentieth century de-
cline in the quebracho extract industry, Puerto Sastre,
Puerto Pinasco and Puerto Guaraní have ceased quebracho operations and are used only as cattle shipping
points.

PUESTO MUÑECA. Chaco concentration camp used for the
detention of persons suspected of anti-government activities during the Morínigo regime of the 1940's, and
reportedly of persons believed to espouse anti-Axis
sympathies.

PUEYRREDON, JUAN MARTIN DE. Supreme director of the
Argentine Confederation during the early years of Dr.
Francia's regime in Paraguay. Alleged to have sent
Colonel Juan Baltázar Vargas to Asunción in 1817-1818
to foment opposition to El Supremo's rule.

PUSINERI SCALA, CARLOS ALBERTO, 1919-   . Paraguay's leading numismatics authority, internationally
known for his research of the republic's monetary system. Dr. Pusineri is also director of the Casa de la
Independencia historical site in downtown Asunción.
His archeological collection is Paraguay's second most
important. Author of several numismatic and archeological studies including La moneda de 1780 a 1956
(1956), and Yacimientos arqueológicos del Paraguay
(1956).

PYNANDI. Name given to the peasant followers of the Colorado Party in the 1947 Revolution. Translated as the
"bare-footed ones." Such irregular troops of rural

peasant origin were a major factor in the defeat of the 1947 movement.

PYRAGUES.   Term dating from the era of Dr. José Gaspar Rodríguez de Francia for secret policemen.   Literally the "soft-footed ones."

- Q -

QUATREFAGES, JEAN LOUIS ARMAND DE   see also LYNCH, ELISA ALICIA.   Frenchman and husband of Mme. Elisa Alicia Lynch.   Though separated from him, Mrs. Lynch was unable to divorce him due to their original Catholic marriage rites.   This factor was apparently a permanent obstacle to legalization of her common-law union in Paraguay with Marshal President Francisco Solano López.

QUEBRACHO.   An extremely hard wood native to Paraguay, growing especially in the eastern zone of the Chaco along the Paraguay River.   The name stems from the Spanish words "quiebra hacha," or "axe-breaker." Discovery that the extract of this wood was an excellent tannin for the curing of leather stimulated large-scale post-Triple Alliance War Argentine and other foreign investment in Chaco land and tannin extract port construction.   Twentieth century invention of extract substitutes has seriously affected this industry.

QUEIROLO, FABIO, 1862-1901.   Journalist and politician. One of the founders of the Centro Democrático, a forerunner of the Liberal Party.   Later a prominent Liberal Party member who was elected president of the party's directorate at the 1895 convention.   Foreign minister during the presidency of Emilio Aceval.

QUELL, HIPOLITO SANCHEZ   see   SANCHEZ QUELL, HIPOLITO.

QUERANDI INDIANS.   Savage tribe encountered by the 1536 Pedro de Mendoza expedition to La Plata.   Engaged in almost constant fighting against the garrison of the first Nuestra Señora de Buen Ayre fort.

QUEVEDO, ROBERTO, 1930-   .   Asunción estanciero also noted for his research of fifteenth and sixteenth century

Paraguayan history, and for specialized studies of the Comunero Revolt period.

QUINTERO, PEDRO. Recorded as a ship's carpenter among the early Spanish arrivals at Asunción in the colonial period.

- R -

RADICAL LIBERAL PARTY see LIBERAL RADICAL PARTY.

RADICALES see also CIVICOS. One of the opposing factions in the 1895 division of the Liberal Party. The Radicales were headed by Cecilio Báez, and published a newspaper called El Pueblo. Differences between them and their opponents, the "Cívicos," were settled in a 1902 convention preceeding the 1904 Revolution.

RAMIREZ, FRANCISCO. Caudillo chieftain of Argentina's Entre Ríos province and former lieutenant of Uruguay's José Gervasio de Artigas who turned against him in 1820. After Artigas was given asylum in Paraguay by Dr. Francia, Ramírez conceived a plan, soon abandoned, of invading Paraguay. Suspected conspirators in the plot were swiftly jailed by El Supremo.

RAMIREZ, DR. ISIDRO. Paraguay's envoy to Brazil who, in April, 1937, signed an agreement providing for expanded commercial and political relations between the two countries. One of a series of agreements negotiated by Colonel Franco's Febrerista government to improve Paraguay's international position.

RAMIREZ, DR. JUAN VICENTE. Paraguay's diplomatic representative in Washington during the 1928-1929 Conference on Conciliation and Arbitration attempting to settle the Chaco problem.

RAMIREZ DE VELASCO, JUAN. Appointed governor in 1597 by the Viceroy at Lima following the departure of Juan Torres Vera y Aragón, last adelantado of La Plata. Succeeded by his lieutenant governor, Hernando Arias de Saavedra, the famed Hernandarias.

RAMIREZ-DIEZ DE MEDINA PROTOCOL see also WASH-

INGTON CONFERENCE OF 1929. Signed at Washington
January 3, 1929. Provided for the study of the growing
Paraguayan-Bolivian Chaco dispute by a conference of
neutral nations. The resulting Washington Conference
of 1929, although it succeeded in promoting temporarily
the reestablishment of diplomatic relations between the
two republics, failed to produce a lasting formula for
peace.

RAMOS, COLONEL ALFREDO. Commander of a rebel col-
umn which unsuccessfully attacked Asunción in the early
stages of the 1947 major revolution.

RAMOS, R. ANTONIO, 1907-   . Prominent Asunción author and history professor at the National University.
Specialist in the independence period and era of Dr.
Francia, and particularly in the field of early diplomatic relations with Brazil.

RAMOS GIMENEZ, LEOPOLDO, 1896-   . Noted poet,
journalist, novelist and historian. Author of works of
a social protest nature concerning the yerba maté plantations similar to those of Rafael Barret. As an historian, he is known for his studies of the Chaco.

RAMSAY, COMMANDER FRANCIS M. American naval officer
aboard the USS Wasp when it removed Minister Charles
Ames Washburn from Paraguay in 1868 during the Triple Alliance War. His later testimony suggested that
George F. Masterman and Cornelius Porter Bliss, two
of Washburn's unofficial aides, had not been tortured by
Francisco Solano López as they claimed.

RAPOSO TAVARES, ANTONIO. Dreaded chieftain of a Brazilian Bandeirante-mameluke band which was especially
ravaging in its 1629 sweeps through the Guairá Jesuit
mission region.

RAVIZZA, ALEJANDRO. Italian architect who with his brother Cayetano arrived in Paraguay in 1854 as a technician
under the program of President Carlos Antonio López
to modernize his country. Responsible for the design-
ing of numerous buildings still existent in Asunción including the customs building, railway station, theatre,
Club Nacional, Panteón Nacional, and the residences of
Francisco Solano, Benigno, and Venancio López. Died
in Paraguay c. 1868.

RAVIZZA, CAYETANO see also RAVIZZA, ALEJANDRO.
Italian painter who with his brother Alejandro arrived
in Paraguay in 1854 under the program of President
Carlos Antonio López for modernization of his country.

REAL CEDULA OF 1617. Famed order from the Spanish
crown dividing the previous jurisdiction of Paraguay to
form the new Provincia del Río de la Plata. Asunción
thus ceased to be the major Spanish center of La Plata.

REAL CEDULA OF AUGUST 8, 1776 see also VICEROY.
Royal order which created the Viceroyalty of La Plata
with headquarters at Buenos Aires. Paraguay became
administratively subject to the viceroy.

REAL CEDULA OF 1801. Ordered the closing of seminaries
in the Spanish colonies to prevent the dissemination of
political theories contrary to Spanish laws and customs.
The Cédula referred to the crown's desire to avoid
further incidents of discussion regarding the "rights of
the people" such as occurred in Paraguay in 1797. Reflected growing royal apprehension over the possible
entry into the colonies of French Revolution philosophy,
and possible renewal and spread of the earlier Comunero movement.

REAL COLEGIO Y SEMINARIO DE SAN CARLOS see also
COLEGIO CAROLINO. Paraguay's first institution of
higher learning, established April 12, 1783, during the
administration of Governor Pedro Melo de Portugal.
Closed in 1822 during the regime of Dr. José Gaspar
Rodríguez de Francia. Its first rector was Dr. Gabino
de Echeverría y Gallo.

REAL ORDENANZA DE INTENDENCIAS OF JANUARY 28,
1782 see also INTENDENCIAS. Royal order which
instituted the Intendency System into South America.
As a result, the extreme southern region became divided into eight jurisdictions including those of Buenos
Aires and Paraguay.

REAL PROVISION OF 1537. Authority granted by the Spanish crown on September 12, 1537, to the conquistadors
and inhabitants of La Plata to elect their own governors
in the event of vacancies. The right became an important issue in later times, especially in the eighteenth
century Comunero period.

REAL SEMINARIO CONCILIAR DE SAN CARLOS   see   REAL
COLEGIO Y SEMINARIO DE SAN CARLOS.

REALES.   Eight small coins or "reales" were equal to a
"patacón" as monetary units in the period from independence to the Triple Alliance War.

REBAUDI, ARTURO, 1859-1926.   Educated in Italy as a medical doctor and resided most of his life at Buenos
Aires.   His father, Antonio Rebaudi, was executed on
suspicions of conspiracy in 1868 during the Triple Alliance War, a circumstance which perhaps engendered the
anti-Francisco Solano López views prevalent in Arturo
Rebaudi's numerous books regarding the war.

RECALDE, JUAN FRANCISCO   see also   CALLEJON HIS-
TORICO, and CASA DE LA INDEPENDENCIA.   Owner
of the residence which existed at Calle 14 de Mayo and
Presidente Franco in downtown Asunción, which was the
meeting place of the patriot conspirators who planned
the May, 1811, independence movement.   The "Callejón
Histórico" and the "Casa de la Independencia" still remaining at the location, are now national historical
sites.

RECOLETA CEMETERY (LA).   Located in the eastern suburbs of Asunción and a veritable permanent archive of
Paraguay's demographic and historical evolution dating
to the early independence period.

REDUCCIONES.   Reductions, or the name given to the missions built by Jesuits in south Paraguay and in neighboring Argentina.   Thirty such missions were constructed during the Jesuit era of which only a few remain as historical sites.   The most prominent in Paraguay are those of San Ignacio, San Cosme, Trinidad,
and Jesús near the Paraná River port of Encarnación.
Their heavy stone structures and massive works of
sculpture are impressive tributes to Jesuit determination and native Guaraní Indian ability.

REDUCTIONS, INDIAN   see   REDUCCIONES.   Name used in
Paraguay, Argentina, and Uruguay for the massive mission stations built by the Jesuits.

REFINARIA PARAGUAYA S. A. (REPSA).   Paraguayan corporation in which foreign capital is invested, and holder

of the concession for the refining and supply of petroleum products, especially gasoline. Inaugurated in 1966. Its production is expected to reduce foreign exchange outlay for petroleum products purchases, and to facilitate steady increase in the nation's highway transport industry.

REGENERACION (LA). One of the most important politically oriented newspapers appearing at Asunción in 1869 at the close of the Triple Alliance War, and one of Paraguay's earliest independent privately-financed papers. Official mouthpiece of the new political organization "Gran Club del Pueblo." Directed by Juan José Decoud. Published between October 1, 1869, and September 23, 1870.

REGIDOR. Aldermen or councilmen elected or appointed to the municipal council at Asunción during the colonial era.

REH, EMMA. American nutrition technician who conducted a research project at Piribebuy, Paraguay, in the 1940's. Her work entitled Paraguayan Rural Life is an expert survey of the dietary and general living customs of Paraguayan residents in interior rural areas.

REINEGG, JOSEPH VON see also SEPP, ANTONIO. German musician and musical instruments maker of the late seventeenth and early eighteenth centuries credited with having introduced the use of musical instruments into the Jesuit Indian reductions of La Plata. Known popularly as "Antonio" or "Padre Sepp."

RENGGER, JOHANN RUDOLPH, 1795-1832 see also LONGCHAMPS, MARCELINE. Rengger and Longchamps were two foreign travelers who reached Paraguay in 1819 and who were forced to remain there by Dr. José Gaspar Rodríguez de Francia for six years. Their Essai historique sur la revolution du Paraguay, published in 1827, is a useful primary source covering El Supremo's early regime.

REPARTIMIENTO see also ENCOMIENDA. Early Spanish term meaning the parceling out of Indians to Spanish conquistadores as the fruits of conquest. Repartimiento subsequently evolved into Encomienda.

REPERTORIO NACIONAL. Appeared during the early phase
   of the Second Consulate in 1841 and regarded as Paraguay's first news journal. Last published in 1851.
   Originally printed at Corrientes, but later published at
   Asunción following acquisition of a printing press, the
   first in Paraguay since that of the Jesuit mission era.
   The Repertorio carried only the texts of official administrative acts and decrees.

REPSA see REFINARIA PARAGUAYA S. A.

REPUBLIC, PROCLAMATION OF see CONGRESS OF 1813,
   and CONSTITUTION OF 1813. Although Paraguay's
   independence dates formally from May 14, 1811, the
   actual use of the term "Republic" and the formal separation of all ties with the Spain of Fernando VII did
   not occur until the convening of the Second National
   Congress in 1813.

RESIDENCIA. Known formally as the "Juicio de Residencia."
   The public board of inquiry required to be undergone
   by all high Spanish colonial administrative officials upon
   being transferred, leaving office or returned to Spain.

RESIDENTAS see also DESTINADAS. Term applied to
   those women who chose to accompany Marshal President López and the survivors of his army in their long
   "via crucis" like retreat in 1869-1870 which finally
   terminated at Cerro Corá, March 1, 1870. Many of
   both the residentas and destinadas succumbed to the
   intense rigors of the long trek through the jungles of
   the Alto Paraná region.

RESQUIN, GENERAL FRANCISCO ISIDORO, 1823-1882.
   Field commander in the Paraguayan army during the
   Triple Alliance War. Loyal to the cause of Francisco
   Solano López, he was among the army's few survivors
   captured at the final action at Cerro Corá, March,
   1870. His Datos históricos de la guerra del Paraguay
   con la Triple Alianza, published in 1896, is one of the
   few eyewitness accounts of the war from the Paraguayan
   side.

REVISTA DEL ATENEO PARAGUAYO. Periodical published
   by the Ateneo Paraguayo, founded at Asunción in 1883.

REVISTA DEL INSTITUTO PARAGUAYO see also INSTITU-

to Paraguayo.   First published in October, 1896.   One
of Paraguay's earliest and most important periodicals
of a cultural nature.

REVOLUCION LIBERTADORA   see also   MOVEMENT OF
FEBRUARY 17, 1936 and FRANCO, GENERAL RAFAEL.
Name given by the Febrerista Party to its revolutionary
movement of February 17, 1936.

REVOLUTION OF MAY 14, 1811   see also   CASA DE LA
INDEPENDENCIA.   Paraguay's bloodless independent
movement.   Commencing the night of May 14 and con-
tinuing during May 15, a group of patriot conspirators
headed by Pedro Juan Caballero, Vicente Ignacio Iturbe
and Mauricio José Troche forced Spanish Governor
Bernardo Velasco to agree to their terms for the organization of a new government for Paraguay.   The en-
suing provisional government, composed by Governor
Velasco, Dr. José Gaspar Rodríguez de Francia (the
future El Supremo), and Captain Juan Valeriano Zeballos,
continued into June, 1811, when the First National Congress approved the separation of Velasco from the government and the formation of a new five-member Junta
Superior Gubernativa, or Superior Governing Board.
A Second National Congress, convened September 30 to
October 12, 1813, authorized the use of "republic" instead of "province" for Paraguay, and authorized the
adoption of a two-member Consulate form of government.   May 14, however, is considered as the nation's
Independence Day.

REVOLUTION OF OCTOBER 18, 1891.   Aborted uprising by
discontented Liberal Party supporters against the administration of Juan G. González, who had introduced
new tax measures to bolster a desperate financial crisis.   González was subsequently forced from office and
the remainder of his term until 1894 was served by
Marcos A. Morínigo.

REVOLUTION OF 1904   see also   PILCOMAYO PACT.   Paraguay's first major, successful and decisive political
uprising in the post-Triple Alliance War period.   Occurring in August, 1904, as a Liberal Party supported
revolt, it eventually toppled the Juan A. Ezcurra Colorado Party and brought the Liberal Party to control
for the first time.   The Pilcomayo Pact ended the hos-
tilities and provided for the assumption to the presi-

dency on December 13, 1904, of Juan Bautista Gaona.

REVOLUTION OF FEBRUARY 17, 1936 see also FRANCO,
COLONEL RAFAEL, and PARTIDO FEBRERISTA.
Movement of discontented Chaco War veterans and oth-
er elements which toppled the liberal government of
President Eusebio Ayala and initiated the short Febre-
rista era of Colonel Rafael Franco.

REVOLUTION OF 1947.   Most serious and prolonged internal
revolt in modern Paraguay's history, lasting from
March to mid-August, 1947.   Known also as the 1947
Civil War and the Concepción Revolution.   Originated
with a troop revolt at the northern Paraguay River port
of Concepción on March 8, 1947, following an assault
attempt on the Asunción Central Police Headquarters
the previous day.   Revolutionary forces, composed of
defecting military units and Febrerista, Liberal and
Communist Party supporters, enjoyed early successes
but were eventually defeated in August by loyal government forces aided by large levies of Colorado Party
peasant supporters.   The revolutionaries were forced
to flee into exile, swelling the exile population at nearby Argentine points to an estimated 400,000 persons.
The revolt ushered in the modern period of Colorado
Party hegemony, stimulated the end of the Higinio Morínigo government, and left scars on Paraguay's political scene which still remain as delicate issues in the
nation's contemporary evolution.

REY BLANCO, EL.   "The White King."   One of a number
of fables which enticed early Spanish explorers in Latin America, this one concerned a fabulously rich king-
dom alleged by Indians to be located far to the west,
across the Chaco.   It mesmerized the early Spanish
La Plata expeditions until conquest proved the nature
of Peru and Bolivia.

REYES, ALONSO.   Appointed president of Paraguay in 1731
by the Comunero Asunción Junta, but resigned shortly
thereafter.

REYES BALMACEDA, DIEGO DE LOS.   Governor of Paraguay at the outbreak of the Comuneros Revolt, and deposed by Dr. José de Antequera y Castro, leader of
the Comuneros.

RHODE ISLAND CO.   see UNITED STATES AND PARA-
GUAY NAVIGATION CO.

RIACHUELO, BATTLE OF. Fought June 11, 1865, this naval action is the most important in Latin American
history. Under command of the Barão de Tàmandaré,
Brazil's naval squadron succeeded in thwarting the
planned boarding tactics conceived by Paraguay's Marshal President López, and planned for the fleet under
command of Captain Pedro Ignacio Meza. The defeat
terminated effective offensive action by Paraguay's
navy in the Triple Alliance War and permitted complete
allied naval control of the Paraná River. The Riachuelo site is located near the Argentine riverport of
Corrientes on the Paraná River south of its confluence
with the Paraguay.

RIART, GERONIMO, 1889-1969. Noted lawyer, politician,
orator and parliamentarian of the first half of the twentieth
century. Prominent director of the Liberal Party during
the Morínigo era who was forced into exile.

RIART, DR. LUIS A.   Influential Liberal Party supporter
of the candidacy for president in 1939 of Chaco War
hero General José Félix Estigarribia.

RIBERA, ANTONIO. Son of a noted Madrid architect who
assisted in the construction of the Jesuit missions or
reductions in the Misiones region.

RIBERA, FRANCISCO DE. Spanish conquistador of the 1543
Alvar Núñez Cabeza de Vaca expedition to the headwaters of the Paraguay River. Used as a scout in the
expedition's probes into the Chaco in search of "El
Dorado."

RIBERA, HERNANDO DE. Member of the 1543 Cabeza de
Vaca expedition to the headwaters of the Paraguay River and the region inhabited by the Xarayes Indians.

RIBERA Y ESPINOSA, LAZARO DE. Successor in 1796 to
Governor Joaquín Alós, and noted for his stimulus to
colonial economic activity. In 1801 Governor Ribera
led an unsuccessful river expedition northward in an
effort to dislodge the Brazilian-Portuguese garrison at
Fort Nueva Coimbra on the Upper Paraguay. Subsequently, he sought actively to promote the absolutist

theory of complete obedience to the Spanish crown
through an unsuccessful effort to centralize all education at Asunción.

RIO BRANCO, VISCONDE DE see PARANHOS, JOSE MA-
RIA DA SILVA. Imperial Brazil's foremost diplomat
and a major figure in La Plata politics during the
Triple Alliance War era.

RIO BRANCO COLLECTION. Notable collection of much of
Paraguay's official archives from independence to 1869
contained in the Biblioteca Nacional at Rio de Janeiro,
Brazil. The archives were seized by the Conde de
Eu's victorious troops after the battle of Piribebuy on
August 12, 1869, and subsequently given to José Maria
da Silva Paranhos, the Visconde do Rio Branco. The
collection, containing 49,313 documents, was taken by
Silva Paranhos to Rio de Janeiro where it was donated
to the Biblioteca Nacional in 1881 after Paranhos'
death. Continued presence of the collection in Brazil
is still a matter of serious concern for Paraguay.

RIO DE LA PLATA, VICEROYALTY OF. Last major viceroyalty of Latin America's colonial era created by the
Spanish Government in 1776. Now roughly equal to
the area comprising Argentina, it then included Paraguay, Uruguay and Alto Perú as well. A cornerstone
of Paraguayan foreign policy since independence has
been that of resistance to Argentine desires to rein-
corporate it within the limits of the former viceroyalty.

RIO GRANDE DO SUL PROVINCE, BRAZIL. Brazil's southernmost state. Prior to the Triple Alliance War,
Paraguay claimed the present Argentine Misiones region which borders on Rio Grande do Sul along the
upper Uruguay River. Paraguay's 1865 eastern invasion force entered this area at São Borja prior to its
defeat at the siege of Uruguayana.

RIO PARAGUAY see PARAGUAY RIVER.

RIO PARANA see PARANA RIVER.

RIOS, ANGEL F., 1903-   . Doctor of medicine attached
to the Paraguayan medical corps during the Chaco War.
Author of several well-documented studies of the war,
among them: La defensa del Chaco--Verdades y men-
tiras de una victoria (1950).

RIOS, JUAN DE LOS. Prominent Asunción citizen implicated
in the alleged conspiracy plot against Dr. José Gaspar
Rodríguez de Francia, and a victim of El Supremo's
1820 wholesale arrests.

RIOS, SATURIO, ? -1921. Illustrator of the Paraguayan
Triple Alliance War newspaper Cabichuí, who studied
painting in Paris prior to the war. A further remarkable exploit was his invention of a transmission device
to substitute the army's old Morse transmitters.

RIQUELME, ADOLFO, 1876-1911. Leader of a Liberal Party revolt in 1911 against the short-lived government of
Colonel Albino Jara. Noted Asunción journalist, founder and president of Paraguay's first press association,
and founder of the "Liga de la Juventud Independiente"
in 1906.

RIQUELME DE GUZMAN Y PONCE DE LEON, ALONSO.
Spanish conquistador and loyal follower of Governor
Alvar Núñez Cabeza de Vaca, employed by him in the
suppression of Indian revolts in the Asunción area.
Married Ursula Irala, mestizo daughter of Martínez de
Irala. His son, Ruy Díaz de Guzmán, wrote La Ar-
gentina, one of the earliest chronicles of the Plata re-
gion.

RIQUELME GARCIA, ANDRES, 1910-   . University professor and historian. Known for his Apuntes para una
historia nacional del Paraguay (1956), and Apuntes para
la historia política y diplomática del Paraguay (1961).

RIQUELME GARCIA, BENIGNO, 1922-   . A staff member of the Archivo Nacional and Casa de la Independencia in Asunción who is noted for his exhaustive historical research projects and published manuscripts of
episodes and events in Paraguay's history. Author of
Cumbre en soledad--vida de Manuel Gondra (1951), and
of numerous historical reviews published regularly in
the Asunción press.

RITTER, RODOLFO, 1864-1946. Born in Moscow and emigrated to Paraguay in 1902. Founder of the periodical
El Economista Paraguayo in 1908, an economic review
which was published until 1923 when Ritter traveled to
Europe. Returning to Asunción in 1925, he continued
to write and lecture on economic matters, especially

those concerning Paraguay, until his death in 1946.
Social protest novelist Rafael Barret called Ritter the
most intelligent and cultured foreigner he had met in
Paraguay.

RIVAROLA, BELISARIO, 1876-1956. Journalist and politician
Director in 1906 of the Revista del Instituto Paraguayo,
and publisher of the newspaper El Liberal. National
deputy, senator, president of the Senate, cabinet minister, and president of the Liberal Party.

RIVAROLA, CIRILO ANTONIO, 1836-1879. Controversial
figure in Paraguay's post Triple Alliance War political
history. Some sources state he was a former political
prisoner who joined the army and was captured by
Brazilian troops after Lomas Valentinas. Others state
that he was a former soldier who deserted from the
army and joined a group of Paraguayan exiles opposed
to Marshal President López. Member of the Triumvirate of 1869, and first president of Paraguay under the
provisions of the Constitution of 1870. Known for his
liberal political ideology. Resigned as president in
1871 in favor of Vice President Salvador Jovellanos.
Rivarola was assassinated in Asunción December 31,
1879.

RIVAROLA, JUAN BAUTISTA, 1790-1857. Active participant
in the revolutionary events of 1811, and member of the
Congresses of 1841 and 1844. Survived both Dr.
Francia and Carlos Antonio López.

RIVAROLA, COLONEL VALOIS. A Triple Alliance War
hero famed for his cavalry exploits. He died at the
Cerro León military camp of wounds suffered at the
battle of Itá-Ybaté in December, 1868.

RIVAROLA, DR. VICENTE. Outspoken Liberal Party leader
forced into exile during the World War II administration
of Higinio Morínigo.

RIVAROLA BOGARIN, JUAN BAUTISTA, 1894-1957. Bacte-
riologist and historian. Author of numerous works in
the field of medical science, and of La Ciudad de la
Asunción y la Cédula Real de 1537--Una lucha por la
Libertad, published in 1952. Known for his research
into the origins and early development of Asunción,
most of which remains unpublished.

RIVEROS, CARLOS, ? -1868. Journalist, educator, congressional deputy and ministry of foreign relations official. Executed at San Fernando during the Triple Alliance War on charges of conspiracy against Marshal President López.

RIVIERE, CARLOS. Printer appointed by Carlos Antonio López as director of an Escuela de Impresores y Litógrafos, a school for printers and lithographers, probably in the late 1850's. A project in the sector of education and literacy sponsored by López as part of his modernization program for Paraguay.

ROA BASTOS, AUGUSTO, 1917-   . Paraguay's most prominent modern author, especially noted for his Hijo de hombre, a novelistic account of a family through epochs of Paraguay's history. Resident of Buenos Aires.

ROBERTSON, J. P. (1792-1843) AND W. P. Enterprising Scottish brothers who were the first British subjects to enter Paraguay. Permitted by Dr. Francia to pursue their business ventures at Asunción, but eventually banished by El Supremo. Their Letters on Paraguay; An Account of a Four-Year's Residence in that Republic, under the Government of the Dictator Francia, published in 3 volumes in 1838, is one of the classic primary sources of the era.

ROBLES, LIEUTENANT EZEQUIEL. Paraguayan Triple Alliance War hero and brother of General Wenceslao Robles. Seriously wounded at the naval battle of Riachuelo in June, 1865, Robles was captured by Brazilians and taken aboard the warship Amazonas where he ripped off his bandages, preferring death to life as a prisoner. His act was subsequently emulated in August, 1868, by Captain José Matías Bado, in whose memory an extreme northeastern frontier village was named.

ROBLES, GENERAL WENCESLAO. One of Paraguay's ranking military officers at the outbreak of the Triple Alliance War, and commander of the Southern Army which was to invade La Plata in 1865 along the Paraná River. Executed in January, 1866, on charges of dereliction of duty and suspected treason.

ROCA, DR. TRISTAN. Exiled Bolivian poet, author and
    journalist who resided in Paraguay during the Triple
    Alliance War and was a major contributor to both El
    Semanario and El Centinela newspapers. Executed
    during the 1868 conspiracy episode.

ROCHA, DARDO. Argentine Senator who sought unsuccess-
    fully during the immediate post-Triple Alliance War
    period to secure Paraguayan acceptance of Argentine
    Chaco claims.

ROCKEFELLER FOUNDATION see also KERR, DR. JOHN
    AUSTIN. Active in the 1920's in the establishment of
    a health campaign in Paraguay to eradicate disease.

RODRIGUEZ, MANUEL. Alleged Portuguese financier whose
    loan of 350,000 gold pesos to Eduardo Schaerer re-
    portedly was a major factor in defraying the expenses
    of the "Comité Revolucionario," the Liberal Party
    splinter faction which supported Schaerer in the 1912
    revolution. Final repayment of the loan and accumu-
    lated interest equalled a sum almost four times greater
    than the original proceeds.

RODRIGUEZ ALCALA, HUGO, 1917-   . Educator, author
    and literary critic resident in the United States since
    1947. Son of Teresa Lamas Carísimo and José Rod-
    ríguez Alcalá, both prominent in Paraguayan cultural
    history. One of the two most important Paraguayan
    intellectuals living in the United States in the twentieth
    century, the other being Dr. Pablo Max Ynsfrán, an
    historian at the University of Texas. Dr. Rodríguez
    Alcalá is currently on the faculty of the University of
    California at Riverside. Author of Historia de la lite-
    ratura paraguaya, a survey of Paraguayan cultural
    evolution published in 1970.

RODRIGUEZ ALCALA, JOSE, ? -1959. Argentine author-
    journalist who emigrated to Paraguay in 1900. Author
    of the novel Ignacia, published in 1906.

RODRIGUEZ DE ASUAGA, ALONSO. Recorded as a sawyer,
    one of the early craftsmen to arrive in the Asunción
    colony.

RODRIGUEZ DE FRANCIA, GARCIA. Died circa 1807 at
    Yaguarón. A Portuguese specializing in tobacco plant-

ing, he migrated to Paraguay and was the father of
El Supremo, Dr. José Gaspar Rodríguez de Francia.
A split between the two in El Supremo's later years
was allegedly never mended.   The Yaguarón home was
reconstructed and is now a well-preserved national
historical site.

RODRIGUEZ DE VERGARA, CAPTAIN GARCIA   see also
   ONTIVEROS.   Spanish conquistador sent on Chaco expeditions in the early colonial period, and founder in
   1554 of the Ontiveros settlement in the Guairá region
   north of the Yguazú Falls.

RODRIGUEZ VALDEZ DE LA BANDA, DIEGO.   Named governor by the Spanish crown in 1599.   Succeeded on his
   death in 1601 by Hernandarias, the first creole in
   Spanish America to be appointed formally as governor
   by the crown.

ROJAS, BLAS JOSE DE.   Commander of an army garrison
   at Corrientes in May, 1811, who was part to a revolt
   planned against the Governor Velasco government at
   Asunción.   His participation was nullified by the May
   14 Revolution which came earlier than the original
   agreed date of May 25.

ROJAS, LIBERATO MARCIAL, 1870-1922.   Journalist and
   politician.   President for a brief nine-month period in
   1911-1912 following the administrations of Manuel
   Gondra and Albino Jara.   His regime was highlighted
   by some of the most serious anarchy and revolt in
   Paraguay's history.   Died in exile at Montevideo.

ROJAS, TEODORO, 1877-1954.   Self-educated botanist whose
   studies of Paraguayan flora in the first half of the
   twentieth century received international recognition.
   Member of commissions to survey Paraguay's boundaries with both Brazil and Argentina.

ROJAS DE ARANDA, LAZARO.   Wealthy Asunción estanciero
   or large ranch owner in Paraguay's early nineteenth
   century history who in some accounts is alleged to be
   the father of Francisco Solano López.   Most Paraguayan
   historians now believe he was rather the national hero's
   god-father.   Evidence indicates that Rojas presented
   the future Iron Marshal with title to the Asunción property now occupied by the National Palace, an occur-

rence which probably stimulated erroneous speculation
regarding relationships between the two.

ROJAS SILVA, LIEUTENANT ADOLFO. Paraguayan officer
killed by Bolivian troops following the capture of his
patrol in the Fortín Sorpresa incident of February 26,
1927. Recorded as the first Paraguayan fatality in the
history of Paraguayan/Bolivian Chaco disputes.

ROLON, GENERAL RAIMUNDO, 1903-   . Professional
soldier, Chaco War veteran, government official, minister of defense, and temporary president of the republic for a 26-day period following the administration
of President Juan Natalicio González. Deposed in February, 1949. Author-editor of a 1940 study of the
Chaco battles of Zenteno, Gondra, Nanawa, and Campo
Via.

ROMERO, FRANCISCO. Recorded in historical accounts as
a Portuguese shoemaker and one of the earliest artisans to reach the new Asunción colony.

ROMERO, JUAN. Early conquistador recorded as the commander of the first settlement of Buenos Aires during
the explorations northward by Martínez de Irala. Later
rejoined Irala and served in Chaco exploration expeditions.

ROMERO PEREIRA, TOMAS, 1886-   . An Asunción architect and prominent leader of the Colorado Party.
Served as president of the republic from May, 1954,
until August, when he promoted a political accord
which supported the candidacy of General Alfredo
Stroessner who became president on August 15. Owner
of the former Cerro León military campsite of the
Triple Alliance War era which is being reconstructed
as a future national monument.

ROOT, JOHN also RUTE, JUAN. Recorded as an English-
man and member of the Pedro de Mendoza expedition
who eventually reached Asunción to become one of the
first artisans capable of making gunpowder.

ROQUE ALONSO, MARIANO, ? -1853. Principal member
of the Comandancia General de Armas of 1841, and
one of the two-member Second Consulate established
by Paraguay's fifth National Congress of March, 1941,
the other being Carlos Antonio López.

ROSARIO. Small Paraguay River port located on the river's east bank approximately half-way between Asunción and Concepción. Nearby Rosario to the east is Itacurubí del Rosario, location of the estancia or ranch owned by Carlos Antonio López.

ROSARIO MIRANDA, JOSE DEL, 1832-1903. Prominent political figure, statesman and diplomat in the post Triple Alliance War era. President of the 1870 constitutional convention, president of the Supreme Court, holder of several ministerial cabinet posts, and vice president in the Patricio Escobar administration. Known popularly for his emotional oratory.

ROSAS, JUAN MANUEL ORTIZ DE, 1793-1877. Governor of Buenos Aires and Director of the United Argentine Provinces from 1829 until his defeat at the battle of Monte Caseros, February, 1852. As one of Latin America's sternest dictators and an ardent advocate of Argentine supremacy in La Plata, Rosas sought to procure Paraguay's retention within Buenos Aires' hegemony. His policies of opening and closing commerce on the Paraná River at his will, and of delaying recognition of independence, were knotty problems for Paraguay's Carlos Antonio López.

ROSENSCHOLD, EBERHARD MUCK AF, 1811-1869. Swedish naturalist who resided in Paraguay 20 years for the purpose of collecting specimens of local flora. Few of his collections ever reached Europe, however, and he disappeared in 1869, apparently a victim of the conspiracy against Marshal President Francisco Solano López.

ROVIRA, GENERAL JUAN. Minister of the Interior in the last 1946 cabinet of President Higinio Morínigo, which reflected a coalition of the Colorado and Febrerista parties. The effort to resolve a growing political crisis disappeared with the outbreak of the major 1947 Revolution.

RUBICHA. Term used by tribal branches of the Guaraní Indians in eastern Paraguay for the leader or chief.

RUBIO ÑU, BATTLE OF see ACOSTA ÑU, BATTLE OF. Name used in some historical accounts for the battle which occurred August 16, 1869, near the interior city

of Eusebio Ayala, formerly Barrero Grande. The last
action of the Cordillera Campaign of the Triple Alliance War, the battle is more widely known as that of
Acosta Ñú.

RUILOBA Y CALDERON, COLONEL MANUEL AGUSTIN DE.
Briefly governor of Paraguay during the high point in
the Comunero Revolt. Arrived at Asunción in July,
1733, but was killed by Comunero forces the following
September 15 at the battle of Guayahibiti.

RUIZ, J. GABRIEL, 1894-1949. Professor of Paraguayan
history at Asunción's Escuela Nacional de Comercio.
Author of several works on the Triple Alliance War,
Dr. Francia and the colonial era.

RUIZ DE ARELLANO, ANTONIO. Briefly president of the
province of Paraguay in the 1730's during the height
of the Comunero Revolt.

RUIZ DE MONTOYA, FATHER ANTONIO. Early seventeenth
century Jesuit missionary from Peru active in the foundation of the first missions in the Guairá region.
Noted for his successful efforts to obtain royal permission to arm mission Indians as a defense against Brazilian mameluke slave raiders, and for his Conquista
espiritual, the first history of Jesuit evangelizing efforts in Paraguay.

RUIZ GALAN, CAPTAIN FRANCISCO. Member of the Pedro
de Mendoza La Plata expedition in 1536, commander
at the first Buenos Aires settlement, and briefly in
1537 a challenger to the position of Martínez de Irala
at the new Asunción colony.

RUTE, JUAN see ROOT, JOHN.

- S -

SAAVEDRA, CAPTAIN CRISTOBAL DE. Messenger who
reached Asunción in 1551 with news of the arrival on
Brazil's Atlantic coast of the Diego de Sanabria-
Mencia Calderón expedition. Sanabria, the newly appointed governor of Paraguay, was lost at sea, however, and Martínez de Irala continued in command at
Asunción.

SAAVEDRA, FORTIN. South central Chaco fortified point
which was the locale of heavy fighting in the early
1932-1933 phase of the Chaco War.

SAAVEDRA, HERNANDO ARIAS DE see HERNANDARIAS,
and ARIAS DE SAAVEDRA, HERNANDO.

SAAVEDRA LAMAS, DR. CARLOS. Argentina's foreign
minister during the Chaco War period whose negotiat-
ing efforts to reach a peace earned him the Nobel
Prize.

SAENZ, SEBASTIAN MARTINEZ. Secretary of Government
during the Dr. Francia/Fulgencio Yegros First Consulate of 1813-1814. Sáenz, a confident of Dr. Francia, was personally selected by the future El Supremo
to assure that his views on government and foreign
affairs would prevail.

SAGASTUME, JOSE VASQUEZ. Uruguayan minister at
Asunción in 1864 who sought to secure Paraguay's in-
tervention in the Uruguayan crisis, the prelude to the
Triple Alliance War.

SAGUIER, ADOLFO. Vice President in the 1878 administration of President Cándido Barreiro. When Barreiro
died in 1880 before completing his term, General Bernardino Caballero organized a revolt which prevented
Saguier from assuming the presidency.

SALAMANCA, DR. DANIEL. President of Bolivia during
most of the era of the Chaco War. Forced to retire
from office in favor of Vice President Tejada Zorzano
following the army's chaotic defeat at Yrendagüe, December, 1934.

SALAZAR, HERNANDO DE. One of Martínez de Irala's
captains who was sent in 1554 with Ñufrio de Chaves
on an expedition to seek a route across the Chaco to
Bolivia.

SALAZAR Y ESPINOSA, JUAN DE, 1508-1560. Member of
the Pedro de Mendoza expedition to La Plata. Sailing
up the Paraná and Paraguay rivers from the Río de la
Plata in 1537, Juan de Salazar founded the city of
Nuestra Señora Santa María de la Asunción on August
15. The date is a major annual national holiday, and

the one on which presidents are formally inaugurated
into office.

SALDIVAR, FRANCISCO DE. Paraguayan intellectual and a
graduate of the University of San Moreno chosen by Governor Hernandarias circa 1604 to inaugurate a modest college at Asunción for the study of mathematics, art and
theology. One of the earliest efforts toward the establishment of an institution of higher learning in Paraguay.

SALONIO, FATHER JUAN. One of the first Jesuits to arrive
in Paraguay in 1588. Credited with commencing the construction of a Jesuit College at Asunción before his death
in 1596.

SALTO, S. S. Paraguayan naval vessel put out of action and
beached at the Triple Alliance War naval battle of
Riachuelo, June, 1865.

SALVADOR JOVELLANOS, JUAN see also JOVELLANOS,
JUAN SALVADOR. Post-Triple Alliance War President
of Paraguay, 1871-1874. Deposed by a coup and succeeded by Juan Bautista Gill.

SAMAKLAY, FORTIN. Paraguayan Chaco outpost attacked
by Bolivian forces in 1931. The incident generated a
bloody riot in Asunción led by students of the Colegio
Nacional and Escuela Normal against the policies of
President José P. Guggiari.

SAMANIEGO, PEDRO PABLO, 1892-1942. Law professor and
government official. Supreme Court president during the
Febrerista regime, 1936-1937. Exiled upon the fall of
the Franco government, he died at Buenos Aires.

SAN ANTONIO, PORT OF. Paraguay River port located between Villeta and Asunción noted as the embarkation point
of meat products of a major American-controlled meat
packing plant. Historically important as the landing site
of the allied army which crossed the Paraguay River from
the Chaco prior to the Lomas Valentinas campaign of the
Triple Alliance War. Nearby are the battlefields of
Ytororó and Avay.

SAN ANTONIO MISSION. Early Jesuit reduction in the Guairá
region, and one of the first attacked by Brazilian mameluke slave raiders in 1629.

SAN BERNARDINO. Located about 30 miles (50 kms) east
of Asunción on the eastern shores of Lake Ypacaray,
this noted summer resort was founded in 1881 during
the presidency of General Bernardino Caballero. Nearby Altos is a small village which was the center of
Paraguay's first German colony, the descendents of
which still reside in the area.

SAN BERNARDO, JUAN DE. Franciscan missionary noted
for his work among Indians and as an accomplished
orator both in Spanish and Guaraní.

SAN BLAS. Proclaimed Patron Saint of Paraguay by the
early Spanish conquistadores due to a victory gained
over an Indian attack at the Corpus Christi outpost,
February 3, 1539, San Blas Day. The Indians were
allegedly frightened into retreat by the apparition on a
tower of the outpost of a man dressed in white and
brandishing a huge gleaming sword.

SAN CARLOS, SEMINARY OF see REAL SEMINARIO
CONCILIAR DE SAN CARLOS.

SAN COSME. Jesuit mission or reduction located near
Encarnación at the terminus of Highway Route One in
extreme southern Paraguay. The only such ruin in
Paraguay which still possesses the original roof construction.

SAN ESTANISLAO MISSION. Founded in 1749, one of the
last Jesuit reductions to be established during the colonial era.

SAN FERNANDO. Small and now uninhabited riverside point
slightly above the mouth of the Tebicuary River into
the Paraguay River south of Asunción. Intermediate
camp site and general headquarters of the Paraguayan
army following the retreat in 1868 from Humaitá, and
the locale for the functioning of the notorious "Tribunales de sangre"--military courts--of the Conspiracy
Period.

SAN IGNACIO GUAZU MISSION. Former Jesuit mission or
reduction located about 70 miles northwest of the river
port of Encarnación in southern Paraguay. Noted for
its museum containing a rich collection of Indian-made
sculptures from the Jesuit era.

SAN ILDEFONSO, TREATY OF see also TRATADO DE
PERMUTA. Boundary limits agreement in 1771 between Spain and Portugal whereby Spain regained possession of the area of the seven former Jesuit missions located along the upper left bank of the Uruguay
River in exchange for Portuguese expansion westward
beyond the line drawn by the Treaty of Tordesillas of
1494.

SAN ISIDRO DE CURUGUATY see also SAN ISIDRO
LABRADOR and ARTIGAS, JOSE GERVASIO. An interior village about 150 miles (250 kms) northeast of
Asunción. Remembered in Paraguayan history as the
residence locale assigned by Dr. Francia to Uruguay's
José Artigas during his more than twenty years exile
in Paraguay, and later as the republic's fourth and
last capital during the Triple Alliance War.

SAN ISIDRO LABRADOR see also ARTIGAS, JOSE GERVA-
SIO. Small inhabited point near the village of Curuguaty (San Isidro de Curuguaty) in east central Paraguay. Site of the residence in exile of Uruguay's national hero José Gervasio Artigas.

SAN JOAQUIN MISSION. Founded in 1746, and one of the
last Jesuit reductions to be established during the colonial era.

SAN JOSE DE FLORES, PACT OF. Agreement of November
10, 1859, between the governments of Buenos Aires
and of Argentina's provinces reached after the successful mediation efforts of Paraguay's Brigadier Francisco
Solano López. For his efforts in aiding to unite Argentina, López received numerous honors attesting to
the "eternal gratitude" of Argentina's peoples.

SAN JUAN BAUTISTA see also REDUCTIONS, MISSIONS.
Administrative capital of Paraguay's Misiones Department located about 125 miles north of the Paraná River port of Encarnación on Highway Route One to Asunción. Noted as the site of a former Jesuit reduction
or mission.

SAN JUST, JAIME. Named governor in 1749. Noted for
having encouraged the introduction of tobacco planting
in the Yaguarón district in 1751, and for his defense
of the northern regions against continued Portuguese

encroachment. Among the tobacco planters coming
from Brazil there probably figured García Rodríguez
Francia, father of Paraguay's future El Supremo, Dr.
José Gaspar Rodríguez de Francia.

SAN LORENZO, BATTLE OF. Encounter near Asunción
between the troops of Bishop Bernardino de Cárdenas
and a Jesuit mission Indian army following the expulsion of the Jesuits from Asunción by Cárdenas in 1649.
The Indian army was victorious, the Jesuits reentered
the capital, and Bishop Cárdenas suffered a temporary
eclipse in his career.

SAN MARCOS. One of two brigantines, the other being the
Todos los Santos, which reached Asunción in 1556.
The cargo carried on their departure probably represented the first foreign-bound shipments from Paraguay.

SAN MARTIN, GENERAL JOSE DE. Argentina's independence hero, national hero of Peru, and regarded as the
Liberator of southern South America as Simón Bolívar
is for the northern half. Several Paraguayan officers
served in his army in the liberation campaigns of Peru
and Chile in the early nineteenth century.

SAN MIGUEL. Only vessel of three incorporating the 1550
Diego de Sanabria expedition to South America. Though
it foundered along the Brazilian coast near Santa Catha-
rina, its survivors, including Doña Mencía de Calderón,
Sanabria's mother, eventually managed to reach Paraguay.

SAN PABLO MISSION. Early Jesuit reduction in the Guairá
region later abandoned due to constant Brazilian mameluke slave raids.

SANABRIA, JUAN AND DIEGO DE. Father and son who
were respectively designated "adelantados" to La Plata
in 1547 and 1549, but who died in Spain before departure to Paraguay.

SANABRIA, MARIA DE see also HERNANDARIAS. Daughter of Doña Mencía Calderón, famed early sixteenth
century woman explorer to Paraguay. María de Sanabria's second marriage to Captain Martín Suárez de
Toledo produced a son, Hernando Arias de Saavedra,

the noted "Hernandarias" of Paraguay's early colonial era.

SANCHEZ, CRISTOBAL DE. Canon and vicar at Asunción appointed by Governor Gregorio de Hinestrosa in 1644 during the tumultous era of Bishop Bernardino de Cárdenas.

SANCHEZ, DOMINGO FRANCISCO, 1795-1870. Long-time minister of foreign relations in the governments of Carlos Antonio and Francisco Solano López, and vice president for the latter from 1865 to 1870. Killed at Cerro Corá with Marshal President López in March, 1870.

SANCHEZ-DORIA CONVENTION see also CANSTATT, SANTIAGO, and BUZZARD, H. M. S. Paraguayan-British Convention negotiated after the 1859 "Canstatt Affair" which served to renew friendly relations between the two countries.

SANCHEZ QUELL, HIPOLITO, 1907-   . Noted educator, statesman, historian and author. Currently Director of Paraguay's National Archives (Archivo Nacional).

SANCTI SPIRITU, FORT. Built by the Sebastián Cabot expedition in 1526 along the lower Paraná River. Later destroyed by Indian attacks. The Cabot expedition was the first to penetrate La Plata and ascend the Paraná-Paraguay rivers nearly to the location of Asunción.

SANTA CRUZ, BOLIVIA. Important eastern Bolivian city located in the Andes mountain foothills near Bolivia's major west Chaco oilfields. Founded by the 1651 Chaco expedition of Ñufrio de Chaves.

SANTA CRUZ, FATHER ROQUE GONZALEZ DE see GONZALEZ DE SANTA CRUZ, FATHER ROQUE.

SANTA FE, ARGENTINA. Important Argentine riverport near the west bank of the lower Paraná River. Founded in 1573 by Juan de Garay descending the Paraguay-Paraná river with a party largely composed of "mancebos de la tierra," mestizos born in Paraguay.

SANTA FE PROVINCE, ARGENTINA. Located on the west bank of the lower Paraná River across from Entre

Ríos province. Its capital of Santa Fe was founded in
1573 by the Juan de Garay expedition from Asunción.

SANTA MARIA DE FE   see also   REDUCTIONS.   Notable
Jesuit mission ruins located near the northern limits
of the Misiones area near the Tebicuary River.

SANTA ROSA   see also   REDUCTIONS.   Site of an old Jesuit mission located in the northern zone of the Misiones
area near the Tebicuary River.   The church was destroyed by fire, but the great tower still stands.

SANTIAGO DE JEREZ.   Aborted settlement project located
to the north of the Apa River, north of Concepción,
on the right bank of the Mbotetey River.   Founded in
1593 by Ruy Díaz de Guzmán, and destroyed in 1632
by a Brazilian bandeirante mameluke raid.

SANTO TOMAS, GRUTAS DE.   Cave located in a rocky hill
near the interior city of Paraguarí on the walls of
which are carved curious and as yet undeciphered
hieroglyphics.

SÃO BORJA, BRAZIL   see   PASSÒ DE SÃO BORJA, AC-
TION AT.   Brazilian riverport on the upper Uruguay
River in Rio Grade do Sul province across from Argentina's Misiones district.   Site of the crossing in
1865 of the eastern arm of the Paraguayan army invasion aimed at La Plata.

SÃO PAULO, BRAZIL.   Brazil's "Chicago of South America, " located immediately inland from the coffee port
of Santos.   A base in the seventeenth and eighteenth
centuries both for Brazilian "bandeirante" exploration
expeditions westward, and for Paulista mameluke slave
raiders penetrating into the Guairá and southern Paraguay Jesuit mission regions.

SÃO VICENTE, BRAZIL.   Early Portuguese settlement located on the south central Brazilian Atlantic coast near
the modern seaport of Santos.   A base for numerous
expeditions arriving from Spain and destined overland
to Paraguay.

SAPENA PASTOR, RAUL, 1908-   . University professor,
jurist and government cabinet minister.   Professor of
history at the Colegio Nacional, dean of the Faculty of

Law of the Universidad Nacional, president of the
Banco del Paraguay, and minister of foreign relations.
Author of several works in the field of international
private law.

"SAPUCAY," LOCOMOTIVE.   The last remaining unit of
the Paraguay Central Railway's original British-made
locomotives.   Now on display at Asunción's Presidente
Carlos Antonio López Railway Station.   Inaugurated
rail service in Paraguay on October 21, 1861, on a
trip from Asunción about five miles to the suburb of
Trinidad.   Recorded as one of the first railways to
operate in South America.

SAPUCAY, VILLAGE OF.   Located along the Presidente
Carlos Antonio López Railway about 55 miles southeast
of Asunción.   The railway's main repair shops are
situated here as well as the government's leper colony.

SARAIVA, JOSE ANTONIO.   Imperial Brazil's special envoy
to Uruguay in early 1864 who sought to negotiate a
formula to prevent war.   His delivery of Brazil's ultimatum to the Uruguayan Blanco government in August,
however, was a significant event leading to the outbreak of the Triple Alliance War.

SARMIENTO, DOMINGO FAUSTINO.   Prominent Argentine
statesman, author and educator.   Replaced Bartolomé
Mitre as president in 1868 following a diplomatic tour
as minister to the United States.   He continued to support Argentina's participation in the Triple Alliance
War, but reduced effective troop participation to nominal size.   His only son was killed at the battle of
Curupaity, September, 1866.   Vociferous in his attacks
against Marshal President López, he nevertheless
chose Asunción as a post-war retirement site.   His
home there, known as the "Solar Sarmiento," is a
well-preserved historic site.

SARMIENTO Y FIGUEROA, ALONSO.   Governor of Paraguay
in 1659 who was forced to use mission Indian help to
quell a major Indian revolt by tribes in the Asunción
area.

SAUVAGEOD DE DUPUIS, FRANCISCO, ? -1861.   French
national and musician whose services were contracted
for by Carlos Antonio López in 1853.   Credited with

having organized the first band in Paraguay, a group with 74 members. Died at Asunción.

SAYAS, PEDRO DE. Probably the first professional in medicine to arrive in Paraguay. Recorded as a surgeon who accompanied the Alvar Núñez Cabeza de Vaca expedition in 1542.

SCHAERER, EDUARDO. Prominent Liberal Party director and president of Paraguay during 1912-1916. Descendent of a German immigrant family of the Colonia San Bernardino near Lake Ypacaray.

SCHAERER, JACOB see also SAN BERNARDINO. Founder in 1881 of the San Bernardino German colony located on the eastern shores of Lake Ypacaray, about 35 miles east of Asunción.

SCHMIDEL, ULRICH see SCHMIDT, ULRICH.

SCHMIDT, ULRICH. German member of the 1535 Pedro de Mendoza expedition to La Plata. His recollections, Viaje al Río de la Plata, probably written before 1554, comprise one of the earliest first-hand accounts of the Spanish penetration of Paraguay.

SCOLASTICA. Servant-mistress of Governor Domingo Martínez de Irala, who bore him a son, Martín Pérez de Irala.

SEBASTOPOL OF SOUTH AMERICA see also HUMAITA. Term used in accounts of the Triple Alliance War referring to Paraguay's major defensive bastion of Humaitá, a fortified position located strategically at a bend of the Paraguay River a few miles above its confluence with the Paraná River. Stubborn and bloody defense of Humaitá during more than three years of siege operations encouraged historians to compare it to Russia's Sebastopol of the Crimean War.

SECRET TREATY OF 1865 see TRIPLE ALLIANCE TREATY.

SEGURA ZAVALA, PEDRO DE. Married Ginebra Martínez de Irala, mestizo daughter of Governor Martínez de Irala by his servant María. Their son, Juan de Irala, was both a prominent government official and a writer during the early colonial period.

SEMANARIO DE AVISOS Y CONOCIMIENTOS UTILES (EL).
Historically Paraguay's second newspaper chronologi-
cally following El Paraguayo independiente. Published
regularly between May, 1853, and November, 1868,
when it was forced to halt operations due to the allied
advance upon Asunción. El Semanario's files are a
major source of information on Paraguayan life, events
and governmental policy during the period.

SEÑORIA DEL COMUN. Name informally adopted by the
Comunero faction at Asunción during the height of the
movement in the early 1730's.

SEPP, ANTONIO, 1655-1733   see also   REINEGG, JOSEPH
VON. German painter and sculptor who assisted in
the construction and furnishing of the large Jesuit mission stations or reductions in the Misiones region.
Also famed as the first to introduce musical instruments into the Indian reductions. His own records in-
dicate he had developed an all-Indian orchestra by
1692.

SERVICE, ELMAN R. AND HELEN S.   see also   TOBATI.
American social science researchers who performed
extensive investigation at the interior village of Tobatí
during 1948-1949 under the auspices of the Social Science Research Council and the Columbia University
Council for Research in the Social Sciences. Their
study, Tobatí, a Paraguayan Town, published in 1954
by the University of Chicago Press, represents not
only the first major sociological study of Paraguay's
people but probably the definitive one as well.

SERVICIO TECNICO INTERAMERICANO DE COOPERACION
AGRICOLA--STICA. Established in 1944 as a joint
United States-Paraguayan official organization to promote improvement to local agriculture and the livestock industry. Credited as one of the most successful international technical assistance projects in Paraguay's history. By 1970 its activities and programs
were assimilated by recently developed Paraguayan
government departments.

SEVEN REDUCTIONS, WAR OF   see   GUARANI WAR.

SEVERINO, DR. BLAS. Rector of the "Convictorio de
Asunción," an officially sponsored project for higher

learning which was organized in 1716 during the governorship of Juan Gregorio Bazán de Pedraza. The project shortly disappeared due to lack of financing and the advent of the Comunero era.

SHAMOKIN, U.S.S. American naval vessel of the South Atlantic squadron under Captain Pierce Crosby, which returned Minister Charles Ames Washburn to Asunción in November, 1866, during the Triple Alliance War.

SIERRA DE LA PLATA. The famed and legendary "mountains of silver" which, like "El Dorado"--the Golden One, enticed early Spanish explorers westward across the Chaco. The "Sierra," of course, eventually turned out to be the gold and silver rich Andes region of Peru and Bolivia.

SILES, HERNANDO. Bolivia's president during 1926-1930, the period in which Bolivian-Paraguayan relations became strained over the growing Chaco dispute.

SILVA PARANHOS, JOSE MARIA DA see PARANHOS, JOSE MARIA DA SILVA, and RIO BRANCO, VISCONDE DO.

SILVA TAVARES, COLONEL JOÃO NUNES DA. Brazilian cavalry commander at the final Cerro Corá action of the Triple Alliance War who allegedly offered a 100-pounds sterling reward to the soldier who killed Paraguay's Francisco Solano López. Although no record exists of who may have received the reward, Corporal "Chico Diabo" Lacerda is the soldier alleged to have mortally wounded the marshal-president.

SIRIPO, CHIEF. Recorded as brother of Chief Mangoré of the Timbú tribe. Responsible for the 1530 destruction and massacre of the settlers of the early Sancti Spíritu fort built on the lower Paraná River by the Sebastián Cabot expedition.

SKINNER, DR. FREDERICK. British physician in Paraguay's army during the Triple Alliance War, and presumed the only foreigner present at Cerro Corá, March 1, 1870, when Marshal President Francisco Solano López was killed in the war's concluding action. Left no known memoirs other than a letter to American Minister Washburn which was condemnatory of López.

SLAVERY, ABOLITION OF, DECREE OF 1842 REGARDING
    FREE BIRTH. A significant achievement of Paraguay's
    Second Consulate, 1841-1844, was the decree which
    provided that, effective as of January 1, 1843, all
    children born of slaves would henceforth be free.

SMITH, COLONEL FEDERICO WESMAN see also FEBRE-
    RISTA REVOLT. Noted Chaco War hero and Command-
    er of a military force at Asunción in February, 1936.
    The military leader who initiated the first armed up-
    rising of the Febrerista movement, but never a mem-
    ber of the Febrerista Party.

SMITH, THOMAS N. British naval engineer whose services
    in Paraguay were contracted for during the Carlos An-
    tonio López administration. Credited with the con-
    struction in 1857 at the new Asunción naval arsenal of
    the 226-ton S.S. Yporá, to become one of Paraguay's
    best naval vessels in the Triple Alliance War. Its
    sunken hull still remains at Vapor Cué inland on the
    Manduvirá River.

SOARES, JOÃO. Brazilian cavalryman from Rio Grande do
    Sul who allegedly shot Marshal President Francisco
    Solano López in the back with a Spencer carbine at
    Cerro Corá, March 1, 1870, the final action of the
    Triple Alliance War.

SOCIEDAD ALEMANA DE GIMNASIA Y DEPORTES. Hitler
    youth-type pro-Nazi social organization at Asunción
    during the World War II period.

SOCIEDAD CIENTIFICA DEL PARAGUAY. Originally founded
    at Asunción January 9, 1921, for research and special
    studies in medicine and the natural sciences. On June
    29, 1929, the Society inaugurated its "Museo Etnográ-
    fico y Histórico Natural," and since then it has con-
    cerned itself principally with ethnographic and linguis-
    tic studies.

SOCIEDAD CULTURA GUARANI see ACADEMIA DE LA
    LENGUA Y CULTURA GUARANI.

SOCIEDAD LIBERTADORA DE LA REPUBLICA DEL PARA-
    GUAY. Early anti-López association of exiled Para-
    guayans founded at Buenos Aires in August, 1858.
    Forerunner of the later Asociación Paraguaya and the

Legión Paraguaya.   Published a periodical entitled El
Grito Paraguayo.

SOCIEDAD PATRIOTICA LITERARIA.   Established in 1812
by order of the Junta Gubernativa (Governing Board)
of 1811 to be responsible for supervision of all public
instruction.   Disappeared in the early stage of the
Dr. Francia era.

SOCIEDAD TRAVASSOS, PATRI Y CIA.   Successful bidder
on March 17, 1877, for the purchase of the railway
from Asunción to Paraguarí at a price of 300,000 gold
pesos.   About a year later the Paraguayan government
decided to buy back the railway from the company at
a cost of 1,200,000 gold pesos, or four times the
amount it received from Travassos and Patri in 1877.

SOCIETE FONCIERE DU PARAGUAY.   French-owned company credited with the establishment of a livestock industry in extreme eastern Paraguay.

SOCIETY OF BROTHERS   see also   PRIMAVERA and
HUTTERITES.   Established the Primavera communal-
type colony in 1941 near the Mennonite Friesland colony in the department of San Pedro north of Asunción.
In 1960-1961 the majority elected to leave Paraguay
for England and the United States apparently due to
the lack of a cultural environment available to their
isolated settlement.   The Society originated in Germany after World War I, and transferred to England before World War II where they were known as the
Cotswold Bruderhof.   The outbreak of war stimulated
them to seek another area where they might live in
peace.

SOCIETY OF JESUS   see also   JESUITS, REDUCCIONES.
The famed Catholic missionary society formed by St.
Ignatius Loyola.

SOLANO, ST. FRANCIS.   Sixteenth century Jesuit missionary
who allegedly performed near-miraculous work among
Chaco Indian tribes.   Some historians suggest that
Francisco Solano López, Paraguay's foremost national
hero, was named after him.

SOLANO ESPINOZA, FATHER FRANCISCO, ? -1870.   Instructor in Latin and an editor of the wartime army

newspaper Cacique Lambaré. Killed at Cerro Corá,
March 1, 1870, the last action of the Triple Alliance
War.

SOLER, ADOLFO R., 1869-1925. Prominent Liberal Party
director, and a prime figure in the staging of the August, 1904, Revolution which brought the Liberal Party to power. Founder and director in 1895 of El Cívico newspaper. Negotiator for Paraguay of the 1907
Soler-Pinilla Protocol with Bolivia regarding Chaco
boundary limits. Minister and aide to President Benigno Ferreira, 1906-1908. Died at Buenos Aires
after extended exile.

SOLER, JUAN JOSE. Son of Adolfo Soler, a principal architect of the August, 1904, Liberal Party revolution,
and a co-founder of the party's El Liberal newspaper.

SOLER-PINILLA PROTOCOL. Signed January 12, 1907; one
of the series of pre-Chaco War efforts to reach a
peaceful settlement of the Paraguay-Bolivia dispute,
this agreement contemplated Argentine mediation and
the maintenance of the status quo in the Chaco. Like
the several other efforts, this agreement was not ratified.

SOLIS, JUAN DIAZ DE. First Spanish explorer to discover
and enter the Plata estuary. His 1515-1516 expedition
seeking a water route to the Pacific was the forerunner
of the subsequent expeditions by Cabot and Mendoza
which led to the founding of Asunción. Solís himself
was killed and devoured by Charrúa Indians when he
landed on the Uruguayan side of La Plata.

SOMELLERA, PEDRO, 1774-1854. Argentine national and
Spanish colonial government official at Asunción in
1807 who, though originally a friend of Dr. José
Gaspar Rodríguez de Francia, favored strong ties
with the new Buenos Aires government. A leader of
the unsuccessful coup against Paraguay's New Junta
government in September, 1811.

SOMMERFELD COLONY. With Bergthal Colony, one of the
most recent Mennonite colonization projects in east
Paraguay. Located about 180 miles east of Asunción
along the highway to Puerto Presidente Stroessner,
and begun in 1948.

SOPA PARAGUAYA.   A heavy cake or tart-like dish which
belies its name, and is composed of ground corn,
cheese, onions, and milk.   One of Paraguay's most
typical dishes.

SOROETA, IGNACIO.   Appointed governor of Paraguay during
the height of the Comunero Revolt, but who was not
permitted by a Comunero army to reach Asunción in
1731.

SORPRESA, FORTIN, INCIDENT AT.   Occurring in February,
1927, near the Bolivian Chaco outpost of Fortín Sorpresa, the incident involved the capture by Bolivian troops
of a Paraguayan patrol and the death of the patrol's
leader, Lieutenant Adolfo Rojas Silva.   A prelude to
the Chaco War.

SOSA, ANTONIO, 1870-1946.   Educator, journalist and statesman.   Professor of Finance at the National University,
dean of the Faculty of Law and Social Sciences, member of the Chamber of Deputies, member of the commission which drafted the 1940 Constitution, and director of numerous Asunción newspapers including La Opinión, La Tribuna, El País, La Libertad, and El Tiempo.

SOSA, JAIME see SOSA ESCALADA, JAIME.

SOSA ESCALADA, JAIME, 1846-1906.   Vice president of
Paraguay's Chamber of Deputies sent to Rio de Janeiro
in 1875 to negotiate a post-Triple Alliance War boundary limits treaty with Argentina.   The resulting Sosa-
Tejedor Treaty of May 20, 1875, was deemed so favorable to Argentina that Paraguay's government refused
to ratify it.   Though not responsible for the treaty,
Sosa was made a scapegoat, publicly disgraced and removed from his position.   Founder of Asunción's Biblioteca Nacional.

SOSA ESCALADA, JUAN MANUEL, 1860-1939.   Educated at
Buenos Aires and returned to Paraguay after the 1865-
1870 war to become an active member of the Liberal
Party.   Figured prominently in the 1904 Revolution
which brought his party to power, but returned to Buenos Aires in 1908 where he resided until his death.
Author of several historical studies, and editor-publish-
er of several periodicals in both Asunción and Buenos
Aires.

SOSA-TEJEDOR TREATY, MAY 20, 1875. Original draft
    treaty negotiated at Rio de Janeiro but later summarily
    rejected by Paraguay, which sought to prescribe Ar-
    gentine-Paraguayan territorial boundaries following the
    Triple Alliance War. Jaime Sosa, the Paraguayan
    negotiator, was denounced and removed from office for
    his actions, although he claimed he had signed the
    draft treaty under duress.

SOUZA, DIEGO DE. Brazil's Captain-general who offered
    to aid Spanish Governor Bernardo de Velasco at Asun-
    ción in May, 1811, provided that Velasco would recog-
    nize the sovereignty of Portugal's Carlota as ruler of
    Spain's provinces. Rumors of the negotiations resulted
    in Velasco's permanent expulsion as Paraguay's gov-
    ernor by the new revolutionary Junta.

SOUZA, MANOEL MARQUES DE see PORTO ALEGRE,
    BARÃO DE. One of Brazil's most able army corps
    commanders during the Triple Alliance War.

SOUZA NETTO, GENERAL FELIPE. Brazilian Rio Grande
    do Sul province politician and landowner who in 1864
    sought to convince the Imperial government to inter-
    vene in Uruguay because of alleged Uruguayan border
    depredations. An incident in the Uruguayan episode
    leading to the Triple Alliance War.

SOYO, OR SOO-YOSOPY. A type of hot meat soup, one of
    Paraguay's most typical dishes.

SPERATTI, ADELA, 1865-1902 see ESCUELA GRADUADA
    DE PERCEPTORES, and SPERATTI, CELSA. First
    director of the Escuela Graduada de Perceptores, a
    teacher-training institution inaugurated at Asunción in
    1890. Also appointed director of the Escuela Normal
    de Maestras. Both Adela and her sister Celsa were
    pioneers in improving teaching methods and introducing
    education for women. Both were trained at the Normal
    School at Concepción del Uruguay, an Argentine institu-
    tion at which the Americans, Isabel and Raquel King,
    were teachers. Both were contracted for by Domingo
    F. Sarmiento, Argentina's educator-president.

SPERATTI, CELSA, 1868-1938 see also SPERATTI,
    ADELA. With her sister Adela, one of the founders
    of Paraguay's normal school system.

STAGNI, COLONEL PABLO see FRENTE DE GUERRA.
Member of the ultra-nationalist and pro-Fascist Frente
de Guerra during the World War II Morínigo administration, and chief of the Paraguayan air force.

STATE OF SIEGE see ESTADO DE SITIO.

STEFANICH, JUAN, 1889-   . Asunción intellectual and
one of the major supporters of the 1936 Febrerista
movement. Served as foreign minister during the short-
lived Febrerista regime of Colonel Rafael Franco, 1936-
1937. One of the founders of the Liga Nacional Independiente. Author of numerous political essays and
historical studies, among them: La guerra del Chaco
(1934), and a series of pro-Febrerista works entitled
Capítulos de la revolución paraguaya.

STEWART, DR. WILLIAM. Former British army doctor who
arrived in Paraguay as a penniless survivor of an ill-
fated colonization experiment prior to the Triple Alliance War. He served on Paraguay's side during most
of the war, but turned against Marshal President López
after capture by allied forces. Later embroiled in the
mystery over the disappearance of monies and other
valuables allegedly entrusted to him by Mrs. Elisa
Alicia Lynch, consort of Marshal President López.

STICA see SERVICIO TECNICO INTERAMERICANO DE
COOPERACION AGRICOLA.

STROESSNER, GENERAL ALFREDO, 1912-   . President
of Paraguay since 1954 and the dean in terms of lon-
gevity in office of all Latin American chief executives.
Native of the southern Paraná River port city of Encarnación whose father was a German immigrant. A dedicated professional soldier, General Stroessner had a
distinguished military career which included service in
the Chaco War and defense of Paraguay's southern frontier during the 1947 major revolution. Promoted to
general-of-division in 1951, he was by 1954 the youngest
and most competent of Paraguay's general officers. In
that year he led the military revolt which toppled the
Federico Chaves government. He assumed the presidency in August, 1954, and has since been reelected
three times, in 1958, 1963, and 1968. Strongly anti-
Communist in his beliefs and policies, he sent a Paraguayan army contingent to the Dominican Republic as a

part of the OAS forces in the 1965 episode. In 1968
he formally visited Washington, the second Paraguayan
president to be invited to the United States. His administration rests upon close cooperation between the
military and the dominant Colorado Party. Its goal
could best be defined as establishing tranquility and
progress with order providing the base for gradually
expanding liberties. Adherents called this policy that
of a "guided democracy." By the 1970's General
Stroessner's long-term presidency had given Paraguay
an unparalleled era of peace, stability and progress.

SUAREZ DE TOLEDO, MARTIN. Interim governor following
the arrest and expulsion of Governor Felipe de Cáceres
in 1572 on charges of suspected lutheranism. Noted
for having encouraged the founding of Santa Fe de la
Vera Cruz in 1573--Argentina's Santa Fe along the
lower Paraná River, and of the original city of Villa
Rica de Espíritu Santo in 1570 east of the upper Paraná River from Yguazú Falls. Married María Ana de
Sanabria, daughter of Diego de Sanabria and widow of
Hernando de Trejo. Their son was the famous creole
governor of Paraguay, Hernando Arias de Saavedra--
Hernandarias.

SUPREMO (EL) see also FRANCIA, DR. JOSE GASPAR
RODRIGUEZ DE, and EL DIFUNTO.

- T -

TABAMPAE. One of three sectors into which land around
Jesuit Indian reductions was divided. Tabampaé, the
largest and most suitable sector, was reserved for
cultivation of crops for consumption by the community
as a whole.

TABAPY, BATTLE OF see TAVAPY, BATTLE OF.

TABARANGUE, CHURCH OF. Located in the Encarnación
area of southern Paraguay near the Trinidad and Jesús
missions. Begun in 1767, the year the Jesuits were
expelled, the church was eventually completed and still
remains an excellent example of the period's architec-
ture.

TABAS. Villages and small inhabited points of the Guaraní

Indian tribes living in the vicinity of Asunción. Commencing in the late sixteenth century, Franciscan missionaries established numerous missions which later became cities at the sites of these "tabas."

TABERE, CHIEF. Chief of a Guaraní tribe north of Asunción in the late 1540's alleged to have been responsible for the death of early Portuguese explorer Aleixo García. On his refusal to inform Governor Alvar Núñez Cabeza de Vaca of circumstances surrounding García and his rumored son, a Spanish force under Alonso Riquelme annihilated Taberé and his followers.

TABOADA, ANTONIO. Post Triple Alliance War era politician credited with the founding in 1887 of Paraguay's Liberal Party.

TACUARI, BATTLE OF. Occurring March 9, 1811, in extreme south Paraguay, against the Argentine invasion forces of Manuel Belgrano, this proved another Paraguayan victory following that of Paraguarí or Cerro Porteño on January 19. Significant for its revelation to Paraguay's force that it could defend itself, and that it could not count upon aid by the Spanish governor, who fled the field of Cerro Porteño. Both factors were decisive in the subsequent May movement for independence.

TACUARI, S.S. Small but modern gunboat purchased in England by Francisco Solano López during his 1853-1854 European mission. Later involved in the Buzzard-Grappler incident of 1859 in which the Tacuarí was stopped by the two British ships from proceeding upstream on the Paraná. Also Paraguay's flagship at the June, 1865, naval battle of Riachuelo in the Triple Alliance War.

TALAVERA, CORPORAL LIBORIO (OLIVERIO) see also PITIANTUTA, LAKE. Commander of a five-man patrol who was killed at Fortín Carlos Antonio López in June, 1932, in an incident which began the Chaco War.

TALAVERA, MANUEL ANTONIO, 1761-1814. One of the most prominent figures among Paraguayan intellectuals of the late colonial era. Educated at Córdoba in Argentina and spent most of his life in Chile. A royalist sympathizer, he specialized in Chilean revolutionary movements in his research and writings.

TALAVERA, NATALICIO DE MARIA, 1839-1867.   Recognized
as the most capable Paraguayan journalist during the
Triple Alliance War.   Educated in Europe and a long-
time staff member of El Semanario, he wrote numerous
articles and essays depicting life in the Humaitá defenses and championing Paraguay's position.

TALAVERA, FATHER RAMON.   Jesuit priest and a vociferous anti-Stroessner spokesman who in 1959 sought to
organize invasion attempts into Paraguay from his exile
in Argentina.   Small invasion parties representing the
dissident 14th of May Movement were easily routed or
captured.

TAM   see   TRANSPORTE AEREO MILITAR.

TAMANDARE, BARÃO DE   see   LISBOA, JOAQUIM MAR-
QUES.   Admiral Joaquim Marques Lisbôa, commander
of Brazil's naval squadron in the Triple Alliance War
until December, 1866.   Foremost Brazilian naval hero
whose birthday anniversary, December 13 (1807), is
still celebrated as Navy Day.   Tamandaré was succeeded in command on the Paraguay River by Admiral
José Joaquim Ignacio.

TAPE AVIRU.   Guaraní Indian name for the Camino Real,
or "Royal Road," which led from São Vicente on the
Brazilian Atlantic coast across the Guairá region to
Paraguay.

TAPE INDIANS.   Guaraní tribe living to the south of Paraguay in the pre-conquest era.   Many of them reportedly
comprised the peoples christianized and encouraged to
live in reductions during the Jesuit mission era.

TAPUA-GUAZU.   Like the legend of El Dorado, a fable
which enticed Spanish explorers to search the Chaco
for gold and silver lodes.   Tapúa-guazú was said by
Indians to be a rocky hill from which a fabulously rich
land could be seen.   Scouts of Alvar Núñez Cabeza de
Vaca's 1543 expedition up the Paraguay River sought
vainly to locate the area.

TAUNAY, CAPTAIN ALFREDO D'ESGRAGNOLLE.   The
Visconde de Taunay, a well-known nineteenth-century
Brazilian novelist, also served in Brazil's army during
the Paraguayan War.   One of his major works, the

Retreat from Laguna, describes the tragedies which befell an army expedition seeking to invade Paraguay south from Mato Grosso province. In the war's later stages, Taunay was editor of the official Brazilian army operations record, Diário do Exército. His memoirs of the war are also a valuable primary information source.

TAVAPY, BATTLE OF see also COMUNERO REVOLT. A battle in January, 1735, occurring about half-way between Asunción and Encarnación, at which Buenos Aires royalist forces decisively beat an irregular Paraguayan Comunero force thus terminating the Comunero Revolt.

TAYI, ACTION AT. Fought November 2, 1867, and an allied victory in the Triple Alliance War which resulted in complete encirclement of the Paraguayan fortified position at Humaitá.

TAYLOR, ALONSO. English stonemason who arrived in Paraguay in 1860 and who was employed during the administration of Carlos Antonio López for work on the Asunción improvement program. Assisted particularly in the construction of the National Palace and railway station, both of which buildings are still principal historic sites. Imprisoned by Marshal President López during the 1868 Conspiracy episode, Taylor managed to live out the war and escape with his life.

TEATRO MUNICIPAL. National Theater. Located in downtown Asunción and constructed in 1863. Now known as the Teatro Municipal Ignacio A. Pane.

TEBICUARY, BATTLE OF THE. Fought August 25, 1724, and an impressive victory of a Comunero army under Dr. José de Antequera y Castro over a mixed Spanish-Jesuit mission Indian army under Baltazar García Ros. Following this high point in his career, Dr. Antequera was subsequently forced to flee from Asunción in 1725 upon the arrival of Bruno Mauricio de Zavala from Buenos Aires.

TEBICUARY RIVER. Runs from east to west and empties into the Paraguay River about 90 miles (150 kms) south of Asunción. Drains the central south region and is the major outlet for the Lake Ypoa system of lakes and swamps.

TEJADA SORZANO, JOSE LUIS. President of Bolivia following resignation in December, 1934, of Daniel Salamanca
due to continued Paraguayan victories in the Chaco War.
Shortly thereafter in January, 1935, Paraguay's advance was stopped at the Parapití River near Villa
Montes.

TEJEDOR, CARLOS see also SOSA ESCALADA, JAIME.
Argentine foreign minister who negotiated the 1875 proposed treaty for Paraguayan-Argentine post Triple Alliance War territorial frontiers.

TELEGRAPH SERVICES see TRUENFELDT, FISCHER
VON. Construction in the immediate pre-Triple Alliance War era of an efficient telegraph line from Asunción to the southern defense bastion of Humaitá represented for Paraguay a distinct "first" and modern in-
novation among the Plata nations. Built by German
engineer Robert Fischer von Truenfeldt, the line provided Marshal President Francisco Solano López with
rapid communications to his government headquarters.
Railroad rails, used as the telegraph posts, may still
be seen in their original positions at the Humaitá area.

TELLEZ, JOSE GABRIEL. Recorded as the director of
Asunción's only public elementary school in 1805 on
the eve of the independence movement and the era of
El Supremo.

TERCIOS. Packages of yerba maté of approximately six
pounds, used similar to currency in the barter trade
of the late colonial and early independence eras.

TERERE see also YERBA MATE. A particularly delicious
version of Paraguay's yerba maté beverage served
cold.

TESTANOVA, BLAS. Genoese physician recorded among
the professionals at Asunción in the early colonial period. Probably the only physician in La Plata in 1541.

TEVEGO. A feared and fearsome prison camp during the
era of Dr. Francia in which political prisoners were
jailed, usually never to return alive. Probably located on the Chaco side of the Paraguay River approximately across from the port city of Concepción.

THOMPSON, COLONEL GEORGE, 1839-1876. Outstanding among the numerous foreign technicians on Paraguay's side during the Triple Alliance War. Thompson came to Paraguay in 1858 as a railway technician, and then became an army engineer officer at the beginning of the war. He served throughout its entire length and was especially noted for his work in preparing the Curupaity trench lines for the army under General José E. Díaz prior to the battle of September 22, 1866. Given command of the Paraguayan garrison at the fortified river post at Angostura in late 1869, he only surrendered to the allies when his position became hopeless. Returning briefly to England, he wrote his famed first-hand account of the war entitled The War in Paraguay (1869). Following Cerro Corá and the death of Francisco Solano López, he returned once more to Paraguay where he settled in Asunción, married, and died in 1876, an official of the Paraguayan Central Railroad. He was the only foreigner to attain field rank in Paraguay's army during the war.

THOMPSON, MAJOR PABLO see also CAMPICHUELO, ACTION AT. Paraguayan commander at the December 19, 1810, skirmish with Manuel Belgrano's Argentine invasion force.

THOMPSON, PAUL see also PARAGUAY CENTRAL RAIL-ROAD. English engineer, probably associated with Burrel, Valpy and Thompson, who constructed the first rail link between Asunción and the suburb of Trinidad, inaugurated on September 21, 1861.

THORNTON, SIR EDWARD. British minister at Buenos Aires responsible for River Plate affairs in the pre-Triple Alliance War period, and later minister to Brazil. Sought to intercede in Uruguay's Blanco-Colorado Party dispute in efforts to prevent the war's outbreak.

TIMBO. Paraguayan river fortification during the Triple Alliance War, located on the Chaco side of the Paraguay River north of the Humaitá defensive position. Abandoned after the 1868 evacuation and surrender of Humaitá.

TOBA INDIANS. Eastern Chaco tribe found along the Paraguay River in the colonial period.

TOBATI see also SERVICE, ELMAN R. Small interior
village located about 40 miles east of Asunción and
about 12 miles north of Caacupé. Site in 1948-1949
of an exhaustive socio/anthropological research project
by the American team of Elman R. and Helen S. Service.

TODOS LOS SANTOS see also SAN MARCOS. One of two
brigantines which reached Asunción in 1556 and took
on cargo which probably represented the first instance
of Paraguayan foreign trade.

TOLDERIA. Spanish term for a native Indian village. An
example is the Makká Indian Toldería along the Paraguay River near Asunción.

TOLEDO, FORTIN. South central Paraguayan Chaco military
post and scene of some of the Chaco War's most desperate fighting in early 1933. The battlefield, inacces-
sible except by small aircraft, still remains in a virgin
state replete with trenches, machine gun posts, dug-
outs, and command posts.

TORDESILLAS, TREATY OF. Agreement between Portugal
and Spain signed June 7, 1494, which provided that all
land discovered west of a north/south line 370 leagues
to the west of the Cape Verde Islands would be regarded as Spanish, while land found to the east would
be Portuguese. Brazil thus became Portuguese territory following Cabral's 1500 discovery voyage.

TORO, COLONEL DAVID. Bolivian field commander in the
late 1934 phase of the Chaco War, who succeeded temporarily in halting Paraguay's advance toward the Andean foothill region.

TORRE, FATHER PEDRO FERNANDEZ DE LA. Bishop of
Asunción, 1556-1571, and credited with the official
beginning of Paraguay's church system. Officiated at
the death of Governor Domingo Martínez de Irala in
1556.

TORRES, FATHER DIEGO DE. Early Jesuit missionary who
arrived in Paraguay in the early seventeenth century,
and established the bases for the future Jesuit mission
system.

TOUNEDOU, FATHER JUAN B. see also COLEGIO DE
SAN JOSE. French priest-educator, member of the
Congregation of the Sacred Heart, and founder in June,
1904, of Asunción's Colegio de San José.

TRANS CHACO HIGHWAY. A 480-mile segment of the Pan
American Highway running from Asunción to the Bolivian border in the Andean foothills. Completed in 1964.
Constructed with American aid, it provides access to
Chaco points previously reached only by air, and especially to the Mennonite colony area around Filadelfia,
a ranching center which supplies much of Asunción's
dairy production requirements.

TRANSPORTE AEREO MILITAR--TAM. Military Air Transport which provides regular scheduled public passenger
and cargo service to most important interior points.
Similar services are also provided by LATN--Lineas
Aéreas de Transporte Nacional, formerly privately
owned and nationalized since 1954.

TRATADO DE PERMUTA. "Treaty of Exchange." Negotiated in 1750 between Portugal and Spain whereby the
former gave up claims to the Río do la Plata port of
Colonia de Sacramento in exchange for possession of
the area occupied by seven Jesuit Guaraní Indian missions along the upper left bank of the Uruguay River.

TREATY OF FRIENDSHIP, COMMERCE AND NAVIGATION;
UNITED STATES AND PARAGUAY. Concluded February 4, 1859, at Asunción during the visit there by the
mission of Special Commissioner James B. Bowlin.
Ratified by Paraguay February 11, 1859, by the United
States on March 7, 1860, and still in force. Supplanted
a previous treaty of 1853 which was ineffective due to
failure to exchange ratifications.

TREATY OF OCTOBER 12, 1811. First treaty signed between Paraguay and the new Buenos Aires Junta providing for conditions of alliance, commerce and friendship.

TREATY OF PEACE OF 1938. Definitive agreement of
peace and frontier limits signed July 21, 1938, between
Paraguay and Bolivia formally terminating the Chaco
War. See also Peace Protocol of June 1935, and
Peace Conference of 1935.

TREJO Y SANABRIA, FATHER HERNANDO DEL, ? -1614.
Bishop Hernando de. Brother of Governor Hernandarias who in 1614 inaugurated the University of Córdoba,
in modern Argentina, and the first institution of higher
learning in La Plata. Many of Paraguay's late colonial
and early independence era leaders, including particularly Dr. José Gaspar Rodríguez de Francia, received
their education at this institution.

TRENCH OF '69 see PIRIBEBUY. The remains of a
trench, still visible until the 1960's, in which Paraguayan defenders resisted allied assaults on the city
of Piribebuy, August 12, 1869, in the late stages of
the Triple Alliance War. Reference to the earthwork
is frequently found in Paraguayan histories of the war.

TRES BOCAS. Three mouths. Frequently used name for
the confluence of the Paraguay and Paraná rivers forming the main Paraná. Located slightly below the Humaitá area in extreme southwestern Paraguay.

TRIBUNA (LA), ASUNCION. Most prominent, impartial and
oldest of modern Paraguay's newspapers, founded December 31, 1925. A daily.

TRIBUNA (LA), BUENOS AIRES. Buenos Aires newspaper
particularly vociferous in its attacks on Paraguay during the immediate pre-Triple Alliance War era.

TRIBUNALES DE SANGRE. Special military courts convened on orders of Marshal President Francisco Solano López in 1868 to try persons suspected of treason
against him. The episode, known as the conspiracy
period, is one of the more controversial matters of
the regime of Paraguay's Iron Marshal. A considerable number of military and civil officials were tried,
imprisoned or executed, and suspicion spread to include even the American Minister Charles A. Washburn. Alleged brutalities were given wide publicity by
the allies. No definitive proof of the existence of a
conspiracy against Paraguay's Marshal President has
yet been established.

TRIFON ROJAS, MANUEL, ? -1869. Young Asunción intellectual who became editor of La Estrella, the army's
last newspaper published briefly at Piribebuy in the
late stages of the Triple Alliance War. Falling into

disgrace, Trifón Rojas was reduced to the ranks and later died of hunger and malnutrition on the retreat to Cerro Corá.

TRINIDAD. Situated in the outskirts of Asunción near the Jardín Botánico, Trinidad is a small township which features a large, ancient and picturesque cathedral in the central crypt of which President Carlos Antonio López was originally buried. Near Trinidad there exists the well-preserved "Ybyraí" estate of Dr. José Gaspar Rodríguez de Francia, the famed El Supremo of Paraguay's early independence era.

TRINIDAD, REDUCTION OF see also JESUITS. Regarded as the most important of several ruins of Jesuit reductions or missions in southeastern Paraguay, this site is located about 20 miles northeast of the Paraná River port of Encarnación. Remarkable for its scenic location, for its considerable size, and for the remaining pieces of Indian-made sculpture still found there. Now a national monument.

TRIPLE ALLIANCE, WAR OF THE see also PARAGUAYAN WAR and GUERRA DE '70. Known in history by its three names, the third one or "Guerra de '70" being preferred in Paraguay. Lasting five and a half years between November, 1864, and March, 1870, it remains a basic water-mark in Paraguay's history, as well as in that of the Plata region. Like the American Civil War, it spelled the end of an age. In Paraguay's case, it terminated the age of the three great authoritarian leaders of the nation's formative era--Dr. Francia, Carlos Antonio López and Francisco Solano López, and thrust a brand of liberal democracy upon a nation which was wholly unprepared for such experiments. It resulted in the loss for Paraguay of a considerable land area in the satisfaction of allied territorial pretensions, and of casualties equal to almost two-thirds of the national population. At its end Paraguay bordered as close to total annihilation as any nation in the world's history. The event left a searing mark which still represents both a socio-economic and a political factor in modern Paraguay's mold.

TRIPLE ALLIANCE TREATY. Formally signed May 1, 1865, at Buenos Aires, this treaty aligned Imperial Brazil with Argentina and Uruguay against Paraguay. Its pro-

visions outline the objectives of the allies in seeking to
remove President Francisco Solano López from power.
A "secret" protocol, however, specifies that each par-
ticipating nation shall have the right to secure the maximum of its territorial claims at Paraguay's expense.
Publication of this proviso in Great Britain through a
copy leaked by Uruguayan sources resulted in intense
protest from other Latin American republics, and generated sympathy for Paraguay's cause.

TRIUMVIRATE OF 1840 see also JUNTA PROVISORIA OF
1840. Organized after the fall of the Provisional Governing Board of 1840, and an interim government after
the death of Dr. Francia until it was overthrown by a
coup of early 1841.

TRIUMVIRATE OF 1869. Formed August 15, 1869, as a
provisional government of Paraguay pending termination
of the Triple Alliance War. Its composition included
Cirilo Antonio Rivarola, Carlos Loizaga and José Díaz
de Bedoya. The latter two were members of the Paraguayan Legion, an association of Paraguayan exiles opposed to Marshal President López and fighting on the
allied side. The Triumvirate dissolved a year later
with the formal promulgation of the Constitution of
1870.

TROCHE, MAURICIO JOSE DE, 1790-1840. Official who
turned over Asunción's barracks to the revolutionaries
the night of May 14, 1811, initiating Paraguay's independence movement from Spain. Probably executed in
1840.

TRUENFELDT, R. FISCHER VON. German technician employed in prewar Paraguay for the installation of the
telegraph line from Asunción to the key defensive bastion at Humaitá. Remained in Paraguay during the
Triple Alliance War as the director of telegraph services, one of the first in South America. Also responsible for the development of Caraguatá pulp (species
of Agave plant) as an ingenious substitute for newsprint
for the publication of newspapers following the allied
blockade of the Paraná River.

TRUJILLO, MANUEL, 1846-1945. Triple Alliance War veteran who published his Gestas guerreras, wartime recollections, in 1911.

TUBAMPAE.   One of three sectors into which land around
    Jesuit Indian reductions was divided.   Tubampaé, or
    "Propriedad de Dios"--God's Property, was utilized
    for the cultivation of products for charity or for the
    limited outside commerce of the mission.

TUPAMAROS.   Modern Castroite terrorist party in Uruguay
    responsible for widespread revolutionary activity, as-
    saults, robberies, assassinations and internationally
    publicized kidnappings in the late 1960's and early
    1970's.   Named after Tupac Amarú, leader of the last
    major Inca Indian revolt against Spanish rule in colo-
    nial Peru.   In spring 1972, the Tupamaros were al-
    leged to have agreed upon a plan to spread their sub-
    versive campaign into Paraguay.

TUPI INDIANS.   Tribe living in the Guairá region along the
    upper Paraná River, subdued by Martínez de Irala dur-
    ing the mid-sixteenth century.

TUPI-GUARANI INDIANS.   Not a specific Indian tribe, but
    rather the term denoting the general Indian family or
    cluster of tribes which inhabited the Amazon and La
    Plata basins at the time of the Spanish conquest.
    Branches of the general family had specific names such
    as Carío, Chiriguano, Tapés, and Itatines.   Most spoke
    a common dialect, unknown to Chaco tribes, and called
    "Guaraní."   The language is still used universally in
    modern Paraguay.

TURCOS.   Spanish term used in Paraguay and elsewhere in
    Spanish America to denote persons of Middle Eastern
    origin, e.g., Syrians, Persians, Lebanese, and Turks.

TURU.   A type of horn emitting a strange, peculiar noise,
    used frequently by Paraguay's soldiers during the siege
    of Humaitá in the Triple Alliance War.   Used derisive-
    ly to note misses by allied artillery fire.   Occasional-
    ly referred to as "turututús."

TUYU-CUE, ACTION AT.   Fought October 3, 1867, and an
    action of the siege of Humaitá in the Triple Alliance
    War prior to the major battle of Second Tuyuty.   Para-
    guayan cavalry under Major Bernardino Caballero, fu-
    ture President of the Republic and founder of the Col-
    orado Party, succeeded in temporarily delaying the al-
    lied envelopment movement around Humaitá.

TUYUTY, BATTLES OF. Two enormously sanguinary battles
of this name in the Humaitá theater of operations on
May 24, 1866, and November 3, 1867, proved the
greatest in terms of casualties in Latin America's history. Strategically, both were allied victories since
the Paraguayan army in each instance was unable to
achieve its objectives. For their impact in slowing allied siege operations at Humaitá, however, they are regarded in Paraguay as victories in the War of the Triple Alliance.

TWITE, CHARLES. British minerology expert contracted
for service in Paraguay during the administration of
Carlos Antonio López. Arriving in 1864, he remained
during the Triple Alliance War. A book containing a
catalog of minerals and his notes was published at Caraguatay in December, 1869, and is included in the
Rio Branco Collection captured by Brazilian troops during the war.

- U -

UGARTE, LOPE DE. Conquistador and follower of Alvar
Núñez Cabeza de Vaca, recorded as present at the
ceremonies inaugurating the latter as governor at Asunción in 1542.

UNION GERMANICA DEL PARAGUAY. Pro-Nazi propaganda
distributing organization during the World War II era.

UNION NACIONAL PARAGUAYA. Type of National Front
political party formed on August 27, 1959, by dissident
Liberal and Febrerista leaders in exile. Strongly opposed to the Alfredo Stroessner government. Though
still existent, its activities have been of minor scope
and importance since the unsuccessful, small-scale invasion attempts of 1959-1960.

UNION NACIONAL REVOLUCIONARIA see also FEBRERIS-
TA PARTY. Founded at Asunción in 1936 as a new
party reflecting the views and platform of the Febrerista Revolt headed by Colonel Rafael Franco. The
party was still not fully organized when Franco was
overthrown in 1937. Subsequently in 1945 at Montevideo, former members of the Unión Nacional reorganized the movement under the name "Concentración

Revolucionaria Febrerista." The present name, Partido Revolutionario Febrerista, was adopted in 1951 during a Buenos Aires convention. Colonel Rafael Franco
has consistently been its president.

UNION PARAGUAYO-ARGENTINA. Joint political-economic
pact signed in 1953 during the apex of close relationships between the government of Federico Chaves and
that of Juan Domingo Perón of Argentina. In 1954
Perón authorized the return to Paraguay of trophies
taken by Argentina during the Triple Alliance War.

UNITED CHRISTIAN MISSIONARY SOCIETY. Society whose
financial support promoted the establishment in 1920 of
Asunción's Colegio Internacional.

UNITED STATES AND PARAGUAY NAVIGATION COMPANY
see also HOPKINS, EDWARD AUGUSTUS. Company
formed with Rhode Island capital in 1852 by Edward
Augustus Hopkins for establishing business in Paraguay.
Hampered from the start by the wreck off the Brazilian
coast of the vessel carrying his supplies and equipment,
Hopkins subsequently had his difficulties compounded by
bad relations with President Carlos Antonio López and
the delicate Water Witch incident of 1855. Expelled
from Paraguay and ruined, Hopkins pressed complaints
in the company's name which became an issue of an
arbitration proceedings in 1860. Though the award was
favorable to Paraguay, Hopkins kept pressing his claims
without success until his death in 1888.

UNIVERSIDAD CATOLICA. Paraguay's currently second
largest institution of higher learning ranking after the
Universidad Nacional de Asunción. Located in Asunción
and founded in April, 1960. Its Faculty of Economics
and Law is located at the site of the old prison dating
from the era of Dr. José Gaspar Rodríguez de Francia.

UNIVERSIDAD NACIONAL DE ASUNCION. Paraguay's foremost institution of higher learning, inaugurated in the
1890's through the initiative principally of José Segundo
Decoud.

UNIVERSITY STUDENT FEDERATION see FEDERACION
DE ESTUDIANTES DEL PARAGUAY.

URBIETA, JUAN GREGORIO. Bishop of Asunción appointed

by the Pope in the later years of the Carlos Antonio López regime.

URBIETA, MAJOR MARTIN. Commander of the Paraguayan force which on December 29, 1864, captured the Brazilian military outpost of Dourados in Mato Grosso at the opening of the Triple Alliance War. The Brazilian commander of the post, Antonio João Ribeiro, who died in the action, became one of Brazil's foremost military heroes. Major Urbieta later figured in Paraguay's defense against Brazil's 1867 attempted invasion which became the famed Retreat from Laguna.

URIARTE, HIGINIO. Vice president to President Juan Bautista Gill. Became provisional president during 1877-1878 following the assassination of the latter in April, 1877, by political opponents. Uriarte was succeeded by Cándido Bareiro.

URQUIZA, JUSTO JOSE. Powerful caudillo chieftain of Argentina's Entre Ríos Province who in 1852 defeated the army of Buenos Aires under Juan Manuel de Rosas at the battle of Caseros. His emissary, Dr. Santiago Derqui, signed a treaty with Paraguay recognizing its independence and establishing national boundaries. Argentina's congress subsequently declined ratification of the treaty. Later in 1858, Urquiza acted as mediator in the dispute between Paraguay and the United States in the Hopkins case. His refusal to join with Paraguay against Mitre's new Argentina, and Uruguay and Brazil, was a discouraging setback to the plans of Francisco Solano López at the outbreak of the Triple Alliance War.

URQUIZA, COLONEL WALDINO. Son of Argentina's Entre Ríos province caudillo, General Justo José de Urquiza. His effort to aid Uruguay's Blanco government with a small Entre Ríos armed band was one of the series of events leading to the Triple Alliance War.

URRUNAGA, JOSE DE. Spanish resident at Asunción involved in a 1719 plot with José de Avalos y Mendoza against Governor Diego de los Reyes Balmaceda. The episode caused Dr. José de Antequera y Castro, member of the Audiencia de Charcas, to be sent as an investigator to Asunción, an event preluding the Comunero movement.

URRUTIA, CAPTAIN MIGUEL DE. Conquistador at Asunción

in the mid-sixteenth century executed by Governor Martínez de Irala for suspected treason against him.

URUGUAY RIVER.   Along with the Paraná-Paraguay system,
the Uruguay flows into the estuary known as the Río
de la Plata.   At its northern headwaters region, the
Uruguay flows only about 50 miles from the Paraná
River at Encarnación-Posadas.   The zone between the
two was selected by the Jesuits as the principal center
for their reduction system.   In the early stages of the
Triple Alliance War, Paraguay's eastern invasion force
proceeded south along the Uruguay River until it was
defeated and forced to surrender at the siege of Uruguayana in 1865.

URUGUAYANA, SIEGE OF.   The eastern arm of Paraguay's
two-pronged offensive toward La Plata suffered a major
defeat with the surrender at Uruguayana, Brazil, on
September 18, 1865, of the forces of Colonel Antonio
de la Cruz Estigarribia.   The remainder of Paraguay's
army was recalled to the fortified bastion of Humaitá.

URUTAU, BIRD.   A curious and nearly extinct nocturnal bird
species in Paraguay.   Noted for its shyness and its
plaintive call.   The subject of the following poem by
Argentina's Carlos Guido y Spano referring to Paraguay's plight after the Triple Alliance War:
  Llora, llora, urutaú
  en las ramas del yatay
  ya no existe el Paraguay
  donde nací como tú
  Llora, llora, urutaú.

- V -

VALDERAS, JUAN DE.   Notary at Asunción before whom
Governor Domingo Martínez de Irala signed his last
will and testament on March 13, 1556.   The document
is a revealing record of the life of one of Paraguay's
most important historical figures.

VALDES, ALFONSO JUAN DE.   Governor of Buenos Aires
who utilized an army of Guaraní mission Indians in
1705 to besiege Portuguese-held Colônia do Sacramento,
a La Plata riverport across from Buenos Aires.

VALDOVINOS, DR. ARNALDO, 1908-   . Poet, novelist,
    journalist and politician. Minister of Agriculture in the
    1946 cabinet of President Higinio Morínigo on the eve
    of the major 1947 Revolution. Represented the growing
    demand of the Febrerista Party for a larger role in the
    government.

VALENZUELA, ALONSO DE. Spanish conquistador recorded
    as present at the 1542 inauguration as governor at
    Asunción of Alvar Núñez Cabeza de Vaca.

VALOIS RIVAROLA, FORTIN. Paraguayan south central
    Chaco army post near which the incident of Fortín
    Mariscal López took place in December, 1928, a pre-
    lude to the Chaco War. Named after a famed Triple
    Alliance War cavalry hero.

VANGUARDIA, FORTIN see also VANGUARDIA INCIDENT.
    Bolivian fortified Chaco outpost north of Bahía Negra,
    attacked by Paraguayan troops on December 5, 1928,
    an incident preluding the Chaco War. Subsequently on
    December 14, Bolivian troops attacked and captured
    Paraguay's Fortín Boquerón in reprisal.

VANGUARDIA INCIDENT. Bolivian Chaco fort near Bahía
    Negra attacked by Paraguayan troops in 1928, an inci-
    dent leading to the Chaco War.

VAPOR-CUE. Located along the Yhaguy River about six
    miles from the city of Caraguatay, this site marks the
    point where the remaining vessels of Paraguay's navy
    were burned and scuttled in the last stages of the Tri-
    ple Alliance War. The remains of several are still
    visible.

VARELA, HECTOR F. Also known by his pen-name "Orion,"
    this Argentine journalist and part-owner of the former
    Buenos Aires newspaper La Tribuna, visited Asunción
    in the pre-Triple Alliance War era. His subsequent
    book, entitled Elisa Lynch, though highly romanticized,
    is a useful source on the peoples and places of that
    period.

VARELA, MARIANO. Argentine foreign minister who in
    1870 proclaimed his nation's position toward defeated
    Paraguay as "la victoria no da derechos"--wartime
    victory does not automatically grant rights to territo-

rial acquisitions. Argentina's position was opposed to that of Brazil which contemplated territorial acquisition according to Triple Alliance Treaty terms. Argentina's position prevailed, but in subsequent treaty negotiations Brazil's claims were satisfied while Argentina's claims were largely rejected by the Hayes Arbitration Award of 1878.

VARGAS, COLONEL JUAN BALTAZAR. Paraguayan national sent by Juan Martín de Pueyrredón, supreme director of the Argentine Confederation, to observe secretly and conspire against the early regime of Dr. José Gaspar Rodríguez de Francia. Arrested and executed in 1818 on the eve of the Conspiracy plot of 1820.

VARGAS MACHUCA, FATHER JUAN JOSE DE. Leader of an unsuccessful last effort in 1747 to promote a re-crudescence of the Comunero movement. Governor Rafael de la Moneda quashed the plot but allowed Father Vargas Machuca to escape alive.

VARGAS MACHUCA, FATHER MIGUEL DE. Prominent Co-munero leader at Asunción during the governorship of Martín de Barua in the period between the flight of Dr. José de Antequera in 1724 and the arrival of Fernando Mompox in 1730.

VARGAS PEÑA, BENJAMIN, 1910-   . Doctor of medicine and historian. Author of numerous books and essays on both medical and historical topics, among them: Vencer o morir (1933), La bandera del Paraguay (1946), Los ideales del Paraguay (1954), and Ensayo sobre la historia del ejército paraguayo.

VASCONSELLOS, VICTOR NATALICIO. Historian and edu-cator. Director of the Colegio Nacional de la Capital, the official high school at Asunción. Author of Leccio-nes de historia Paraguaya, the most widely used and up-to-date government-approved text on Paraguay's his-torical evolution.

VASQUEZ, JOSE ANTONIO, 1924-   . Poet, cinema critic-reviewer and historian. Author of several works on world history topics as well as of Paraguayan history. Founder of the "Club Universitario del Ciné-arts," first organization of its nature in Paraguay. Noted particu-larly for his 1961 study, El Dr. Francia visto y oído

por sus contempóraneos (Dr. Francia, as seen and
heard by his contemporaries.

VASQUEZ, NICOLAS. Paraguayan foreign minister in the
Carlos Antonio López administration who, in 1856, ex-
plained to U.S. Commissioner Richard Fitzpatrick that
the 1853 U.S.-Paraguayan treaty could not be altered
since it had been ratified by Paraguay.

VELASCO Y HUIDOBRO, BERNARDO DE. Last Spanish governor of Paraguay, deposed by the revolutionary movement of May, 1811.

VELASCO Y YEGROS, MARIA JOSEFA FABIANA. Cousin
of Fulgencio Yegros y Ledesma, former governor of
Paraguay, and mother of Dr. José Gaspar Rodríguez de
Francia.

VELASQUEZ, RAFAEL ELADIO, 1926-   . University professor, jurist, politician and historian. Professor of
colonial era history at the Universidad Nacional. Contributor to several academic periodicals and author of
numerous studies of Paraguayan history, particularly of
the colonial era and of the Comunero Revolt. Noted
particularly for his El Paraguay en 1811, published in
1962.

VELAZCO, FATHER J.M. Paraguayan priest resident at
Buenos Aires who allegedly issued a strong anti-Dr.
Francia proclamation when El Supremo was named perpetual dictator of Paraguay. No similar opposition, of
course, was possible or permissible in Paraguay itself.

VELILLA, BENJAMIN, 1888-   . Journalist, politician and
historian. Editor for El Nacional, La Defensa and El
Diario. Author of numerous monographs of a historical
nature, particularly regarding the early independence
era and the Triple Alliance War.

VELLOSO, GUILLERMO ENCISO. Prominent member of the
"Democrático" faction of the Colorado Party in the late
1940's and 1950's.

VENCER O MORIR! TO WIN OR DIE! A famed semi-offi-
cial Paraguayan motto used during the Triple Alliance
War, especially by Marshal President Francisco Solano
López, whose sword bore this inscription.

VENEGAS, CAPTAIN GARCIA. Follower of Domingo Martínez de Irala and opponent of Alvar Núñez Cabeza de
Vaca. Accompanied the latter back to Spain in 1545
after his arrest and removal from his position as governor.

VERA, CAPTAIN EDUARDO see also GENES, IGNACIO.
One of the commanders of the unsuccessful but ingenious Paraguayan canoe boarding attack against the Brazilian fleet at Humaitá in March, 1868, during the Triple Alliance War.

VERA Y ARAGON, ALONSO DE. Credited with the founding
in 1585 of Concepción de la Buena Esperanza del Río
Bermejo, a short-lived early colonial settlement located
on the Bermejo River west of the Paraguay River near
the riverport of Pilar.

VERA Y ARAGON, JUAN TORRES DE. Last adelantado at
Asunción. Married the daughter of Juan Ortiz de Zárate, arrived at Asunción in 1587, and traveled the following year to Spain from where he never returned.

VERGARA, CAPTAIN see IRALA, DOMINGO MARTINEZ
DE. Name by which Paraguay's Founding Father was
popularly known among his comrades; stemming from
the name of his village birthplace in the Spanish Basque
provinces.

VERGARA, FRANCISCO ORTIZ DE see ORTIZ DE VERGA-
RA, FRANCISCO.

VERGARA, JUAN see ORTIZ DE VERGARA, JUAN.

VERSEN, MAX VON. An enterprising Prussian army officer
who took leave of absence from his duties to visit privately the scene of the Triple Alliance War. Unbelieved
by both sides, he eventually became a prisoner of Paraguay. His account of his experiences is a fascinating
prime informational source of wartime conditions.

VERTIZ, JUAN JOSE. First viceroy of the new Viceroyalty
of La Plata, created in 1776 and including Paraguay
within its jurisdiction.

VIANNA DE LIMA, CESAR SAUVAN. Minister Resident of
Imperial Brazil in Asunción at the outbreak of the Tri-

ple Alliance War. Received and answered the Note of
Protest of August 30, 1864, regarded by the Paraguayan
government as its ultimatum to Brazil in the light of
that nation's intervention in Uruguayan affairs.

VICEROY (OR VIRREY). The Viceroy, personal representative of the Spanish kings in the New World. From
1542 to 1777, Paraguay was a province of the Viceroyalty or "Virreinato" of Peru. From 1777 to 1811,
it was included in the "Virreinato y Audiencia del Río
de la Plata."

VICTORIA, ANTONIO. Appointed governor of Paraguay in
1717 but renounced the appointment in favor of Diego de
los Reyes Balmaceda, during whose regime the Comunero movement began.

VICTORICA, JULIO. Private representative of Argentina's
General Justo José de Urquiza sent to Asunción on a
special mission in February, 1865, to persuade Francisco Solano López not to impair friendly relationships
with President Bartolomé Mitre of Argentina. López,
who had sought unsuccessfully to obtain Mitre's permission to cross Misiones in order to attack Brazil, rejected Victorica's advice and subsequently declared war
on Argentina.

VIEIRA, TORRENNI. Paraguayan army unit commander during the late 1933 Paraguayan Nanawa offensive in the
Chaco War.

VIENTO NORTE. An especially enervating hot north wind
occurring in the Paraguayan summers. Its effects are
said to have been so deleterious to morale in Dr.
Francia's time that El Supremo was willing to pardon
even murderers who committed their crimes during the
wind's incidence.

VILLA DEL SALTO, S.S. Uruguayan river steamer fired
on by Brazil naval units in September, 1864, while proceeding up the Uruguay River with Blanco Party rein-
forcements aboard. The attack produced a protest by
Francisco Solano López to Brazil, and represented another in the series of events which preluded the Triple
Alliance War.

VILLA HAYES see also NUEVA BURDEOS. Located about

15 miles north of Asunción on the right bank of the
Paraguay River, and the site of the ill-fated Nueva
Burdeos French colonization experiment of the 1850's.
The river port and terminal of the Trans Chaco high-
way, it received its present name from the arbitration
proceedings conducted by U. S. President Rutherford B.
Hayes in 1878. The Hayes arbitral award favored Para-
guay's position and rejected post Triple Alliance War
Argentine claims to the Chaco.

VILLA MONTES. Bolivian Andean foothill city menaced by
Paraguay's late 1934 offensive in the Chaco War.

VILLA OCCIDENTAL see VILLA HAYES and NUEVA BUR-
DEOS. Pre-Triple Alliance War name for the former
and original French colony site of Nueva Burdeos. Re-
named Villa Hayes after the arbital award of 1878.

VILLA RICA DE ESPIRITU SANTO see also VILLARRICA.
One of the earliest Spanish settlements in the eastern
Guairá region, founded by Ruy Díaz de Melgarejo in
1570. Originally located about 150 miles east of Yguazú in Brazilian territory, the site was moved repeated-
ly because of Indian and mameluke slave attacks until
1676 when it became established at its present location
in eastern Paraguay.

VILLAREJO, JOSE S. , 1907-   . Journalist, jurist and
novelist. Regarded as the author who initiated the
novel of the Chaco War, for his works Ocho hombres
(1934) and Ojhóo la Sayoiby (1935).

VILLARRICA. Situated about 110 miles (175 kms) east of
Asunción, this is one of the oldest and most important
inhabited points in extreme eastern Paraguay. Founded
originally in the Guairá region in 1570 by Ruy Díaz de
Melgarejo on orders of Juan de Garay, it became a
major colonial center which attracted invading Brazilian
mameluke and bandeirante forces, and later, large-
scale European colonization projects.

VILLAZON-IRENDAGUE, BATTLE OF. Fought in November,
1934, and the most important victory for Colonel David
Toro's late Chaco War Bolivian offensive campaign.
The gains, however, were subsequently wiped out by
the smashing Paraguayan victory at El Carmen.

VILLEGO VILLASANTI, JUAN DE. Leader of a movement
    in 1649, during the provisional government of Bishop
    Bernardino de Cárdenas, which resulted in the mob
    destruction of Asunción's Jesuit College.

VILLETA. About 25 miles (45 kms) south of Asunción along
    the Paraguay River, this river port was founded in
    1774 by Governor Juan Bazán de Pedraza. Commercial-
    ly, it is noted as a free port for Spain from which lum-
    ber and orange exports are major items. Historically,
    Villeta is ringed by famed battlefields of the Triple Al-
    liance War including Ytororó, Avay, Itá Ybaté, Pikysyry,
    and Angostura.

VISITA see also VISITADOR. An unusual Spanish colonial
    administrative device involving the investigation, usually
    in secret, of the conduct in office of colonial officials.

VISITADOR see also VISITA. The secret agent of the
    Spanish government who in colonial times performed
    the "Visita," or investigation of the conduct in office
    of public officials.

VITORIA, ANTONIO. Nominee as governor of Paraguay who
    allegedly sold his patent with the King's approval to
    Diego de los Reyes Balmaceda in 1717. Reyes Balma-
    ceda, partial to the Jesuits, was disliked at Asunción,
    and the city Cabildo protested his nomination to the
    Audiencia of Charcas. The action produced the inves-
    tigation mission to Asunción of Dr. José de Antequera
    y Castro and is thus held as the immediate cause of
    the Comunero Revolt.

VITTONE, LUIS. Contemporary historian and noted for his
    El Paraguay en la lucha por la independencia (1961)
    and Guerra de la Triple Alianza contra el Paraguay
    (1962).

VOIGT, CARLOS. Immigrant from southern Brazil whose
    viticulture experiments in the area of Villarrica after
    1907 served to revive Paraguay's grape-growing and
    wine industry.

VOLLENDAM, MENNONITE COLONY OF. Small Mennonite
    colony located about 200 miles north of Asunción along
    the Paraguay River. Locale in the 1960's of a planned
    project for the construction of a sugar refinery with
    German financial aid.

VOLUNTARIOS DA PATRIA.   The volunteers and conscripts
    who comprised the major part of Imperial Brazil's
    army in the Triple Alliance War.   Largely Negro and
    Mulatto in racial composition.   Known as "cambá" by
    Paraguayans.

VOZ DEL PUEBLO (LA).   Post-Triple Alliance War Asun-
    ción newspaper.

- W -

WANDERLEY, JOÃO MAURICIO DE.   Brazil's Barão de
    Cotegipe and representative at Asunción after the close
    of the Triple Alliance War.   Negotiated the Loizaga-
    Cotegipe Treaty of 1872 which fixed the new frontier
    boundaries between Paraguay and Brazil.

WAR OF THE SEVEN REDUCTIONS   see   GUARANI WAR.

WARS   see   GUARANI WAR, TRIPLE ALLIANCE WAR,
    CHACO WAR, WORLD WAR II.

WASHBURN, CHARLES AMES, 1822-1889.   First American
    minister appointed to Paraguay where he resided until
    replaced by Major General Martin T. McMahon in late
    1868.   A keen observor and originally friendly with
    Marshal President Francisco Solano López, Washburn
    developed a penetrating knowledge of Paraguay which
    he used to prepare his History of Paraguay, a two-
    volume comprehensive study published at Boston in 1871.
    By early 1868 he fell into the Paraguayan president's
    bad graces for alleged connections with the conspiracy
    episode.   He was permitted to leave Paraguay only after
    a series of acrimonious incidents which distorted his
    reporting of the era and which provided the background
    for a subsequent 1869 U.S. Senate investigation into
    Paraguayan affairs.

WASHINGTON CONFERENCE OF 1929   see   RAMIREZ-DIEZ
    DE MEDINA PROTOCOL and CONCILIATION AND AR-
    BITRATION CONFERENCE OF 1929.

WASP, U.S.S.   American naval vessel of the South Atlantic
    squadron, commanded by Captain W.A. Kirkland, which
    proceeded to Asunción in August, 1868, during the Tri-
    ple Alliance War, to embark Minister Charles Ames

Washburn. Later in December, the Wasp carried new
Minister Martin T. McMahon to Paraguay.

WATER WITCH, U.S.S. United States naval gunboat under
the command of Lieutenant Thomas Jefferson Page which
visited Paraguay in 1853-1855 on a hydrographic mission. In 1855 while sailing near the Paraguayan river
fort of Itapirú on the Paraná River above its confluence
with the Paraguay River, the Water Witch was fired
upon and its helmsman was killed. Coupled with the
Hopkins affair, the incident brought a rupture in United
States-Paraguayan relations. The subsequent dispatch
in 1858 by President Buchanan of the powerful Bowlin
naval mission, and the successful mediation efforts of
Argentina's Justo José de Urquiza, encouraged a re-
conciliation. President Carlos Antonio López agreed
to remuneration for the family of the deceased U.S.
sailor, appropriate ceremonies, and a note of apology.
The episode was the most delicate of the several international incidents of his administration.

WATTS, JOHN. One of the several unsung but notable British technicians in Paraguay's service during the Triple
Alliance War. Watts arrived in Paraguay as engineer-
officer aboard the new Paraguarí, naval vessel built in
England under the J. and H. Blyth contract. He served
in her at the June, 1865, river battle of Riachuelo, was
decorated for his actions, but was subsequently executed
in 1868 during the period of the alleged conspiracy
against Francisco Solano López.

WEBB, GENERAL JAMES WATSON. American minister to
Brazil during the Triple Alliance War period. Inter-
vened to obtain permission for the U.S.S. Wasp to pass
allied lines in order to remove Minister Charles Ames
Washburn from Paraguay.

WEGENER, WILHELM. An unsung and seldom mentioned
German technician in Paraguay apparently during the
last phases of the Triple Alliance War. His one known
contribution was the construction of an ingenious Con-
gréve multiple rocket launcher found by victorious Brazilian troops after the battle of Acosta Ñú, August 16,
1869. Evidence that he may actually have participated
in the battle is suggested by a small grove of trees
in the area known locally as Isla Cohete, or Island of
the Rockets.

WHITE, EDWARD LUCAS. American author whose novel, El Supremo, a Romance of the Great Dictator of Paraguay, published in New York in 1916, remains one of the most engaging reproductions of the life and times of Dr. José Gaspar Rodríguez de Francia.

WHITE, FRANCIS. American assistant secretary of state who headed the five member neutral government commission in 1929-1932 seeking to reach a formula for solution of the Chaco dispute.

WHITEHEAD, JOHN WILLIAM see also WHYTEHEAD, WILLIAM. British naval architect and engineer whose services were contracted for during the Carlos Antonio López administration. As director of Asunción's naval arsenal, he provided Paraguay's armed forces with river vessels, field guns and large caliber siege artillery. His early wartime death was a serious blow to Paraguay's cause.

WHYTEHEAD, WILLIAM. British technician who with his countrymen Colonel George Thompson, John Watts, Alonso Taylor, George Masterman, and Dr. William Stewart, rendered valuable services to Paraguay's cause during the Triple Alliance War. Whytehead was first director of Asunción's arsenal, and achieved the remarkable feat of producing heavy caliber field and siege guns used by the army at Humaitá. His death in the first year of the war, according to George Masterman, was a severe set-back for Paraguay's victory hopes.

WILLIAM COOPER AND NEPHEWS. British firm which established a quebracho processing port and factory at Puerto Cooper in the early twentieth century. The plant has since closed operations.

WISNER DE MORGENSTERN, ENRIQUE see MORGENSTERN, COLONEL ENRIQUE WISNER VON. Also referred to as Francisco Wisner de Morgenstern. One of the more notable foreign technicians contracted for service in Paraguay during the Carlos Antonio López administration.

WORKERS' COUNCIL see CONSEJO OBRERO.

WORLD WAR II. The period was practically concurrent with that of the regime of President Higinio Morínigo, Sep-

tember 1940 to June 1948.   Though Paraguay joined
with most other Latin America republics in severing
ties with the Axis nations (January, 1942) and in declaring war on them (February, 1945), there were in-
dications and some evidence that at least in part its
government reflected some of the pro-Axis sympathy
which characterized neighboring Argentina in the same
period.   German propaganda and propagandists appeared
to enjoy more freedom from controls than did allied
sympathizers, and in the post-war period Paraguay was
and is still occasionally claimed to be a haven for
wanted Axis escapees.   In general, World War II for
Paraguay was a prosperous period due to increased
prices for its export products and the availability of
United States loans and other assistance.   A highlight
of the period was President Morínigo's formal visit to
the United States in June, 1943, representing the first
visit by a Paraguayan chief executive.

XARAYES, LAKE.   A system of swamps and lagoons in the
northern area of Brazil's Mato Grosso state which is
given semi-legendary status as the headwaters of the
Paraguay River.

XARAYES INDIANS.   Tribe found by early Spanish expeditions
in the Lake Xarayes region, the headwaters area of the
Paraguay River in Brazil's Mato Grosso province.   Subsequently obliterated by Spanish attacks and mameluke
slaving raids.

- Y -

YAGUARIGUAY, CHIEF RODRIGO.   Chief of a Guaraní tribe
at Arecayá pueblo near Asunción, who figured in a
large-scale Indian revolt of 1659-1660, finally quelled
by the aid of mission Indian forces.

YAGUARON.   Founded in 1539 by Domingo Martínez de Irala,
this old city was one of the earliest established in the
interior by Spanish colonists from Asunción.   It is located about 30 miles (48 kms) southeast of Asunción
on highway Route One.   A major center of Franciscan
missionary activity, it is noted for its immense old
church built by Guaraní Indians under Franciscan direction and holding a vast collection of Indian-made religious sculptures.   The reconstructed colonial-style home

of Captain García Rodríguez Francia, father of Dr.
José Gaspar Rodríguez de Francia, Paraguay's famed
El Supremo, is likewise a noted Yaguarón historic site.

YANACONA. Term used in colonial Paraguay referring to
perpetual servitude by Indians in the large "estancias,"
as compared to the "mita" type which involved only
periodic labor for the "estanciero" or "encomendero."

YATAITY-CORA, PEACE CONFERENCE OF. Locale near
the Humaitá positions at which on September 13, 1866,
Marshal President López conferred with allied commander General Bartolomé Mitre in a fruitless effort
to reach peace terms. The allies, at Brazil's insist-
ance, declined to negotiate with López. The most important effort at securing peace during the Triple Alliance War.

YATAY, BATTLE OF see also DUARTE, MAJOR PEDRO.
Fought August 17, 1865, on the Argentine side of the
Uruguay River across from Uruguayana, Uruguay. An
allied victory in the early stages of the Triple Alliance
War, it resulted in annihilation of the Paraguayan force
of Major Pedro Duarte, and in the siege of Uruguayana
and the subsequent surrender of the remainder of Paraguay's invasion force under Colonel Antonio de la Cruz
Estigarribia.

YBICUI see also YNSFRAN, CAPTAIN JULIAN. Situated
about 60 miles southeast of Asunción, and historically
important for the site there in the prewar era of Paraguay's only iron works. Permanently destroyed by allied troops in 1869.

YBIRAI see also FRANCIA, DR. JOSE GASPAR RODRI-
GUEZ DE. The well-preserved home of Paraguay's
famed El Supremo, located in the suburb of Trinidad,
about three miles north of Asunción. Still used as a
private residence.

YBYBOBO, BATTLE OF. One of the last battles of the
Chaco War, a Paraguayan victory, fought near the Parapití River on the Bolivian border, December 30, 1934.

YEGROS, ANTONIO TOMAS, 1783-1866. Prominent officer
in Paraguay's contingent at the defense of Montevideo
and Buenos Aires against the British, and a participant

in the 1811 battles of Paraguarí and Tacuarí against
Belgrano's Argentine force. Personal friend of Dr.
José Gaspar Rodríguez de Francia, and El Supremo's
military and security chief. Survived both Dr. Francia
and Carlos Antonio López. Later exhumed and deposited
in the Pantheon of the Heroes, his remains are the only
ones positively authenticated of Paraguay's founding fathers.

YEGROS, FULGENCIO, 1780-1821. Recognized as the leader
of the Revolution of May, 1811, he was an experienced
soldier having served with Paraguay's contingent at the
defense of Buenos Aires and Montevideo against the
British invasions, and in Paraguay's army which defeated Manuel Belgrano's Argentine forces. President
of the Supreme Governing Board in 1811, and later
Consul with Dr. José Gaspar Rodríguez de Francia.
Executed on El Supremo's orders in 1821 on charges of
complicity in the treason plot of 1820. His grandfather
was Fulgencio Yegros y Ledesma, captain general and
provisional governor of Paraguay.

YEGROS, LIEUTENANT ROMULO. Member of the Francisco
Solano López 1853-1854 European mission, and author
of a source record of the mission Diario de viaje. Also
wrote an account of his travels on horseback as an official courier between Asunción and Rio de Janeiro.

YEGROS Y LEDESMA, FULGENCIO DE. Governor of Paraguay, 1764-1766, and a relative of María Josefa de
Velasco y Yegros, mother of Dr. José Gaspar Rodríguez de Francia, Paraguay's famed El Supremo.

YERBA MATE. Ilex paraguayenis. A bush-like tree native
to eastern and southern Paraguay from the leaves of
which Paraguayan tea is prepared. The trees are commonly referred to as yerba or yerba maté trees.

YERBALES see also YERBA MATE. Forests or groves of
yerba trees from the leaves of which yerba maté is
prepared.

YGABAS. Long canoes fashioned from logs, and used by the
Guaraní Indians.

YGATIMI RIVER. Small stream in northeast Paraguay, the
locale in the early 1770's of a Portuguese attempt at

further encroachment into Spanish territory. Forced
to depart in 1777 by Governor Agustín Fernando de
Pinedo.

YGUAZU FALLS. One of the world's largest and most scenic cataracts located near the juncture of the Yguazú
and Paraná Rivers slightly south of Puerto Presidente
Stroessner and Foz do Iguassú about 225 miles east of
Asunción. Nearby is the point known as "Trés Fronte-
ras," one of the only two points in South America where
the borders of three republics coincide. The falls are
largely on the Argentine side of the Iguassú River, but
are best visible from the Brazilian side.

YNSFRAN, EDGAR LINNEO. Born 1920 in Asunción. Prominent lawyer and historian. Minister of the Interior in
the cabinet of President Stroessner, 1956-1966, and
distinguished director of the Colorado Party. Noted for
having founded in 1957 the frontier city of Puerto Presidente Stroessner along the Paraná River in the vicinity
of Yguazú Falls. Possessor of one of Paraguay's most
complete history libraries, notably covering the Triple
Alliance War. Author of numerous essays and monographs on historical topics, including Fin de la fábrica
de fierro de Ybycuí, 1972.

YNSFRAN, FACUNDO, 1861-1902. Distinguished physician
and statesman. Vice president of Paraguay, 1894-
1898, and founder of the Faculty of Medicine of Asunción. One of the first Paraguayan physicians to obtain
the academic doctorate in medicine.

YNSFRAN, CAPTAIN JULIAN. Commander/director of Paraguay's only iron foundry located at Ybicuí, about 60
miles southeast of Asunción. Executed by attacking allied forces on May 19, 1869, prior to the final Cordillera Campaign of the Triple Alliance War.

YNSFRAN, PABLO MAX, 1894-1972. Historian, poet, statesman, and educator. Minister of Public Works during
the administration of President José Félix Estigarribia.
Left Paraguay in 1940 in exile, to become professor of
Latin American studies at the University of Texas.
Noted for his translation of General Estigarribia's Chaco War memoirs, The Epic of the Chaco, published in
1950, and for his study of the Hopkins and Water Witch
incidents entitled La expedición norteamericana contra

el Paraguay, 1858-1859, published in 1954. Died at
Austin, May, 1972.

YNSFRAN DE LOPEZ, MELCHORA.   Wife of Cirilo López
and mother of President Carlos Antonio López.

YNSFRAN DE MARTINEZ, JULIANA.   Cousin of Francisco
Solano López, intimate friend of Mme. Elisa Alicia
Lynch, and wife of Colonel Francisco Martínez, last
commander of the Paraguayan army garrison during the
siege of Humaitá.   Executed in 1868 for alleged complicity in the conspiracy rumored to exist against Paraguay's marshal president.

YPACARAY (ALSO IPACARAI).   This lake, located about 25
miles east of Asunción, is possibly the most scenic natural feature in Paraguay.   On its shores are the summer resorts of San Bernardino and Areguá.   Nearby
are Altos, one of the first sites of German colonization, and the Cordillera de los Altos, the abrupt escarpment marking the western end of the Paraná plateau.

YPANE RIVER see IPANE RIVER.   One of the northern
tributaries of the Paraguay River, entering it near the
riverport of Concepción.

YPOA, LAKE.   A connected system of lakes, lagoons and
swamps in southwestern Paraguay, approximately 50
miles south of Asunción, which becomes a heavily inun-
dated area during the rainy season.   Its major drainage
stream into the Paraguay River is the Tebicuary River.

YPORA, S.S.   Paraguayan naval vessel, part of the fleet at
the naval battle of Riachuelo, June, 1865, during the
Triple Alliance War.   Finally put afire and scuttled at
Vapor Cué in 1869 by the retreating Paraguayan army
to prevent capture by the allies.   Remains are still
visible.

YRENDAGUE, BATTLE OF see also IRENDAGUE, BATTLE
OF, and PICUIBA-CARANDAYTY, BATTLE OF.   One
of the Chaco War's last and most decisive battles, occurring on December 8, 1934.   A small Paraguayan
detachment under Colonel Eugenio A. Garay performed
a spectacular route march under superhuman conditions
to seize the region's only water wells at Yrendagüe.
Cut off from a water supply and abandoned by their of-

ficers, some 4,000 Bolivian soldiers surrendered and an additional estimated 8,000 died of thirst and heat prostration in the arid Chaco zone. The grim defeat triggered an army coup which forced the renunciation of Bolivia's President Daniel Salamanca.

YTORORO, BATTLE OF. Fought December 6, 1869, and the opening battle of the Pikysyry or Lomas Valentinas campaign. Known as Paraguay's Thermopylae, the holding action by Paraguay's army at a bridge over the Arroyo Ytororó near the riverport of Villeta, was a bloody defeat which nevertheless slowed the allied advance toward the main Itá-Ybaté positions.

- Z -

ZALDIVAR VILLAGRA, COLONEL FABIAN see REVOLUTION OF 1947. Commander of the rebel forces in the major 1947 Revolution.

ZARATE, FERNANDO DE. Briefly governor by appointment of the viceroy at Lima during the late sixteenth century era of Hernandarias.

ZARATE, JUAN ORTIZ DE see ORTIZ DE ZARATE, JUAN.

ZAVALA, BRUNO MAURICIO DE. Governor of Buenos Aires and a nemesis for the Comunero movement. In 1725, with an army which included many mission Indians, he forced Dr. José de Antequera y Castro into exile and eventual execution in 1731 at Lima. In 1735 he again led an army to Paraguay and brought a complete end to the Comunero episode.

ZAVALA, PETRONA. Allegedly a young lady who attracted Dr. José Gaspar Rodríguez de Francia, the future El Supremo, but who spurned him for a rival, Estanislao Machaín. The event is held as the sole evidence of romance in El Supremo's austere life.

ZAVALA Y DELGADILLO, COLONEL JOSE ANTONIO DE see also FUERTE BORBON. Founder in 1792 of Fuerte de Borbón, a north Chaco outpost along the Paraguay River designed to stop Brazilian settlement southward.

ZEBALLOS, CAPTAIN JUAN VALERIANO DE.   Spanish national and a member of the first provisional revolutionary government following the movement of May,
1811.

ZENTENO-GONDRA, BATTLE OF   see   ALIGUATA-ZENTE-
NO, BATTLE OF

ZIPOLI, DOMENICO.   Recorded as an Italian Jesuit music
composer who stimulated an interest in music among
mission Indians.

ZUBIZARRETA, CARLOS, 1904-   .   Novelist, short story
author, journalist and historian.   Author of two well-
researched historical works: Capitanes de la aventura
(1957), biographic studies of Alvar Núñez Cabeza de
Vaca and Martínez de Irala; and Cien vidas paraguayas
(1961), a useful and complete biographic study of 100
of Paraguay's most important historical figures.

ZUBIZARRETA, DR. GERONIMO, 1880-1952.   Distinguished
jurist and statesman.   Paraguay's minister of foreign
affairs during the Chaco War, noted for his presenta-
tion of evidence indicating that Bolivia was being sup-
plied with war equipment obtained from Armstrong-
Vickers of England.   Representative to the Buenos
Aires postwar Peace Conference.   Prominent Liberal
Party member, and party president from 1946 until his
death at Asunción on May 14, 1952.

ZUBIZARRETA Y ZULUETA, RAMON, 1840-1902.   Born at
Burgos, Spain, and emigrated to Paraguay via Argentina
in 1871.   Major contributor to the development of a
law school system and the structure of new, modern
penal codes.   One of the organizers of the Colegio Nacional de Asunción, founded in 1877, and of the Universidad Nacional, founded in 1889.   Rector of the university from then until his death on August 16, 1902.

APPENDIX I

The governors, governments and presidents of Paraguay during the colonial and independence eras are indicated in the following listing:

I. Colonial Era

Governors

1534	Adelantado Pedro de Mendoza
1537	Juan de Ayolas
1539	Capitán Domingo Martínez de Irala
1542	Adelantado Alvar Núñez Cabeza de Vaca
1544	Capitán Domingo Martínez de Irala
1556	Gonzalo de Mendoza
1557	Francisco Ortiz de Vergara
1567	General Felipe de Cáceres
1572	Martín Suárez de Toledo
1575	Adelantado Juan Ortiz de Zárate
1576	Diego Ortiz de Zárate Mendieta
1576	Juan de Garay
1583	Juan de Torres Navarrete
1587	Adelantado Juan Torres de Vera y Aragón
1592	General Hernando Arias o Hernandarias de Saavedra
1599	Diego Valdez de la Banda
1602	General Hernando Arias o Hernandarias de Saavedra
1609	Diego Marín de Negrón
1615	General Hernando Arias o Hernandarias de Saavedra
1621	Capitán Manuel de Frías
1626	Diego de Rego y Mendoza
1627	Capitán Manuel de Frías
1631	Luis de Céspedes García Xería
1633	General Martín de Ledesma Valderrama
1636	Pedro de Lugo y Navarra
1641	Gregorio de Hinestrosa
1647	Diego de Escobar Osorio
1649	Bernardino de Cárdenas
1649	General Sebastián de León y Zárate
1650	Andrés Garavito de León

1653	Cristóbal de Garay y Saavedra
1656	Juan Blásquez de Valverde
1659	Alonso Sarmiento de Sotomayor y Figueroa
1663	Juan Diez de Andino
1671	Felipe Rege Corvalán
1676	Diego Ibáñez de Faría
1676	Felipe Rege Corvalán
1681	Juan Diez de Andino
1684	Antonio de Vera Mugica
1691	Francisco de Monforte
1691	Sebastián Félix de Mendiola
1696	Juan Rodríguez Cota
1702	Antonio de Escobar y Gutiérrez
1705	Sebastián Félix de Mendiola
1706	Baltasar García Ros
1707	Manuel de Robles Lorenzana
1713	Juan Gregorio Bazán de Pedraza
1717	Diego de los Reyes Balmaceda
1721	José de Antequera y Castro
1725	Ramón de las Llamas
1725	Martín de Barua
1730	Ignacio de Soroeta
1730	El Común (Fernando de Mompox, Matías de Saldivar, Francisco de Roa, José Luis Barreiro, Pedro Bogarín)
1731	Junta Gubernativa. José Luis Barreiro, Presidente de la Provincia del Paraguay
1731	Junta Gubernativa. Capitán Miguel de Garay, Presidente de la Provincia del Paraguay.
1732	Junta Gubernativa. Antonio Ruíz de Arellano, Presidente de la Provincia del Paraguay
1733	Coronel Manuel Agustín de Ruiloba y Calderón
1733	Fray Juan de Arregui
1734	General Cristóbal Domínguez de Ovelar
1735	Bruno Mauricio de Zavala
1735	Martín José de Echauri
1741	José de la Moneda
1747	Coronel José Marcos de Larrazábal
1750	Brigadier Jaime de Sanjust
1761	José Martínez Fontes
1764	Capitán Fulgencio Yegros y Ledesma
1766	Carlos Morphi
1772	Coronel Agustín Fernando de Pinedo
1778	Pedro Melo de Portugal y Villena
1785	Joaquín Alós y Brú
1796	Lázaro de la Rivera y Espinoza de los Monteros
1806	Brigadier Bernardo de Velazco y Huidobro
1807	Manuel Gutiérrez

1807   Brigadier Bernardo de Velazco y Huidobro
1809   Eustaqui Gianini
1809   Brigadier Bernardo de Velazco y Huidobro

II. Independence Era

First Provisional Government

1811   Brigadier Bernardo de Velazco y Huidobro - Capitán Juan Valeriano de Zevallos - Doctor José Gaspar Rodríguez de Francia

Superior Governing Board

1811   Teniente Coronel Fulgencio Yegros - Doctor José Gaspar Rodríguez de Francia - Capitán Pedro Juan Caballero - Doctor Francisco Javier Bogarín - Fernando de la Mora

First Consulate

1813   Coronel Fulgencio Yegros - Doctor José Gaspar Rodríguez de Francia

Temporary Dictatorship

1814   Doctor José Gaspar Rodríguez de Francia

Perpetual Dictatorship

1816   Doctor José Gaspar Rodríguez de Francia

First Board of Government

1840   Doctor Manuel Antonio Ortiz - Agustín Cañete - Pablo Ferreira - Miguel Maldonado - Gabino Arroyo

Second Board of Government

1841   Juan José Medina - José Gregorio Benítez - José Domingo Campos

Comandancia General de Armas

1841   Coronel Mariano Roque Alonso - Carlos Antonio López

Second Consulate

1841   Coronel Mariano Roque Alonso - Carlos Antonio
        López

Presidents of the Republic

1844   Carlos Antonio López
1862   Mariscal Francisco Solano López

Second Provisional Republic

1870   Carlos Loizaga - Cirilo Antonio Rivarola - José
        Díaz de Bedoya

Presidents of the Republic

1870   Cirilo Antonio Rivarola
1871   Salvador Jovellanos
1874   Juan Bautista Gill
1877   Higinio Uriarte
1878   Cándido Bareiro
1880   General Bernardino Caballero
1886   General Patricio Escobar
1890   Juan G. González
1894   Marcos Morínigo
1894   General Juan Bautista Egusquiza
1898   Emilio Aceval
1902   Andrés Héctor Carballo
1902   Coronel Juan A. Escurra
1904   Juan B. Gaona
1905   Doctor Cecilio Báez
1906   General Benigno Ferreira
1908   Emiliano González Navero
1910   Manuel Gondra
1911   Coronel Albino Jara
1911   Liberato M. Rojas
1912   Doctor Pedro Peña
1912   Emiliano González Navero
1912   Eduardo Schaerer
1916   Doctor Manuel Franco
1919   Doctor José P. Montero
1920   Manuel Gondra
1921   Doctor Félix Paiva
1921   Doctor Eusebio Ayala
1923   Doctor Eligio Ayala
1924   Doctor Luis Alberto Riart
1924   Doctor Eligio Ayala

1928	Doctor José P. Guggiari
1931	Emiliano González Navero
1932	Doctor José P. Guggiari
1932	Doctor Eusebio Ayala
1936	Coronel Rafael Franco
1937	Doctor Félix Paiva
1939	General José Félix Estigarribia
1940	General Higinio Morínigo M.
1948	Doctor Juan Manuel Frutos
1948	Juan Natalicio González
1949	General Raimundo Rolón
1949	Doctor Felipe Molas López
1949	Federico Chaves
1954	Tomás Romero Pereira
1954	General Alfredo Stroessner

APPENDIX II

Historiography

Paraguayan historians included in the dictionary who
have published works on their nation's development or who
have contributed significantly to the evolution of their profession, are listed as follows. See also individual dictionary
entries.

Aguirre, Andrés
Amarilla Fretes, Eduardo
Báez, Cecilio
Báez, Pedro
Báez Allende, Amadeo
Benítez, Luis G.
Bray, Arturo
Brugada, Arturo
Cardozo, Efraím
Centurión, Carlos R.
Chaves, Julio César
Civils, Manuel
Codas Papalucá, Alcides
Decoud, Héctor F.
Delgado, Nicolás
Díaz de Guzmán, Ruy
Domínguez, Manuel
Falcón, José
Gaona, Silvio
Garay, Blas
Gill Aguínaga, Juan Bautista
Godoi, Juansilvano
Gómez Ríos, Emiliano
González, Antonio E.
González, Luis
Ibarra, Alonso
Irala Burgos, Jerónimo
Jaeggli, Alfredo
Laconich, Marco Antonio
Lara Castro, Mariano Luis

Marín Iglesias, Alejandro
Molas, Mariano Antonio
Moreno, Fulgencio R.
Moreno González, José Antonio
O'Leary, Juan Emiliano
Otaño, Juan Bernardo
Pastore, Carlos A.
Pastor Benítez, Justo
Pérez Acosta, Juan Francisco
Pesoa, Manuel
Prieto, Justo
Pusineri, Carlos Alberto
Quevedo, Roberto
Ramos, R. Antonio
Ramos Giménez, Leopoldo
Rebaudi, Arturo
Ríos, Angel F.
Riquelme García, Andrés
Riquelme García, Benigno
Rivarola Bogarín, Juan Bau-
    tista
Ruiz, J. Gabriel
Sánchez Quell, Hipólito
Sosa Escalada, Juan Manuel
Stefanich, Juan
Vargas Peña, Benjamín
Vasconsellos, Víctor Natalicio
Vásquez, José Antonio
Velásquez, Rafael Eladio
Velilla, Benjamín

275

Vittoni, Luis
Ynsfrán, Pablo Max
Ynsfrán, Edgar L.
Zubizarreta, Carlos

SELECTED BIBLIOGRAPHY

Academia Paraguaya de la Historia. Historia paraguaya. Anuario de la Academia Paraguaya de la Historia, Vols. 1-12, Asunción.

Aguirre, Andrés. Curuzú infante. Asunción: n. d.

Archivo Nacional, Asunción. Publications, files and records.

Aveiro, Coronel Silvestre. Memorias militares, 1864-1870. Asunción: Ediciones Comuneros, 1970.

Barrett, William E. Woman on Horseback. Garden City: Doubleday and Co., 1952.

Benítez, Luis G. Manual de historia paraguaya. Asunción: El Arte S. A., 1970.

Bourne, Richard. Political Leaders of Latin America. Baltimore: Penguin Books, 1969.

Box, Pelham Horton. The Origins of the Paraguayan War. 2 vols. Urbana, 1927.

Bray, Arturo. Hombres y épocas del Paraguay. Asunción: Ediciones Nizza, n. d.

Cardozo, Efraím. Apuntes de historia cultural del Paraguay. 2 vols. Asunción: Colegio San José, n. d.

_____. Breve historia del Paraguay. Buenos Aires: Editorial Universitaria de Buenos Aires, 1965.

_____. Efemérides de la historia del Paraguay. Asunción: Ediciones Nizza, 1967.

_____. Hace 100 años: crónicas de la guerra de 1864-1870. Vols. 1-5. Asunción: Ediciones EMASA, 1961-1971.

277

_____. Historiografía paraguaya. Mexico: Instituto Panamericano de Geografía y Historia, 1959.

Centurión, Carlos R. Historia de la cultura paraguaya. 2 vols. Asuncion: Biblioteca Ortiz Guerrero, 1961.

Ceuppens, Henry D. Paraguay, año 2000. Asunción: Artes Gráficas Zamphiropolos, 1971.

Chaves, Julio César. El General Díaz. Asunción: Ediciones Nizza, 1957.

_____. El Presidente López, vida y gobierno de Don Carlos. Buenos Aires: Ediciones Depalma, 1968.

_____. La revolución del 14 y 15 de mayo. Asunción: Editorial Asunción, 1961.

_____. El Supremo Dictador. 4th ed. Madrid: Gráficas Yagües, 1964.

Estigarribia, José Félix. Memorias del Mariscal Estigarribia. Asunción: Imprenta Nacional, 1972.

Ferguson, J. Halcro. The River Plate Republics. New York: Time, Inc., 1965.

Ferreira Gubitich, Hugo. Geografía del Paraguay. Asunción: La Colmena, S. A., 1971.

Fretz, Joseph Winfield. Immigrant Group Settlements in Paraguay. North Newton, Kansas: Bethel College, 1962.

García Mellid, Atilio. Proceso a los falsificadores de la historia del Paraguay. 2 vols. Buenos Aires: Ediciones Theoría, 1964.

Gill Aguinaga, Juan B. La asociación paraguaya en la guerra de la Triple Alianza. Asunción: Ediciones Nizza, n. d.

Godoi, Juan Silvano. Monografías históricas. Buenos Aires: 1893.

Gómez Ríos, Emiliano. El Paraguay y su historia. 5th ed. Buenos Aires: Americalee Editora, 1963.

González, Juan Natalicio. Geografía del Paraguay. Mexico: Editorial Guarania, 1964.

Gunther, John. Inside South America, New York: Harper and Row, 1967.

James, Preston E. Latin America. New York: The Odyssey Press, 1959.

Kolinski, Charles J. Independence or Death: The Story of the Paraguayan War. Gainesville: University of Florida Press, 1965.

_____. "Paraguay." Worldmark Encyclopedia of the Nations. 4th ed. Vol. 3. New York: Harper and Row, 1971.

Lewis, Paul H. The Politics of Exile: Paraguay's Febrerista Party. Chapel Hill: University of North Carolina Press, 1968.

Maiz, Fidel. Etapas de mi vida. Asunción: Imprenta La Mundial, 1919.

Meyer, Gordon. The River and the People. London: Methuen, 1965.

Ministry of the Interior, Government of Paraguay. Los restos mortales del Dr. José Gaspar Rodríguez de Francia. Asunción: Imprenta Nacional, 1962.

Ministry of National Defense, Government of Paraguay. Museum, publications, records, and files covering the Triple Alliance and Chaco Wars.

Mörner, Magnus (ed.). The Expulsion of the Jesuits from Latin America. New York: Knopf, 1965.

O'Leary, Juan E. La alianza de 1845 con Corrientes. Asunción: Imprenta Militar, 1944.

_____. El libro de los héroes. Asunción: Librería La Mundial, 1922.

_____. El Mariscal Solano López. Asunción: Casa América, 1970.

Pan American Union. Paraguay. American Republics Series, No. 17. Washington, D.C.: Pan American Union, 1965.

279

Paraguay en America. Monthly review. Vols. 1-4. Buenos
Aires, 1969.

Pastor Benítez, Justo. Estigarribia, el soldado del Chaco.
Asunción: Ediciones Nizza, n. d.

_____. El solar guaraní. Buenos Aires, 1947.

Patria. Asunción daily newspaper. Files and records.

Pendle, George. Paraguay, A Riverside Nation. 2nd. ed.
New York, 1956.

Pérez Acosta, Ernesto. La contienda del Chaco. Asunción,
1962.

Pincus, Joseph. The Economy of Paraguay. New York:
Praeger, 1968.

Pitaud, Henri. Madama Lynch. Asunción: Ediciones
SEE FP, 1958.

Pomer, León. La guerra del Paraguay. Buenos Aires:
Centro Editor de América Latina, 1971.

Pusineri Scala, Carlos Alberto. La moneda de 1780 a 1956.
Asunción, 1956.

Raine, Philip. Paraguay. New Brunswick: Scarecrow
Press, 1956.

Reh, Emma. Paraguayan Rural Life. Washington, D. C.,
1946.

Riquelme García, Benigno. Cumbre en soledad: vida de
Manuel Gondra. Buenos Aires, 1951.

Robertson, J. P. and W. P. Letters on Paraguay: Comprising an Account of a Four Years' Residence in that Republic under the Government of the Dictator Francia.
2 vols. London, 1838.

Rodríguez-Alcalá, Hugo. "Hijo de hombre, de Roa Bastos
y la intra-historia del Paraguay." Cuadernos Ameri-
canos, No. 2, March-April, 1963.

_____. Historia de la literatura paraguaya. Mexico:
Ediciones de Andrea, 1970.

_____. "La narrativa paraguaya desde comienzos del siglo XX." Cahiers du Monde Hispanique et Luso-Bresilien, Caravelle 14, 1970.

_____. "Official Truth and True Truth: Augusto Roa Bastos, borrador de un informe." Studies in Short Fiction, VIII, No. 1, Winter, 1971.

Rout, Jr., Leslie B. Politics of the Chaco Peace Conference, 1935-1939. Austin: University of Texas Press, 1970.

Saguier Caballero, Raul. Paraguay. Asunción: Presidencia de la República, 1964.

Sánchez Quell, Hipólito. Estructura y función del Paraguay Colonial. Buenos Aires, 1944.

Service, Elman R. and Helen S. Tobatí: Paraguayan Town. Chicago: University of Chicago Press, 1954.

Severin, Kurt. "Guns in the Green Hell of the Chaco." Guns, Vol. VI, No. 11-71, November, 1960.

Sherbinin, Betty de. The River Plate Republics. New York, 1947.

Stewart, Norman R. Japanese Colonization in Eastern Paraguay. Washington, D.C.: National Academy of Sciences, Publication No. 1490, 1967.

Taylor, Alice. (ed.) "Paraguay." Focus, The American Geographical Society, Vol. XVIII, No. 4, December, 1967.

Thompson, George. The War in Paraguay. London, 1869.

Tribuna (La). Asunción daily newspaper. Files and records.

Vasconsellos, Victor Natalicio. Lecciones de historia paraguaya. 6th ed. Rio de Janeiro: Livraria Freitas Bastos, S.A., 1970.

Warren, Harris Gaylord. Paraguay, an Informal History. Norman: University of Oklahoma Press, 1949.

Washburn, Charles A. The History of Paraguay. 2 vols. Boston, 1871.

Wendt, Herbert. The Red, White and Black Continent. Garden City: Doubleday and Co., 1966.

Wisner de Morgenstern, Francisco. El dictador del Paraguay. 2nd ed. Asunción: Ediciones Nizza, n. d.

Ynsfrán, Edgar L. "Fin de la fábrica de fierro de Ybycuí." La Tribuna, Asunción, May 28, 1972.

Ynsfrán, Pablo Max. The Epic of the Chaco (Memoirs of General Estigarribia). Austin: University of Texas, 1950.

_____. La expedición norteamericana contra el Paraguay, 1858-1859. 2 vols. Mexico, 1958.

Zook, D. H. The Conduct of the Chaco War. New York, 1960.

Zubizarreta, Carlos. Cien vidas paraguayas. Buenos Aires: Ediciones Nizza, 1961.